D1231530

# LATIN AMERICAN TRAVEL

# NEW GRANADA:

## Twenty Months in the Andes

BY ISAAC F. HOLTON

*Edited with an Introduction*
*by C. Harvey Gardiner*

SOUTHERN ILLINOIS UNIVERSITY PRESS
*Carbondale and Edwardsville*

FEFFER AND SIMONS, INC.
*London and Amsterdam*

# Contents

# Introduction

In mid-nineteenth-century years New Granada, as it had been earlier and would be later under other names,* was a land of contradictions—of contradictory terrains and climates, contradictory flora, and contradictory political personalities and outlooks.

The 1820's, the initial decade of independence, had featured clashes between the great liberator, Simón Bolívar, and Francisco de Paula Santander. In the next decade, after Venezuela and Ecuador had detached themselves from the authority seated in Bogotá, the clashes between Liberals and Conservatives created numerous unbridgeable chasms in New Granada. In time, as strong personalities mesmerized their followers and principles meant little, the labels would spell ideological confusion, but initially one of the major differences between the two camps was the fiercely anticlerical outlook of the Liberals and the stanchly loyal Catholic position of the Conservatives. Behind differing religious postures were unreconcilable policies in reference to many areas of everyday life —the jurisdiction of courts, the management of cemeteries, the operation of schools, and others.

In the 1840's the new Conservative constitution accorded the president absolute powers and, as expected, the old order of church-state relations flourished, including the return of the banished Jesuits. Some economic prosperity came to New Granada in the form of increased trade and expanded coffee production. However, transportation remained inadequate for the needs of both man and freight as successive efforts to establish steamboat

*In late stages of the colonial era the area was known as the Viceroyalty of New Granada; in independence it successively became Gran Colombia (1819–30), New Granada (1830–63), and Colombia (since 1863).

operations on the Magdalena failed to fulfill the hopes of the nation and the promises of the promoters. In 1846, when New Granada granted the United States transit privileges across the Isthmus of Panama, the South American state benefited but little. On the other hand, the increased movement of citizens of the United States via Panama and the railroad it boasted by the mid-1850's did rivet American attention on that peripheral portion of New Granada.

In 1849 the Liberals won the presidency and placed José Hilario López in that office. Again the Jesuits were expelled and many areas of authority which previously had been centralized in Bogotá were divided among the provinces. Suffrage was extended, slavery ended, and freedom of the press proclaimed. Political bitterness and administrative fumbling were widespread and persistent. When bishop and archbishop protested the anticlericalism, they were summarily exiled. In sum, as the Liberals moved rapidly on many fronts simultaneously, New Granada was turned topsy-turvy, making the 1850's, with which R. L. Gilmore associates the term "Socialist mirage," one of the most restless decades in all Colombian history. Revolution and threat of revolution stalked the land; and the people, despite their desire for peace, knew little peace.

As did all of newly independent Latin America, New Granada attracted her share of inquisitive foreigners who felt compelled to record their experiences for the amusement and edification of others. When Charles Stuart Cochrane of the British navy published his *Journal of a Residence and Travels in Colombia, During the Years 1823 and 1824* (2 volumes, London, 1825), he showed himself to be the aloof and removed observer rather than a participant in the way of life he reported. He saw a landscape that invited the federal system of government and a people whose happiness might best be obtained under a limited monarchy. Cochrane was haunted by the rich beauty of the land and the complacency of its unlettered people.

Endless curiosity, intensified by novelty, characterized book after book about the South American republic. Also issued early by London publishers were G. T. Mollien's *Travels in the Republic of Colombia, in the Years 1822 and 1823* (1824), Francis Hall's *Colombia: Its Present State and Inducements to Emigration* (1825) and Colonel J. P. Hamilton's *Travels through the Interior Provinces of Colombia* (1827).

In 1822–23 Colonel William Duane of Philadelphia visited Colombia "on behalf of persons in the United States, having claims against the government." Like many other travelers who visited Colombia later, Duane was intrigued by the drama of Holy Week in Bogotá and the tumbling waters of Tequendama Falls—activities of the people and the grandeur of the landscape. His descent of that river of hope and heartbreak, the unpredictable Magdalena, also figures in *A Visit to Colombia, in the Years 1822 & 1823* (Philadelphia, 1826). Another early account by an American, *Notes on Colombia in the Years 1822–3* (Philadelphia, 1827), derived from the experiences of Captain Richard Bache.

A decade later, when foreign interest had sagged under mounting disillusionment, Charles Empson included New Granada in his *Narratives of South America; Illustrating Manners, Customs, and Scenery . . .* (London, 1836). Kaleidoscopic and impressionistic, his writing entwined truth with legend. Naturalist Empson, lured from Yorkshire to South America by the writings of Humboldt, was the kind of person that like-minded Isaac Holton would have understood.

Amid varying degrees of approval and disapproval of life in contemporary New Granada, all of the first generation of foreign writers underscored many of the unchanging ingredients in that way of life.

At mid-century New Granada was off the agenda of intense concern. Then the traveler was not blazing the trails of initial commercial concessions, nor was he trying to settle claims or press other great interests, political or economic. Then it was, with no narrow range of duty or outlook prompting his travel, that Isaac F. Holton produced a book, *New Granada: Twenty Months in the Andes*, that exceeded the standards of reliability, breadth of coverage, and readability achieved by most of his predecessors and successors.

*New Granada: Twenty Months in the Andes* is the fullest and best-written assessment of that country at mid-century by a foreign observer. Based on a diary but structured so that it represents a lot of extra labor, *New Granada* is almost totally the fresh eyewitness account of a patiently sympathetic and intelligently curious traveler. No theme— geographical, climatic, transportational, economic, social, religious, educational, or political failed to interest and inspire its author. At all times the specific and the general are so intermingled as to avoid the narrowness of the former and the fuzziness of the latter. As novelty is attended by curiosity, so, too, Holton's facts are accompanied by reflection. Even as the text informally instructs the general reader, so the appendixes exhibit to scholars the scientific precision to which the writer also aspired. Because the writing is both casual and precise, it merits the high praise it has repeatedly received from students of Colombian life.

Holton's adaptable nature is evident in his assessment of a trip he made to Ibagué. "Although in these five days I saw no floor but earth, and but few tables (those not spread, except with my coarse utensils), no beds but dried hides, neither teacup, tumbler, metal spoon, looking glass, newspaper, book, or pamphlet," he declared, "it was one of the most delightful trips I have ever taken." Afloat on the Magdalena on a tedious trip upstream, Holton was remembering the Connecticut, the Hudson, the Ohio, and the Mississippi Rivers when he wrote, "I cannot understand how these fertile banks can remain, washed almost weekly by the waves from steamboats, but without commerce, and nearly without inhabitant."

Because he never became a good judge of horseflesh, the North American suffered many torments in overland travel but when it came to nighttime relaxation he enthused about one of his Colombian discoveries, the hammock. "I am ready to pronounce it," he declared, "one of the cheapest luxuries known."

A capacity for producing thumbnail sketches of people, places, and circumstances definitely enriches his writing. Months of residence in Bogotá led Holton to observe, "The normal way of living here is to hire a house or a 'habitation,' and either eat at a fonda, have your meals sent in to you from a fonda, or hire a cook. This last implies either that you also go to market and have your provisions stolen at home, or send your cook to market to steal your money." His low estimate of servants persisted, as when he wrote, "It is not wise to turn off a servant for peculation, for you may get in his place one who has been long out of employment, and who, consequently, has some months' back stealing to do."

The fountain in the plaza of Guaduas attracted the attention of the male visitor. "The water girls," Holton noted, "come here with a large earthen jar—múcura—slung so as to rest on their hips, and a long tube in their hand. The múcura is placed on the low wall, one end of the long reed—often terminating in a cow's horn—applied to the mouth of one of the iron tubes, and thus the stream conducted to the múcura. When a múcura is nearly full, a struggle often occurs between two expectants, each desirous to fit her horn to the spout as soon as the other leaves it."

Humorous understatement enlivens many experiences, including one in Bogotá. "While here," Holton recalled, "I paid the common matriculation fee to a residence—an attack of the diarrhea." At Paila, on 9 July 1853, a diary entry tersely proclaimed, "Had a capital day. Dreamed of home last night; had recent beef for dinner; got a new plant, caught a butterfly, and *killed a flea.*"

A botanist, Holton was forever pouncing on green things—in patios, along the trail, even over the brink of a waterfall. A teacher, Holton visited schools wherever he went. "I volunteered some suggestions," he wrote of a visit to a girls' school, "among which were to get the garden cultivated, to fix the chimney in the kitchen so that it could be used, to pray less, and sing more."

In one of his recurring moments of political pessimism, he declared, "Perhaps New Granada is governed too much." The behavior of native visitors in the halls of the congress in Bogotá further depressed him. "The spectators are called the barra," he wrote. "Their conduct is outrageous, often disturbing the proceedings with cries and insults against some of the members, and always with impunity."

An active Presbyterian, Holton disapproved of many aspects of the religious life but no surge of evangelical zeal ever led him to assume the role of missionary. Many fiesta activities disgusted him, among others those encountered on St. John's Day. "My conclusion from all this is, that the beloved disciple was fond of horse racing, dram drinking, shouting, and gunpowder. . . ." Concerning church bells, unprejudiced timelessness attends his remark, "There is no tolling, no solemn peals, but a rang-a-tang-tang on all occasions, and as in all the city there must be over one hundred of them, they can make considerable noise."

To most towns he reacted negatively. Of one river community he remarked, "Honda is all stone and tile, so that never had an obsolete old place harder work to tumble down, and it would not have succeeded without the respectable aid of a few earthquakes." Of another town he wrote, "Melgar is one of those market towns whose existence is a nut for politico-economists. Imagine, in the middle of an uncultivated plain a large town of mud and thatch, with a church, chapel, and a public square, without a trace of industry."

In addition to camera-like portraits of Colombian

life, Holton reflected about many matters. Of travelers, he remarked, "A man needs to be a year in a country before he can begin the study of the character of its inhabitants to advantage." Of Colombian life, he remarked, "The key to all this is a want of education in the masses. They are tolerant of hunger; of comforts they know nothing, and desire none." After regaling his readers with a dawn-to-dusk recital of activities on a Colombian ranch, Holton concluded, "If some Rip Van Winkle should wake from a sleep of two centuries, the only thing to surprise him would be the dawn of civil and religious liberty."

One century later a long-term sleeper might awaken to challenge those conclusions, but unchallenged is the essential worth of Holton's writing about an alien and complex culture.

Carrying a preface dated in the autumn of 1856, *New Granada: Twenty Months in the Andes* was published early in 1857 by Harper and Brothers. Although the title remained in print for many years, no other edition was ever printed.

Isaac Farwell Holton was born 30 August 1812 in the Connecticut River country of southeastern Vermont. There, at the edge of Westminster, he spent his early youth on "a rocky little farm." His early formal education included four years (1824–28) at Berwick Academy in South Berwick, Maine, a brief interval at the Limerick (Maine) Academy, and finally the year 1831–32 at Amherst Academy. At all of these institutions young Holton assisted the teaching staff as well as pursuing his own studies.

A freshman at Amherst College in 1832, Holton remained there until he received his A.B. degree, in 1836. Little is known of his interests and activities in that period, except that his formal commencement contribution was a disputation: "Ought the attempts to civilize the Indians of this country to be abandoned?" We do not know which side he upheld but in terms of those later years which found him concerned about the spiritual well-being of mankind and the glories of nature, he might have argued either the affirmative or the negative with conviction.

Moving south to New York City, Holton continued his education at Union Theological Seminary from 1837 to 1839. Licensed by the Third Presbytery of New York on 1 August 1839, the young Presbyterian churchman soon set out for home missionary duty in sparsely settled Illinois. Much of the way he trudged on foot, carrying his limited belongings. Between 1840 and 1845 Holton was situated in west central Illinois, teaching Greek and natural history at the Reverend David Nelson's Mission Institute at Quincy, and serving as a missionary in McDonough, Adams, and Pike Counties. In this period, as well as during a brief stint as principal of a school near Natchez, Mississippi, Holton came to know steamboats and river life, both of which he recalled time and again during his stay in New Granada.

Unmarried, footloose, and endlessly curious, Holton continued to move about, both physically and intellectually. Recipient of an M.A. degree from Amherst in 1846, he may or may not have been on that campus that year. The mathematical turn of Holton's mind shone through in his "Essay on Musical Intonation and Temperament" in the *Annals of the Lyceum of Natural History of New York* (January, 1847). Between 1848 and 1852 he was professor of botany at the New York College of Pharmacy and sexton of the Houston Street Presbyterian Church. Whether the latter duty was a labor of love or proof of the inadequacy of his teaching salary remains unknown. During this time in New York, Holton formed a lifelong friendship with Dr. John Torrey. Sixteen years older than Holton and initially trained in medicine, Torrey had for many years dedicated his leisure to scientific pursuits, especially botany. The older man's interests and achievements, including a remarkable aptitude for descriptive botany, challenged Holton. Torrey's laborious survey of the flora of the state of New York, as well as his systematic study of the flora of North America at large, quite possibly shaped Holton's approach to New Granada and its plant life.

"The botanist cannot study the productions of the torrid zone," Holton later wrote, "without a strong desire to see with his own eyes the regions of perpetual summer." The scanty information available concerning New Granada, combined with its botanical wealth, led Holton to focus his attention on that country.

On 21 August 1852 the bespectacled, bachelor botanist, carrying two bales of paper for drying plants but no passport for himself, first glimpsed a tropical landscape. He had read Acosta, Boussingault, Steuart, Duane, and Humboldt and Bonpland; and he was carrying an expensive and treasured copy of one of S. F. L. Endlicher's botanical works as well as a number of letters of introduction. For twenty unhurried months on itineraries of his own choosing, he traveled widely, visiting many areas more than once. When he bade farewell to New Granada in mid-May, 1854, his luggage contained approximately 1,800 botanical specimens, a diary crowded with details and vast quantities of data concerning political subdivisions, mail routes, altitude, climate, weights and measures, etc.

Returning to the United States, Holton served the College of New Jersey, at Princeton, as lecturer in chemistry and natural history during the single academic year 1854–55. In 1855–56 he preached irregularly at Meredith Village, in central New Hampshire. During these first two years following his stay in South America, Holton, in addition to his duties as teacher and clergyman, was busy composing an account of his experiences in New Granada. By the time he went to Vermont to assume his responsibilities as Burr Professor of Chemistry and Natural History at Middlebury College in the autumn of 1856 his hefty manuscript was complete.

During Holton's year at Middlebury his book was published and he met and wooed Susanne Warner of nearby Cornwall. Simultaneous with his venture upon the sea of matrimony, forty-six-year-old Isaac Holton again turned from teaching to the ministry. He and his bride journeyed to northernmost Illinois where, between 1858 and 1863, he preached in McHenry County at the small communities of Lawrence, Chemung and Alden. At Lawrence, on 1 May 1860, he was ordained by the Presbytery of Belvidere. After five years of service he again moved, this time to the McDonough County he had known in 1840.

Pastor of a small church at Hillsgrove, Illinois, and father of the growing family that came to count two sons and two daughters, Holton was barely eking out a living. To supplement his slender income, he again turned to writing. Very briefly the *New York Observer* offered him $4.00 per column. Next, without pay, he contributed book reviews and other minor items to a newspaper in Portsmouth, New Hampshire. A crowning economic blow came late in 1864 when he learned that without expensive litigation he could not obtain title to the small plot of land that he had cleared and cultivated. Willing to turn his back once more on Illinois, he applied for a chaplaincy in a colored regiment. During these months of despair a renewed correspondence with an old friend who had recently become joint owner and editor of the *Boston Recorder* presented Holton with a favorable prospect.

In mid-1865 the Holton family moved to Boston, where Isaac entered upon his duties with the *Recorder*. When the *Congregationalist* absorbed that publication, he continued on the staff of the new paper. Likewise when the *Daily News* began publication, Holton became one of its editors. When, in 1872, Amherst College sent questionnaires to her alumni, Holton filled the blank left for "any other facts that may be of special interest to classmates," by inserting, "Own a house and garden (precisely three miles due north of Bunker Hill Monument) in the town of Everett, corner of Belmont and Hancock Streets, where we shall be happy to see any of them." In excellent health and seemingly rid of the wanderlust which previously had never found him in any one place as long as five years, Holton collapsed and died early in 1874.

One of the finest and most accurate tributes paid Holton came from famed botanist Asa Gray, who wrote, "Professor Holton was a very able scientific man, who would have been eminent as a botanist if he could have followed his bent in this direction. His pursuits and tastes were too multifarious, and his life too unselfish for achieving the distinction and worldly success which he well deserved. His ambition mainly showed itself in his zeal for helping others, and in forwarding their interests without regard to his own."

The man who had been many things—teacher, missionary, traveler, scientist, minister, and journalist—left as the finest monument to his endless quest for knowledge his book *New Granada: Twenty Months in the Andes.*

The editor's role, in addition to the Introduction, has included the following: deletion of the original preface, maps, illustrations, hearsay, repetitious and historical passages, and the appendix; the restructuring of the table of contents and the chapter headings and the consolidation of some chapters; and some corrections in punctuation and spelling. The words are always those of author Holton. This abridged edition has been derived from the American edition of 1857.

The kind assistance of Rena Durkan, Curatrix, at Amherst College and Lockwood Merriman, College Archivist, at Middlebury College is gratefully acknowledged. Information which they provided has helped to reveal an otherwise obscure author.

C. HARVEY GARDINER

"The Oaks"
Murphysboro, Illinois
March 1, 1967

# New Granada:
## *Twenty Months in the Andes*

# I

## SANTA MARTA, SABANILLA, AND BARRANQUILLA

The unfortunate traveler bound for Bogotá, whose impatience leads him to leave his vessel at Santa Marta, has first some leagues to go by land, then to take a canoe or small boat over ponds and through narrow channels, till he counts himself happy to reach Remolino. Brief happiness, if he finds no steamer there! I have seen Remolino, and should judge that a detention there would be worse than a residence in one of our prisons in dog days. The town, when I visited it, had been recently overflowed—no uncommon occurrence, I should judge, by the eight-inch dike that promises defense to the town from the river.

Santa Marta, I am told, has no good harbor. Though sheltered from the prevailing wind from the northeast, still ships will drag their anchors rather than face the gusts that come down the mountains back of the town. As for piers, where a ship may lie to discharge and take in freight, you must not expect such a thing in South America.

At Santa Marta you leave the mountains, and at length, in following on west, you lose the land entirely if the weather is not very clear. After some hours, a fringe of bushes appears on your left, suggesting rather the idea of a submerged thicket than a shore. At length the ship enters muddy water—she is sailing across the mouth of the Magdalena. The fresh water, even when surcharged with mud, is lighter than sea water, and floats on the surface; but here may be seen a rare phenomenon. The tawny flood that is spreading over the top of the sea strikes against the south side of the vessel, but cannot pass under. In place of it boils up clear sea water on the north side. It remains unmixed with the fresh water so long as you can see it.

At length there appears over the low trees a large

white building. It is the customhouse (aduana) of Sabanilla. It gives you good hopes of the country to see so fine
a building, for it appears, at least, good enough for a
second-rate port in the United States.

The flag of our Union is hoisted to call a pilot, and
in due time a boat is seen approaching. It is something to
see a new face after a voyage of twenty days; but to see
one of another race and nation in his own home, un-
altered by travel, is enough to excite a deep interest in
anyone who is just beginning his foreign wanderings. The
boat contained the pilot, his little son, and a Negro. The
pilot and his boy had on enough clothes, and dirty enough,
but the Negro was half-naked, and of a stupid, vacant
countenance. I could not refer the other two to any one
of the five races of man, but it seemed as if three of them,
at least, had contributed to the blood in their veins.

Now the word is given, and the anchor is let go! It is
an event in a man's life, when, for weeks, he has been
moving, with no visible object to mark his progress or fix
his situation, whose ideas of locality have all been cooped
into the space of a few yards, to find his ship, so long a
world by itself, again part of the great world. Yes, our
position is fixed, and what we see now we shall see tomorrow in the same places. We are twenty or thirty rods
from a shore that runs north and south along the foot of
a low, green hill, covered with sparse woods. On that hill,
southwest of us, is the pretentious, unoccupied customhouse, and at the foot a group of sheds, and a little wharf
where boats can land; there is none for ships. I ask for the
town, and they show me a few acres of low flat land and
low thatched roofs two miles south. There is Sabanilla,
and the nearest residences of men.

Scarcely had the anchor reached the bottom, when
another boat approached, with a more numerous company of health officers and customhouse men. Contrary to
all the predictions of the captain, they pronounced me
free to go ashore when I liked. For a fortnight, no occasion
had been lost of impressing on my mind that I was to be

taken off the ship by a file of soldiers, carried to prison, kept there till the vessel was ready to leave, and then put aboard again. So much was the captain's mind exercised by this, that he declared he would never carry another passenger without seeing that his passport was in due form, and the first item of his report to the collector, of the contents of his ship, was, "One passenger without a passport."

The town of Sabanilla is as dense as any factory village, and as much more homely than they can be as mud and thatch is worse than brick and slate. Not a tree, bush, or weed is found in the streets; but a few steps brought me to an opening in a fence, where I pounced upon a bush in flower—the first green thing within reach of my hands. It was Laguncularia racemosa, a common Antillan Combretate shrub. I fell at once to dissecting its peculiar fruit. It left a permanent mark on my bright new knife from its corrosive juice.

A little farther on I saw the papaya—Carica Papaya —well translated by the word papaw. Unfortunately, we have applied the name to a very different plant, the Asiminia triloba, that has nothing in common with the true papaw. The branchless tree, ten feet high, with the flowers, often unisexual, clustered about the summit of the almost hollow stem, is at once recognized by anyone who has a previous idea of this peculiar genus. I find there are other species of them, but if any of them have the strange property of making meat tender, it is unsuspected here. I found later a Jamaica gentleman, who "knew of a man" who used the leaves to pack meat in for this purpose, but I would like to see the matter made the subject of scientific experiment.

The next thing that caught my eye was huge Cactate stems, on the sandhill back of the town. They are triangular, and ten feet high. I have never found flowers on them, but one of them must be the famous night-blooming Cereus grandiflorus, or an allied species.

It seems as if all the houses or huts of Sabanilla might

be taverns or stores. A remarkable prevalence of bottles
and absence of casks strikes you on entering the stores.
The first place I went into was a large, almost vacant
room, the house, perhaps, of some customhouse officer.
I saw an object on the floor that I took for a large monkey
at the first glance, but, to my disgust, a second view
showed it to be a baby, naked, and of the precise color of
the earth of the floor on which it was crawling. A similar
specimen of the same species I saw in another house
swinging in a hammock, a piece of dry hide being placed
under the child.

The next house I entered was formally "placed at my
disposition," which simply means that I am welcome. Its
inhabitants seemed to be a woman, who may have been
a widow (you can never tell widows here); her son, a
customs' guard; and Joaquín Calvo, M.D., a customhouse officer. They kindly proposed to procure me a horse
to go next day to Barranquilla, distant about eight miles,
directly up the river.

Some horsemen rode past while I was sitting with
them, and fairly started me to my feet with the flaming
colors of their ruanas. Those of the better class may be
regarded as striped shawls, woven of thread cotton, with
a few inches of seam left unsewed in the center to admit
the head. The name of poncho, by which we best know
them, must not be used in some parts of the country, and
is little used anywhere. The heavier article, made of two
thicknesses of flannel or blanket, often thick enough to
shed water, is called a bayetón. Ruanas may cost from
two to five dollars; a good bayetón, an article no traveler
should be without, costs about eight dollars. When made
of India-rubber cloth it is called an encauchado.

One hut of two rooms had the shop in one room, and
the other served as a family room and for the public
school. This consisted of about a dozen boys. It is contrary
to law to have girls and boys in the same school, and as
it is only large places that can maintain two public
schools, girls must generally learn as they can at home,

or, as is too often the case, go ignorant. I now look at Sabanilla with a more experienced eye, and conclude that it is the meanest town that I have seen in New Granada, and its school is also the poorest. Here I saw naked boys in school. Elsewhere it would not be allowed. The teacher was a mere boy, and the school was almost completely destitute of books. But it is a credit to such a town to have a school at all, when it has no church.

Under the hill, at the wharf, the low sheds belong to a foreign firm in New Granada, and are rented to the government. Here I saw the collector and inspector passing goods. Their swords and pistols were lying on the table by them, and their attendants were ripping open every bale, broaching every cask, opening every box, and weighing all things, wet and dry. Such is the law. The inspector placed the weights on the scale, and the collector recorded their several weights. If the weights of the several parcels were nearly equal, the vigilance of the officers would relax a little after probing, ripping, and broaching some fifty parcels.

I do not suppose smuggling is impossible at Sabanilla, but its chief difficulty is not in the seal on the main hatch and the watchman on board, but rather in the uninhabited state of the country around the landing. Much, however, may be done by bribery, and many officers will be found open to it. In the short interval that our vessel lay in the harbor, I believe nearly all the officers of the port were changed. The displaced collector asked my certificate that he was not intoxicated when he visited us, and I readily gave it.

The next day was my ride to Barranquilla. I started early to avoid the heat, and took a cup of coffee at the house where they offered me the horse. I never tasted so good coffee before in my life, and I am sorry to say that, in all my subsequent travels, I have not seen another cup like it. There was a fragrance about it that I should like to meet again.

This ride might be called one of the epochs of my life.

A botanist feels a growing desire to visit the tropics every time that he examines or arranges plants from the sunny lands. The difficulty of gratifying the desire generally grows with its growth and strengthens with its strength, and remains for life a case of stable equilibrium or equal balance of centrifugal and centripetal forces. In my case the centripetal force had proved too weak, and here I was traversing the space I had so long desired to enter. It was like an illimitable conservatory.

It is said that the traveler retains for life a peculiar affection for the first spot where his feet have pressed a tropical soil. Certain it is that my mind turns back with strong longings from the happier scenes that now surround me to the lower Magdalena. I may be obliged to confess it is a dry, sterile, desolate region, with inhabitants few and far between, and of the ruder cast of Granadinos; but I love it, and always shall, next to the rocky little farm that I first called home. But what a contrast!

The farm in Westminster, Vermont, could boast the best assortment of rocks, the finest and tallest snowdrifts, and the most diminutive trout I ever knew, while my new love was blazing with a tropical drought and burning sand, a very paradise for lizards.

In the day's ride I found no houses except at a small town called La Playa—the beach. It has a small plaza— the almost universal center of a Spanish town, with a few miserable huts ranged around it. Sabanilla has no plaza. Towns here are laid out by authority, and are rarely irregular or straggling. The plaza is sometimes paved, and is generally the seat of a weekly market, almost always on the Sabbath, so as to secure a better attendance on the church on that day.

Soon after leaving La Playa, I fell in with the mail carrier. He was on a mule, on a saddle somewhat resembling a saw horse. The four horns were very convenient to hang things on. On one of them hung perhaps the cheapest pair of shoes possible. They call them albarcas. They were mere soles of raw hide, with a loop to put the great toe through, and perhaps some leather thongs to tie them on with. His hammock helped to cushion his sawhorse, and from one side projected his sword. He was bearer of the weekly mail from Barranquilla to the customhouse at Sabanilla.

In all my ride I saw nothing of the river, and but one field, and that contained nothing but maize. The first symptom of approaching Barranquilla was that my companion stopped by the roadside to dress himself. Next, the heads of palms appeared, the first I had seen in my trip, except a low species. Those now before me were cocoas growing in the gardens of Barranquilla. Like the mail carrier, I too had my toilet to make; for the lady at Sabanilla had taught me to roll my coat up in my handkerchief, wrapping it in diagonally, and tying the two free corners around my waist. I stopped at the very edge of the town to put it on.

Barranquilla looks much better than Sabanilla, for the houses are all whitewashed, according to law, and some of them are of two stories. I did not at once learn the first radical distinction between houses as tiled or thatched. It seems to be thought that the best possible thatched house is inferior to the poorest tiled one. At this place the thatch appeared to be cattail flag—Typha; but farther up, it is of the same leaves as the Panama hats— iraca, Carludovica palmata. In all cases thatch is called paja, straw.

I came up mainly to deliver letters of introduction from the Granadan minister in the United States to the governor, and to Señor José María Pino, one of the chief merchants of this region. I found the latter in his warehouse, where he received me very politely, offering me a glass of wine. I capitulated for lemonade. He insisted on my spending the night in town, and furnished me a guide to Mrs. Creighton's house, the only decent stopping place in town, where I paid at the rate of eighty cents a day. Here he did me the honor of a call in the evening.

Barranquilla boasts a private school and a public

school for boys, but no school for girls that we could call
one. Even two girls, taught in the same house, would make
a school, according to the governor's report, which states
the number of female schools in the province to be about
five, and the number of scholars some twenty or twenty-
five. The public schools are all professedly on the Lancasterian plan, and the variations are deteriorations, not
improvements. A great clumsy wheel, five feet in diameter, with the written alphabet on its circumference, is
the most useless part of the furniture. The teacher here is
a young man, but of some education, and, among other
accomplishments, can read a little English.

New Granada is divided into one state, twenty-two
provinces, and three territories; in 1851 these contained
one hundred and thirty cantons, subdivided into eight
hundred and sixteen districts, and seventy aldeas or ham-
lets. These last have the local government concentrated
into fewer hands than in the districts.

The national government is called gobierno, its executive presidente, and its legislature congreso. The provincial government is gobernación, its executive gobernador, and its legislature cámara provincial. The executive of a canton is jefe político; it has no legislature.
The executive of a district is the alcalde, and the legislature cabildo. The district is distrito, formerly called
distrito parroquial and parroquia, or parish. Vice-par-
roquia is a parish dependent on another for occasional
services of its cura, or parish priest, who was, till Sep-
tember, 1853, an officer of the distrito as much as the
alcalde is. There are no parroquias nor vice-parroquias
now.

Aldea is a partially organized distrito; territorio is a
partially organized provincia; both are thinly inhabited,
while the Estado de Panamá has conceded to it more independence from the central authority than have the
provinces.

Barranquilla is the seat of gobernación or provincial
government for the province of Sabanilla. I had a letter

for the previous governor, and called with it on the present incumbent, Señor Julián Ponce, and had a very interesting call, but declined his invitation to dine with him, fearing to incommode him.

The gobernación always gives employment to one or two men besides the governor. He was appointed by the president formerly, and appointed the head of the government of the canton (jefe político), and he, in his turn, the chief of the district (alcalde). Perhaps New Granada is governed too much. The gobernación here occupies the lower story of the governor's house.

This has been the arrangement, but much is changed in the new constitution. The cantones have no legal existence or officers. Many officers appointed are now to be elected. Among these are the governors who are still to be the agents of the president, though they may be his personal enemies. Thus they may interfere in any national matter, as mails or military movements. I fear this cannot last.

I visited also the provincial prison. It has a hall with two rooms on each side. The keeper (alcaide) was at work making shoes. He was the first man that I saw at work on land in the country. If I saw any other work here, it was sawing boards, by two men, using a rude contrivance to elevate one end of the log so that one could stand partly beneath it. The prison was not very full or very clean, but the most objectionable feature was that the windows of two rooms opened on the street. No prison here is made of anything stronger than rammed earth or unburned bricks. Of course, the volition of the prisoner must have much to do with the duration of his captivity in such a pen. The laws of different provinces differ as to whether the prisoners shall be fed at the cost of the province. In all, they beg from the windows whenever they can.

My only other call of interest was at the church. I was first conducted to an old priest, who had a sort of study in an upper room of the church. He assures me that things have gone wrong ever since the king of Spain lost his power here. He is the only man that I have found that had the frankness or imprudence to avow this opinion. As the Cuban government is now the only remaining specimen of Spanish domination in the New World, we cannot easily appreciate too highly the loss that New Granada suffered at the overthrow of the power of Spain.

We descended to the church, my hat being carefully removed before crossing the threshold. It is a vast shell, with an earth floor. The principal altar is at one end, but along both sides are placed secondary altars that are rarely used for mass. There are no seats in this church. The priest stated that the town greatly needed a larger and better church, though this is but half-filled even on special occasions.

The organ particularly attracted my attention. It was of parlor size, but had outside it two huge pairs of bellows that require two men to blow them. The carpentry around the organ was rather coarse, but it was ornamented with a row of trumpet-shaped pipes, projecting horizontally from the front, and the front row of the remaining pipes had faces painted on them, long and narrow, like the reflection of the face from the back of a spoon. The cura has an assistant.

## II

## CARTAGENA AND BEYOND

The navigator who sails from Sabanilla to Cartagena has both wind and current in his favor. As he nears its white walls, he wonders to have finished his voyage so soon. He has not finished it. He must pass the town entirely to reach Boca Grande, the large mouth of the harbor.

You anchor at an inconvenient distance from town. Will commerce never demand decent wharves here? What would Boston or New York be without wharves? How would Liverpool dispense with her docks? You land on a boat wharf as free from commerce, perhaps, as the Battery at New York; passing through a thick wall, you are at last in Cartagena.

It is the first and only walled town I have ever seen. I look at its defenses with amazement. They seem to have cost as much as all the buildings within them. A good, well-equipped railroad to the Magdalena would have cost much less. First, here is an island entirely walled in, except that certain waste grounds, that would have made the wall too irregular in its form, were left between it and the sea.

I can only speak of these works as a layman. Next to their cost, the most observable thing is the compactness they give the town. Cartagena is finished—has been so a long time; it looks as if it might have been a hundred years. Room is precious within fortifications, so the streets are narrow, the houses of two stories, and the plazas small. Withal, there is an air of neatness about it, notwithstanding that rainwater is sold by the cask, that really does one good to see.

Scarce as space is within the city, the walls furnish an exceedingly delightful promenade. Everywhere you find water on one hand, and the old, sleepy town on the other. There is another fine walk on the beach, between the

13

walls and the water, where those who do not fear sharks too much may take a nice sea bath. I saw little use made of either of these facilities, perhaps because my stay was so short. For the same reason, I saw none of the many pretty drives that there are in the neighborhood of the city. If you are to go to the interior, you must here take leave of all wheeled conveyances, unless it may be in Bogotá.

I love Cartagena, and for many reasons. Not the least is, that it is the residence of that model of American consuls, Ramón León Sánchez. Mr. Sánchez is an annexed citizen of the United States, having been a Spanish subject in Florida. Speaking both languages with facility, for a long time a resident of Cartagena, an experienced merchant and a polished gentleman, if anything is wanted to enable him to serve his countrymen, it must be the will to do so, and of this will I have never heard of anyone that has yet found him lacking. Never had I more need of a friend than when I arrived in Cartagena without a single letter, for I had not anticipated a visit to this city; but letters would be of little use if all men were like Mr. Sánchez. From all the letters that I carried to South America, there did not result one half so much pleasure or profit as I have experienced in the bosom of that excellent family. Mr. Sánchez has long been consul here. Were the office a more profitable one, it would doubtless, ere this, have been taken from him to reward some maker of stump speeches or puller of wires, who, leaving his family and interests in the United States, would hastily come and gather as many dollars as the length of his harvest would permit.

I took leave of Cartagena with great regret, and a strong desire to revisit it, or to meet elsewhere Mr. and Mrs. Sánchez, and the amiable sister of the latter; and my memory of those brief happy days stands in strong contrast with much that I have seen this side of there. To one who arrives here inexperienced in wheelless traveling, the advice and assistance of the good consul is invaluable. It seems incredible that your two trunks will ever be mounted on the back of a mule. You are told to have them even in number, each pair of equal size and weight, and not much to exceed one hundred pounds each; and if you neglect this, dear is the penalty you pay. An article of freight may exceed the ordinary limits, and, with time and money, it will reach its destination, but to the traveler such detention would be worse than the entire sacrifice of his baggage.

Every trunk ought to have a waterproof cap, covering it entirely except the bottom, or, in default of this, it must be encumbered with an encerado. This is a stiff, sticky cloth, waterproof with pitch or paint. It is tied on with a rope that you do not pretend to untie with your own hands. I have paid eighty cents per trunk for encerados and ropes.

You must own the ropes that tie on the encerados. The peons will steal them if they can, for they have a great propensity to stealing anything of the nature of string. Nothing would be secure from them, from a needleful of thread to a cable. The ropes for the hammocks and encerados are called incorrectly lazo, which means running knot or noose. Ropes of rawhide, rejo, are sometimes used to tie encerados, and always to tie the cargas to the mule. These ropes are furnished with the beasts. Whiplashes are made generally of slender rejo, so the lash is translated by rejo.

Provisions for the journey are often put in cubical cases of nearly two feet on a side, made of leather, and lined within; these are called petacas. If roughly made and not lined, they are atillos.

Your next concern is to secure cattle—bestias—a term that includes horses, oxen, female mules (mulas), and male mules (machos). If the number you require be five or more, you pay for the number you hire, and the hired man—peon—is paid by the owner of the cattle; if the number be less, the peon is paid for as an additional bestia. Thus four beasts cost you the same as five. It would be difficult to force them to make an exception to the rule, if not impossible. The peon is to feed himself and his cattle from his employer's purse; he is also your servant to bring you water to wash, hang your hammock, etc.; indeed, the limits of his rights and duties are not well defined. At the ferry you pay your fare and that of your baggage; he pays his and that of the cattle, if the boat helps them to swim.

Your peon cannot load his mules alone, but only in an emergency will call on you to hold one trunk against the side of the animal while he puts on its fellow and ties them together. A load is called a carga, and its two component halves, tercios. The peon throws his ruana over the mule's head to cover his eyes so that he will stand still. Then he puts on a pair of cushions called an enjalma. Next he brings one tercio or half-load, and places it against the animal's side, where someone must hold it while he places its fellow—compañero—on the opposite side, and ties them together.

When all are loaded, it will be prudent for you to see the peon and cargas safe off before losing sight of them. You need not keep with them all day, but it makes a great difference whether you are before or behind them. If you go before, they travel rather better; but it may happen, if you pass at five o'clock a place where there is to be a ball or a frolic, that something will happen to some of the cargas that will render it impossible for them to reach the place where you are innocently waiting for them. Your best remedy will be to believe all the peon says, but watch him better next time; and count yourself happy if your bedding do not line his nest on a night you have to do without it, or if you get it again uninfested with blood-thirsty parasites.

Turbaco is called nearly two and a half leguas from Cartagena. Unless you can find two measures given, you can in no case be sure of what league is used. I follow this rule: understand all leagues to be common Castilian ones unless there is evidence to the contrary. A league is an hour's journey of a baggage mule in good weather, with an ordinary load and no drawbacks. You can never calculate on performing more than this, but you will find a thousand good reasons for making less. So I call Turbaco eight miles from Cartagena.

A long night-ride, in which a French gentleman in the India-rubber business was fortunately my companion, and unfortunately my baggage was not, brought me to Arjona. As I never saw the place, having entered long after dark, and left it before daylight, I can say little, except that it has a plaza and quite a number of houses, and a posada, or stopping place, where it was quite difficult to make a supper. We gave our horses postmeat, the usual treatment of hired horses in New Granada. In plain English, we left them tied, starving, as we could do no better. A man who lets you his horse never expects you to feed it more than to sustain life, and the letting of a horse is often prudently coupled with the condition that, if it die from any cause whatever, the loss shall be yours. I would not like to lend or let a horse to a Granadino without this slight provision for the animal's comfort.

Our posada, or stopping place for the night, was a tienda or small shop. These tiendas may be considered as a house with two rooms, one of which has a counter run across it before the front door, and behind the counter another door, opening into the other room—sala, or parlor, as I will call it. The sala is the dancing room and sleeping room, and generally also the dining room. We ate, as an exception, in a sort of shed, which connected the house with the kitchen.

I had first slept in a hammock in Barranquilla, and I am ready to pronounce it one of the cheapest luxuries known. To read in, by day or night, no bed can equal it. You can vary your posture as you please, on your back or side, diagonally or parallel, and you never find it hard, and I, for one, never tire of it. Many complain that the constant use of the hammock injures their chest, tending to roll them up into a ball; but I have thus far experienced no such inconvenience. And although they say that there are in this country bedbugs more formidable than any we know, they never molest one in a hammock; nor do fleas, with all their agility, manage so often to take up their quarters with you as in a bed.

Apropos to fleas and bedbugs, I propose to do justice to the former when I bring my narrative up to Cartago in this happy valley, but as to bedbugs I have not seen one. The Cimex lectularius is said not to live at a greater altitude than 5817 feet. Nor have I, with all annoyances, goats included, suffered so much in any night in New Granada as in my penultimate night in our dear native land, when I relighted my candle in the small hours, held it under my tormentors, and, to use the words of a poet whom I can not quote well from memory, I "gave to grease and vengeance" so many of these hateful creatures as nearly to extinguish it. For the convenience of more unfortunate travelers, I will mention that the Spanish call these novelties that disturb our peace chinches.

Beds are unknown in this country except, so far as I have seen, in Cartagena or near Bogotá. The traveler's usual bed is to lay his bayetón and ruana on the poyo, or bench that runs round the principal apartment of a house —the sala. At the very best, he has a square frame allowed for a bedstead, and nothing more on it than a thickness of the estera—matting used for carpets—laid on a rawhide, stretched as tight as a drumhead. All the addition your host thinks of offering you is a red pillow in a pillowcase open at both ends, trimmed doubtless with some sort of edging or embroidery.

Our bill here was sixty cents for our supper; nothing for the hammock they lent me, and nothing for the posts to which our horses were tied. Early indeed were we on our way, and had not my companion been a baquiano, as they call a man familiar with a road or with any operation (in law-English, an expert), my great haste would have been bad speed. As it is, some five leagues beyond Arjona represent themselves to my mind as a series of man traps and horse traps, with one pond of the most stupendous frogs I ever heard or heard of.

The first thing we shall recognize on the road will be the Dique. So they name a crooked canal that they have laid out from Calamar, on the Magdalena, to the tidewater near Cartagena. At the Dique is a ferry, where every passer who does not live in the province of Cartagena is obliged to pay a dime. When the canal is low and fordable, as now, this tax is called peaje; were the canoe necessary, it would be pasaje; and, were the water bridged, it would be pontazgo. Its chief use is to replenish the provincial treasury, and to drive off commerce and travel to the rival ports of Sabanilla and Santa Marta. These tolls were once part of the national revenue; now, with great imprudence, they are put into the power of the provinces, and they often, as in the present instance, use them to their own detriment.

Mahates or Mate, as they generally call it, is quite a place, thirty-four miles from Cartagena. It is cabecera of a canton. It lies on low ground, and the traveler who thinks of stopping overnight must be forewarned that the Dique keeps them well stocked with mosquitoes. At Arjona there were none. I found a poor dinner rather dear there too.

At Mahates I discovered once the most amusing imposition by which I was ever victimized. I must tell it to you, though you laugh at me. Well, at nine o'clock one night, I leaped off a steamboat that was about making fast at Calamar, on her way down the Magdalena. Breathless, I sought Joaquín Duque, with a letter for him in my hand. In a quarter of a minute I found him, put the letter into his hands, telling him, at the same time, I was a "cabinet courier" of the United States, and that I must be in Cartagena without loss of time.

"How many animals do you need?" he asked.

"Three."

"Three animals, Catalina," he said, turning to his wife; "quick! find Lorenzo!"

Catalina ran one way, and Joaquín another, and in two minutes more both cattle and peon were engaged.

"Will you start now?" asked the "duke."

"No; but at three in the morning."

By this time the boat had been fastened, the plank put out, and leisurely up came a congressman on his way home from Bogotá. He was a personal friend of Duque, and they had a good hearty hug. Then came two more congressmen, then three more, all friends of Joaquín Duque, and all needing animals for saddle and carga. I had not been any too quick in engaging mine.

I hung my hammock and mosquito net in Duque's house, and slept till three, and then found nobody within call. Daylight came—six, seven, and eight. I stormed, and the "Duke" answered presently. The truth was, he had so many animals to get off that he could not find enough. Saddles, too, were wanting, as many of the travelers had brought none. He dared not offend his personal friends by sending me off before them on so frivolous a pretext as that his word was pledged.

But animals (horses and asses—no mules) were assembling, and I took some strange substitute for breakfast. It may have been an enormous quantity of chocolate, with boiled eggs, without bread or anything else. It did not occupy my attention. I paid well for it—twenty cents. Just then Duque inquired if I did not want a gentle horse. I replied, "A gentle horse for a cabinet courier, forsooth! Vaya!" Then I found a man who had a carga and a half was about fixing his half-carga as a sobre-carga, a middle load, over the top of one of my light cargas.

I called out, "To whom am I indebted for this present, and what shall I do with it when I get home?" They took it off.

My horse was saddled, and I saw a peon putting my bridle on another horse. I called to him to put it on my horse.

"I know it is your bridle," said the "duke," "but your horse is not used to such. I will give her the bridle she is used to."

I was too mad at the delay to notice anything else.

We were off at nine. I paid $4.80 each for my carga beasts, and $5.60 for that which I rode.

Well, at Mahates I took off the saddle to rest her a bit, and I was horrified. She was a walking skeleton—skin and bone—minus a good piece of skin on the back.

"Your horse never will reach Arjona," said a by-stander. "She is destroncada."

I know of no English for destroncada, but I knew its meaning too well. It might designate the condition a gun would be in after it had successively lost its stock, lock, barrel, and ramrod.

Just then a peon of Duque's arrived. He brought the pleasing intelligence that one of my baggage beasts had given out, and that one of my cargas was some leagues behind.

"Tell me nothing of my cargas," I replied; "but if you do not wish it to cost Señor Duque all he is worth, do you look me out a horse without a moment's delay."

This was precisely what he was going to do. The price of an animal from Mahates to Cartagena is perhaps $1.50, and better animals at that than at Calamar at $5.60. So the duke gained some $4.00 by the services of poor Rackabones, who really had gone remarkably well considering her condition. I confess I was angry enough for an instant, but my wrath gave place to mirth when I discovered what sort of "bridle she had been used to." It was no bridle at all, but merely a headstall with reins attached to it! Duque had got short of bridles for some of his friends who had neglected to bring their own, and, not daring to offer them this thing, had ingeniously borrowed mine.

As to my cargas I never took pains to inquire. I never doubted that it was not my beast that gave out, as my cargas were considerably under weight. Either they selected for mine the weaker beasts, or, one of the others failing, they changed him for mine. Now I have told my story, not for the amusement of those who sit at home to laugh at me, but for the benefit of any poor wight that may have to follow my steps. Let such "avoid entangling alliances" when he is in a hurry, and see that his peon has nothing to do with any man with whom he is unacquainted, and particularly let him learn to be, what I shall never become, a judge of horseflesh.

But let us be off from Mahates, a place of dear dinners and cheap horses. We enter next a rolling country, covered with wood all the way to Arroyo Hondo. Arroyo Hondo is not worthy of the name of a village; but the remaining cluster of houses, bearing the lovely name of Sapo (toad), is altogether poorer yet. There was not another house till we came to Calamar. We are now on level ground.

*III*

# The Magdalena Steamer

Steam on the Magdalena has a long infancy. Bolívar arbitrarily rescinded the first contract, giving a monopoly of it to Mr. Elbers; a second was afterward given him, which he forfeited by delays in the execution of it.

It has been since open to free competition, but the boats were all owned at this time by two companies. The Santa Marta Company had the government for a partner, and, whenever it overtook a mail canoe, carried the mail. The rival interests of Cartagena and Barranquilla maintained the other line, which had no aid from government. Both have since gone down, and an English company, which put on boats wholly unfit for the river, and mismanaged them as none but nonresidents could do, must probably follow.

Still, the enterprise will succeed whenever it shall be put in the right hands. The fare up is ninety-six dollars from Barranquilla to Honda, and the returning fare twenty-four dollars. Freight enough can be had for several boats at nineteen dollars per ton up, and sixteen dollars down.

No happier sight can greet the eyes of a traveler in a dull, mean village like Calamar, on a flat plain, with uninteresting vegetation, than the approach of the steamer he is waiting for. The little naked urchins, clothed in their own skins of nankeen variegated with dirt, shout "Vapor!" the women get their bottles ready, and the lords of creation slowly rise from a recumbent posture and walk down to the bank.

It fell to my lot to be passenger in the "Barranquilla," then under the command of Captain Chapman, an experienced navigator of the sea with sails, but little versed in river craft. Like the Mississippi boats, those of the

Magdalena have but one story for passengers. The deck belongs to the engineers, firemen, and bogas. These last make capital deckhands. Their chief is called contra-maestro; ours bore the name of Pedro, and a strange combination he was of savage and civilized man. He could talk a little English. You are at once brought in contact with him, as he takes charge of the baggage, all of which he will put in his hold. As a particular favor from Captain Chapman, mine was rescued from his clutches and carried up to the cabin.

You should be aware of this arrangement of your baggage before entering the boat. It will often be nearly as much as a thing is worth to get it out of a trunk in a hold that has only a notched timber, at most, for a ladder. If there be much baggage—and every man has a right to two cargas, four trunks—yours may be deeply buried up sometimes, and moved about, from time to time, as un-fortunate passengers, seething in that damp, dark oven, with a dim light, tumble it over in search of some stray trunk. These visits to the bodega, as they call the hold, are terrible. You are covered with perspiration, and ready to drop, and at length make up your mind to do without the most indispensable articles rather than go to that pur-gatory for them.

The "Manzanares" has a ladies' cabin on the same floor as the deck, and, if there are ladies there, they remain by themselves, and eat with the gentlemen of their com-pany. The "Barranquilla" has a little triangular space at the stern that bears the name of ladies' cabin. It is very small indeed, but, as they have very rarely any female pas-sengers, they make it answer. We had only two little girls and their servant, and these slept in the principal cabin. There are no berths. They would impede the cir-culation of air. They give you a cot bedstead, and, if you need any bedding, you will probably have it with you. In a large boatful there will always be some scrambling for the best places, and, if the captain does not interfere actively, the whole cabin will be obstructed by beds soon after six. The rule is not to locate any beds before eight. I hung my hammock, with its mosquito net, and had a very comfortable night's rest. The mosquito net of a hammock is a large bag inverted, with a couple of sleeves for the cords of the hammock to pass through.

We are early risers on steamers. We first roll up our bedding, and put it where it will not be in danger of being disturbed. An attendant takes away the cot. Next comes, with us, the washing; but the Granadinos are not in a hurry for this operation, nor is it always essential to them. It is a little difficult to get water, and often more so to obtain a towel, here not called toalla, but only paño de manos. They are generally made of sheeting, but are embroidered with red at the ends.

You are next invited to take a drink of anisado. Omitting the *d* in words terminating in *ado*, they unite the *a* and *o* into a diphthong like *ou* in *thou*. Anisado is thus clipped into anisáu. It is a sort of rum, distilled, I am told, from the seed of Anethum Fœniculum, called anis. It is much used on the Magdalena. It takes the place of a cup of chocolate, which is not easily prepared on board at this hour. I have seen coffee used as a better substitute.

Breakfast comes about ten. It is spread in a small space between the cabin and the captain's house, that has a roof over it, but is open at the sides. Among other luxuries, they put on the table some square soda biscuit, and butter, that is eagerly dipped out with spoons by persons who scarcely know the article by name. It is universally called, in New Granada, mantequilla, a diminutive of manteca, its lawful name, here reserved entirely for lard. There is an infinite variety of stews, of beef, kid, fowl, etc. The most essential vegetable with me was rice, for plantains were dealt out to us with a very sparing hand, while the bogas were denied rice and bread altogether, and compelled to eat plantains.

It was interesting to see the bogas preparing their dinner. The beef they used is cut up, when on the carcass of the ox, into ropes of meat, that are rubbed in salt, and hung on a pole to dry. This they call tasajo, and a pile of it is enough to sicken one by the mere sight of it. This they cut up in pieces, and stewed in a large iron pot mounted on three stones on a fire built on deck. Three stones thus arranged—tulpas—are the ordinary fireplace of the peasantry here; in a boat they are, of course, placed on a box of earth. They threw in pieces of green plantain till the disgusting broth threatened to run over. When done, they used the carapax of a turtle for a platter, and dipped out the mess, and attacked it with fingers and wooden spoons, till soon they would be scraping the ribs of the turtle. Nothing could sicken me more unless it were a cannibal feast; but one of the passengers told me he would rather have a part of their dinner than of ours. Fish is a popular food here, but seen rarely on the boat; it is too cheap. On the rivers it is only surpassed in cheapness by plantains.

We have not yet been over the whole boat. The captain's house is a little room, with two little closets, between the dining space and the chimney. The dining space would accommodate about twenty, but they seldom have so many passengers. There is a considerable space of open air around the chimney, and then succeeds the pilot-house. The pilots are picked out from among the bogas, and are utterly incompetent for their duties. The captain and the engineer divide the pilot's responsibility between them. The pilots are chosen because they know the river, its rocks and channel, but the engineer keeps a lookout, and stops and reverses without waiting for orders to do so. Forward of the pilothouse is a large space covered with awning; this is the general sitting room of the passengers. They sometimes annoy the pilot by cutting off his lookout, or, rather, he annoys them by calling on them to move.

The engineer has a little house of his own down on deck. His name was Salt, and he was a man far superior to what we expect of such a post. On another boat, whenever it was lying still, we had the pleasure of the company at table of the American engineer, his English mate, and his

Irish mate's assistant, together with a nice-looking Negro that was employed on the boat in some capacity. The captain cannot put himself high above his engineers when they can command nearly equal wages and need equal abilities; but they err exceedingly in taking captains that have no river experience, good seamen on merchantmen, but who have never seen Council Bluffs.

Dinner, when it comes, is but a repetition of breakfast. It is hasty judging of national character by the conduct at the table of a steamboat, especially when so many nations are represented as here. I have seen boats on western waters with as much piggishness at table; but it could hardly be worse served. Richard, the steward, was a well-meaning Jamaica Negro, but his two assistants are very stupid Indian boys. I heard a passenger scolding one of them, and I asked him what he had done. He replied, "I called for a knife, and, as he was bringing it, he used it to scrape his arm with; when I complained of that, he wiped it on his pantaloons." It is exceedingly difficult to secure good waiters. Ours can hardly understand good Spanish, or make themselves understood.

The river banks present little variety. It seems much like the scenery or want of scenery of the lower Mississippi, but the water, I think, is never so low as to show such elevated banks as we see there. We conclude, then, that at high water the Mississippi immensely exceeds the Magdalena in depth. It is also wider, and its width is more uniform, and its channel far more crooked. After this lapse of time I can recollect no difference of color between the Magdalena and the lower Mississippi. We make no stops except for wood, or so rarely that each one will be chronicled as an event.

On Wednesday the boat set out from Barranquilla, and tied up for the night at Remolino, the station of the Santa Marta boats. They call the distance six leagues. My rule makes it twenty-one miles; but if the leagues are new ones, it is much less. They attribute the smallness of the journey to a late start, and delays in getting out of that little arm of the river on which Barranquilla stands. On Thursday, before reaching Calamar, they came eight and one-half leagues, say twenty-eight miles.

They wood but about once a day, and at woodpiles of their own. A wood agent on board discharged so much of the clerk's duties as he was going up, that I long mistook the real clerk for a passenger. At night they often tied up to a bank far from any house. We come to more signs of cultivation as we ascend the river.

On Friday we stopped at a small town on the west bank. We found here the head of the distrito represented by a barnlike edifice, with a roof of thatch and walls of sticks, designed to let in the light and air, but keep out all animals as large as a hog. In this last office they failed for want of a door. So I saw in this very prison a mother with about the same number of offspring that John Rodgers had. The grunting parent of little swine lay stretched in the abundant black dust, contented with her lot. Happy the prison that witnesses no sadder scenes! But when a biped is detained here, it is, of course, with his locomotive apparatus locked in between two logs—the stocks. So, as a man that does not possess "the thumb and first finger of the right hand" cannot vote, a man that has lost both legs cannot be imprisoned here until a new apparatus is invented to hold him.

A group of various colors, all ages, and both sexes, and in every possible stage of nudity, gathered on shore to look at us. From these I select the wife and child of a fustic-cutter as a favorable example. She is carrying two baskets of ivory nuts in positions which the reader is challenged to imitate. The sleeveless garment that covers as much of her as she thinks necessary is called a camisón, an augmentative of the word camisa, as it is nearly twice as long as that garment, which would be useless without another garment to eke out its scantiness.

By Saturday noon we reached the head of the island opposite Mompós, formerly spelled Mompox. This is stated as forty and one-half leagues from Barranquilla, say one hundred forty-eight miles in four days (for we went no farther that day), or, throwing out a day for hinderances and stoppages, fifty miles a day.

Mompós is called the hottest place on the river. Up to here some little influence of the sea breeze is felt, and above, the increase of altitude diminshes the heat; here the sum of these restraining influences on the sun's power is at a minimum. The population is about the same in number as at Barranquilla, but very different. It is a very old town, and a very religious one. The churches are quite numerous, and in a far higher condition than the solitary barnlike edifice in Barranquilla. The schools are not correspondingly advanced, though a girls' school of the higher class was to open the day I left (Sunday).

I visited the cemetery, one of the best in New Granada. The iron fence in front of it is of Granadan workmanship, and was much admired by Bolívar. The inscription over it signifies, Here are the limits between life and eternity. (Aquí confina la vida con la eternidad.) There is within it a very small chapel, as there is in every cemetery of the least pretensions. Most of the best tombs were brick vaults, called bóvedas, built like ovens, with the foot against the wall. Some of them are beautifully set off with miniature steeples. There are some monuments in the ground also, but none of either are of a high class of merit.

Mompós is a town of jewelers and bogas. It stands on an island. Perhaps its insular position, making so much land accessible to it by canoes, has been the origin of its greatness. The steamboat landing is at the upper extremity of the town, above the head of an uninhabited island. Farther down, in front of the older part of the town, is the ordinary landing of market boats. An open space adjoining is protected on the river side by a wall three feet high, the use of which I cannot conjecture. It is the marketplace.

At this spot I once witnessed an exciting scene. A French lady was going up the river in the steamer "Nueva Granada" to join her husband in Bogotá. A French family

with which she was acquainted was descending, on their
way to "la belle France." She came on board the "Manzanares" to chat with them, as the boats lay side by side
all night. They talked in the morning till, before any of
them were aware of it, her boat had left and was beyond
hail. Poor woman! She had not even a bonnet to her head
nor a dollar in her pocket. Two remedies were suggested:
one, to take a canoe and follow after the "Nueva Granada"
with the vain hope of overtaking her. The other appeared
more feasible—to take a horse and ride up on shore, as
there was a slight bend in the river above; but there was
no horse at hand. Hundreds became interested in her case,
and I in their sympathy. She was unknown and a foreigner
—nothing but *a passenger left*. It might have moved the
mirth of a crowd on our docks, but here all were anxious.
For half an hour nothing else was thought of, and all eyes
were turned up the river. At length the "Nueva Granada"
appeared round the point, and one universal viva broke
from the anxious crowd. Whether you take this as a
testimony in favor of poor human nature, which has many
amiable traits in common with that of gregarious animals,
or in favor of Granadan nature in particular, it is honor-
able to the Momposinos.

Here we saw the last of certain loaves of bread more
than a foot in diameter, and about a quarter of an inch
thick, very white and tender, but quite insipid. They are
cassava, made of the starch of a poisonous Euphorbiate
root. The root also comes on the table quartered and
boiled, under the name of yuca, but is not to be confound-
ed with the Liliate genus Yucca. It is a slow-growing herb
or herbaceous shrub, and is nearly a year in coming to
perfection. It rarely flowers, and I have never seen them
digging its roots. For a substitute for flour, it is grated and
then washed in cold water.

I went into two gardens in Mompós, and was surprised to see so many familiar things. These gardens were
the courts of two-story houses. Most of the plants were in
pots around the court or patio. Perhaps, as these were the

first regular houses I was in, I may as well describe them. A house with but one entrance from the street is called a casa claustrada. That one grand entrance is the portón, and the space that leads to the inner door is the zaguán. The zaguán is always paved. The pavement is often of brick. Sometimes it is of small stones, with mosaic figures in it of vertebræ of oxen or swine. It leads into one corner of a square space within the house that has no roof. In the Bible this is called the court, and here the patio. A walk —the corredor—runs entirely around it. The corredor is separated from the patio by a balustrade called pretil. The rooms generally open into the corredor, and only the front has windows that do not look into the patio. If the house be of two stories, the stairs, which are of brick edged with wood, are placed in a recess in one corner of the corredor. In a two-story house, casa alta, the lower rooms facing on a street are either used for stores or rented to poor people, and then they have no connection with the patio. These families, who have no rights out of their narrow rooms save in the streets, are a nuisance to the neighborhood. Poor things! decency is a luxury beyond their means.

No houses have more than two stories. The casa baja one-story house—is more common and more convenient, if not damp; but the casa alta is more pretentious, and is preferred. Another radical distinction is into tiled and thatched houses. Thatch is cooler, but exposed to fire, and sure to decay and let in the rain when you are unprepared for it. Tile is called teja, and in the plural tejas or texas. Thatch is called paja, straw, because in Spain it was made of the culms of grasses. Here it is generally of the leaves of a pandanate plant, Carludovica palmata, which bears the names of iraca, jipijapa, and nacuma. The so-called Panama hats are made of the young leaves of this plant, which are split fine and dipped in boiling water to make the shreds cylindrical.

These hats are generally a week in braiding, and the fineness and price are in proportion to the skill of the braider. The average price, as first sold, is estimated at eighty cents. The finest have been sold at fifty dollars, and even one hundred dollars. The mature leaves are sold standing by the proprietors of the ground for thatch. They spring from the ground on smooth petioles eight feet long. The blade looks like that of a palm leaf, but the flowers have a striking resemblance to ears of maize. I know of no warm lands in New Granada where this useful plant does not grow.

We left Mompós about eight on Sunday morning, instead of six, as had been intended. They often have to hunt up slack and careless passengers who would otherwise be left. Such delays astonish, amuse, and vex. We took in tow a champán—a large flatboat with an arched thatched roof. It had its crew of bogas. Their women came down to see them off. As they sat on the shore, I was struck with the fact that their skirts were all blue. I soon found that this color is almost universal in New Granada among the lower classes, whether from taste or from the abundance of indigo I know not; but this row of women probably had cause for looking blue. It is likely that they had danced all night, and mayhap attended mass this morning, and now had come down to take farewell of the men whose last cuartillo they had helped spend, and who were now taking to the river for more money to be spent in the same way.

Before the day of steam, it used to be impossible to engage a crew from below to go above Mompós, nor would any from above go lower down, so that every champán was delayed at Mompós till a new crew had been shipped, provisioned, and got off with no small ado.

More than thirty miles now pass with no noticeable place, but amazing multitudes of children at the waterside under the green trees. Then we come to Banco, on the east side of the river, fifty miles above Mompós. Here we arrived in the afternoon, and stopped to wood. A large, unfinished church, roofless and floorless, filled with vegetation, stands as a monument of ambition, and perhaps to date the decline of Romish power.

Here I saw a great curiosity. It was a long procession of ants, every one with a bit of green leaf in his mouth. I understate the matter. There ran through the grass a well-beaten road, like a sheep path, six inches wide—a very Cumberland road for ants. It was thronged with busy travelers, all of whom were hastening from home, or returning with about half an inch square sheared out of a leaf. I followed on to see their nest. It was curious to see their broad highway passing under logs, stones, and brush heaps. I followed it for a long distance into the woods, and then gave up in despair. These ants are called arrieros—the same word that means muleteer. They are a terrible pest. It is thought that ant-eating animals generally reject this species, on account of four strong, sharp projections on the body. They can carry a grain of maize, and I am sure that to load a whole colony would demand many bushels. Woe to the orange tree that they have determined to shear of its leaves! The best, if not the only defense, is to make the trunk inaccessible to them by water. Some even manage to surround their house with a stream of water, and others are driven to despair by domiciliary visits, clearly in violation of the Constitution of 1843, but which neither parchment nor architecture have strength to resist.

I was once sitting in the evening in a house near Tuluá, and fancied I saw something whitish moving on the floor. I examined, and found a broad stream of rice flowing from a large jar under a bed; each grain was in the jaws of an arriero. Long before morning the jar would have been empty, for the diligent thieves work night and day, without even stopping Sunday. The only hope for the rice was to hang it up in what the sailors call a true-lover's knot by a hair rope. In the end, the jar fell and broke, and the enemy bore off the contents. But, on the whole, I am surprised that so resistless an enemy should do no more damage in a country.

I saw where the ants' highway crossed a human footpath. Of course, many of the little folk must be crushed under the feet of the lords of creation. There their green loads were left, for no ant picks up the load of another. I found that if the antennæ of one of these ants were removed, he no longer had the power of finding his way. Whether it is by smell, or by some analogous sense, I know not, but it is not by sight. I have effaced the path of ants with a little chocolate oil, too little to impede the feet of the insect, and only for an ant's length in extent. On each side were gathered a crowd, at a loss to find their way, although their antennæ could nearly meet in the middle. At length some formic Columbus set the example, others followed, and the way was reestablished.

But let us go back to the boat.

"Do you see that handsome young man—buen mozo —leaning against the post?" asked a fellow traveler.

I looked, and saw a nice young man, with a sort of stock on. It is called sotacuella. It is a plain parallelogram, about two inches wide, more fit for a badge than anything else, and is often, if not always, of what is called worsted work. This, and the tonsure—a carefully shaved spot on the crown as large as a dollar—are intended to be permanent marks of the sacred position of the wearer.

"Well," he continued, "that is the Cura of Banco. Young as he is, they tell me that he has twelve children that are known to be his."

And a friend that passed Banco some time after mentioned incidentally that he witnessed the baptism of a newborn child of the cura there.

I have asked two persons just now what proportion of the priests are unfaithful to their vow. One replied, "About 99 per cent." I knew him to be a friend to the priests. I knew that the other was not, and his reply must be received with a grain of allowance. It was, "Of the secular clergy (parish priests), 98 per cent; of the regulars (monks), 102 per cent. Thus," says he, "the excessive licentiousness of the monks is enough to offset any casual instance of chastity in the seculars."

Up the stream we go. Settlements become thinner, and the groups of children rarer and smaller. At last we stop and make fast to the bank. The forest is so dense that there is hardly a place for the boga to set foot when he leaps ashore to make fast. Here grows an immense quantity of a Heliconia, called by the people lengua de vaca—cowtongue. It is of that group of families including the plantain, arrowroot, and ginger.

On again the next day. All day we go without stopping except to wood. I cannot understand how these fertile banks can remain, washed almost weekly by the waves of steamboats, but without commerce, and nearly without inhabitant. No American would have anticipated such a state of things, so do we cling to the maxim of political economy that travel begets traffic.

Now comes another entire day, with only one stop in the edge of the dense forest for wood. Above here no steamer can safely run at night. At dark we made fast to the western bank in tall grass, where they cautioned me against snakes, and I knew no better then than to heed their counsel. I succeeded, however, in bringing down a stem of caña brava, which should mean wild cane. It is a gigantic grass, the stem of which is herbaceous and not hollow. Sections of it, when young and juicy, make admirable pickles, crisp and tender, having no taste except what they derive from the vinegar and other condiments. The ripe stems serve to make fences and houses, being more than an inch in diameter. When in fruit, the panicle at the top of the stem is of great beauty, particularly when the wind carries all the peduncles to one side, waving them like a streamer of a lance. The whole height of the stem is from twelve to twenty feet.

I have said nothing about the alligators; but now, as we are soon to take leave of that abundant and interesting animal, I must give him a paragraph. The caiman is an animal of the same genus with the crocodile and the alligator. They infest the middle Magdalena to an incredible extent, and in the lower part they are as common as the alligator is in our southern waters. They disappear entirely before reaching Honda; but on the sandbars here there were sometimes half a dozen to be seen at once. Swimming is not to be thought of; and even women washing on the shore, unprotected by a fence, are sometimes carried off. Mosquitoes also reach a maximum in the middle Magdalena, and disappear entirely before reaching Nare.

For some time after leaving San Pablo our voyage seemed to be without events to chronicle. Day passes after day without receiving or leaving a passenger or an article of freight. Once a day we stop for wood. Perhaps the space of an acre has been cut over, and may have been cultivated, but has again run up to weeds. Two miserable sheds—ranchos—serve to protect the occupants, who cannot be called a family, from dew and rain. A part of a raceme of plantains, the staff of life, hang under one roof, and a few ears of maize constitute the remainder of their store. All their furniture is summed up in a few coarse earthen vessels (perhaps made on the spot), and some of totuma or calabaza. This last is a huge fruit of the gourd family, and has given origin to the English word calabash. The name ought not to be applied to the totuma, which is a much smaller fruit, made only into dishes and spoons, all made of half a fruit or less; but the calabaza needs but a small opening made into it, and it is cleaned out by rinsing with water if the orifice be too small for the hand. In a word, calabashes are substitutes for kegs, jugs, and bottles; totumas for dishes, bowls, and spoons. Ask for a totuma of water, and they will give you what you need to drink. Ask for a calabaza of water, and they will propose to lend you or sell you a calabaza to hold a supply of water to take with you.

As you ascend the river population decreases. The villages grow smaller, and you forget to inquire their names, even when they are few and far between. There is also a sensible diminution in the proportion of children, suggesting an infant mortality equaled only in the vicinity of still-slops and "pure country milk."

Mountains appear in the distance, now on one hand and now on the other, gradually coming nearer and nearer, till at length they are seen on both sides at once, a sure indication that the alluvial region of the Magdalena is narrowing as we ascend. There is now and then a bluff of thirty feet in height, but I have generally seen the banks of a height varying from eight feet to two or three. The width of the river has diminished one half, till it is less than the Ohio or the Hudson at Albany. The current has been growing a little more rapid, but here at last is something new. The river is compressed by rocks on both sides, and for a few rods is quite rapid. This is the Angostura de Nare—the Narrows of Nare. It is the eleventh day of the trip, and our confinement has just reached the term of a Liverpool voyage.

There are no houses at the mouth of the Nare. There were only a storehouse—bodega—and a woodshed. Both are since leveled to the ground, and boats now stop only at the town, half a mile or so above. While waiting for dinner I went up to the town. It is the last mentionable place before you get to Honda. It is a desolate range of mud huts, and a wretched plaza, with a small church on it, as usual. It is all the worse for having a back street and cross streets. We found the people dressed up because it was Saint Somebody's day. This made the bad place look somewhat better. One little fellow, who was too small to need clothes, attracted my attention as a remarkably fine specimen of a frequent disease, said to be produced by earth-eating, called jipitera; such a person is called a barrigón, from the great enlargement of the abdomen. No sooner did he see my four eyes (spectacles included) bent on him, than he ran bellowing into the house. After dinner I went out to look for plants. I went far and found few.

We had left Nare three hours behind us when we ran plump into a sandbank. Here I did injustice to Captain Chapman, and I am sorry for it. He was a good seaman, and had omitted nothing he could contribute to the comfort of his passengers, and to mine especially; but he knew nothing of low water on the Ohio. I, who have been on more bars than I hope ever to be again, looked on his

operations with perfect amazement, till I came to the
conclusion that he wished to stay there. Once we were
fairly afloat, but one awkward manœuver fixed us. The
next that I saw, twenty bogas stood in three feet of water,
on the lower side of the boat—which lay obliquely to the
stream—pushing against the current. They carried out
hawsers, and they slipped. They tied them better, and
broke them. The spar with which a resolute Ohio captain
would crawl over two feet of dry bar, was unknown to
them. There we lay, and we lay all day.

At night we were notified that we were to leave the
boat early next morning in the champán that had been
towing more than a week at our stern filled with idle bogas.
Now commenced a packing-up, and it was like the sack
of a city for confusion. All languages were put in requisi-
tion. One question would begin with "Where is——," the
next with "Dónde está——," another with "Ou est——,"
"Wo ist——." Only the Italian was precluded from the
use of his mother tongue. It was at bedtime only that the
Babel became quiet, and our twelfth day on the boat was
at an end.

*IV*

## Afloat and Ashore

It is time now to describe the champán. It is much larger than a bongo, being, in fact, a flatboat with an arched roof—toldo (the same word describes also a mosquito bar, a bed-curtain, and a tent), woven of poles and thatched with palm leaf. The ends are open to the air; the width of the boat is about seven feet, and the length of the covered part may have been fifteen or twenty feet. It contained but one article of freight, a hogshead of crockery, but our baggage seemed to nearly fill it. One passenger, however, contrived to keep a portion of the floor free from trunks by spreading his bed down upon it. As for myself, I paid little attention to matters, as I was suffering from a distressing diarrhea, the result, perhaps, of the beautifully clear Nare water with which we regaled ourselves. I ate nothing this morning before starting; the others took only a cup of chocolate.

A Bogotá Yankee and his son remained with his large and varied lot of freight on board the steamer. There were eight of us, then, consigned to the tender mercies of an uncivilized horde of bogas, most of them absolutely naked, governed by a patrón of a little higher grade, who, with his woman—patrona—occupied the open stern—popa—of the boat; and all that represented the owners of the boat —captain, clerk, steward, cook—all was supplied by Richard (the steward—a Jamaica Negro) and Manuel, a stupid Indian boy, who scarce understood any Spanish! I complained of this to the captain, but he told me that even what he did was a favor and not an obligation, done at a great expense, and that it was optional to take the champán or wait the rise of the river in the boat. My complaint, then, was groundless.

It is time now to introduce to the reader these seven

fellow prisoners and victims with whom I was now brought into so close and involuntary an intimacy. They were,

1. A little Granadan of the name of Lara, who lived in Honda. He spoke Spanish only.

2. A Frenchman who had been in Jamaica, and spoke English and Spanish well. He was a sort of apothecary.

3. His son, a thievish little rascal, speaking Spanish and French. He would read all the children's tracts I would lend him, and stole from under my mattress some anti-Catholic tracts I had there, which I did not think best to lend.

4. Another Frenchman, a Bogotá tailor—a nice man —speaking French and Spanish.

5. A fine young Italian, named Dordelli, nephew to a merchant in Bogotá. He was going from there to establish a branch of his house in Cúcuta. He was a naturalist and my especial friend. He spoke French and Spanish.

6. A Dutch violinist, who had been in the United States with Sivori, and was now going through the American tropics. He was a gentlemanly man, but unprincipled and miserly to excess. He spoke Low Dutch, German, English, French, and a little Spanish.

7. His companion, a pianist, an easy, overgenerous man, who had given up all the financiering operations to his more penurious partner; he spoke the same languages, and also Latin to me when we wished the Frenchman, No. 2, not to understand us.

There never had been very strict discipline on the steamboat. Here there was and could be none except that of the patrón over the bogas. These all assembled in the front open space, the proa—forecastle; and one of them began a prayer, which all the rest finished. I could never determine whether this prayer was in Latin, Spanish, or lingua franca.

Then most of them sprung to the roof, seized their palancas and commenced pushing against the bottom of the river, and walking toward the stern, shouting, Us! us! us! us! us! us! us! till they could go no farther. Their cry was tremendous. Oh for some method incapable of exaggeration, like the photographic process, to record it and compel belief! A pack of hounds may make as much noise in some given half hour as a crew of bogas, but these continue it, only with the intermissions of eating and crossing the river, from daybreak till night. They shout, and jump on the toldo over your head till you might fancy them in battle and repelling boarders.

Sad indeed was the sight to me, sick and dispirited, to see the boat slowly disappearing around a bend of the river. Barbarism was carrying me away from civilization, and when or how was I destined to see its like again? I turned and went in, for a horizontal position and quiet were the only remedies in my power. Horizontal position and quiet! how could I obtain either? I found Lara's bed empty, and I lay down on it. I lay there till he came, and, fearing to lose his ill-founded claim, requested me to leave it. I found another space as large, which Richard had been busy in, now unoccupied, and I would have at once spread my hammock on it as a bed, but the little French boy was asleep on it, and I would not disturb him. While waiting for him to waken, his father took formal possession of the spot in question by unrolling his bed on it. None had leisure to sympathize with me, and I roused myself, and roused the boy too, and called to Richard to sling my hammock.

"No hammock can be slung in this champán," says the Frenchman.

"But I must lie down, for it is impossible for me to remain up longer," I replied.

No others offered any objection, and the hammock was soon slung, in nobody's way, close up under the toldo, over a pile of baggage at the side of the boat, and I was in it. I wish my best friend might some day receive, in recompense for some great and good action, an equal gratification. I was as much out of the way of all the rest as though I had fallen overboard and drowned, and it was all the same to them. I remained in my hammock, with little intermission, twenty hours, and rose entirely recovered.

A boat thirty or forty feet long, with baggage piled on both sides, with an alleyway of less than three feet in the middle, would be a tolerable prison for seven men, a boy, two servants, the patrón, the patrona, and an uncounted lot of bogas, although these last had no rights under or aft of the toldo. But there was a sad drawback on this. There were three beams running across the top of the boat, from side to side, too low to creep under and too high to step over, so that, in fact, we were penned up like animals in a cattle show.

Such was our home, or our prison, from Monday till Saturday. Once or twice a day we came to land when the bogas' dinner was boiled enough, but as soon as it was eaten they prayed again, and on they went again with an us! us! us! us! us! us! uh! jumping and screaming. One black rascal had a string tied round his waist, and tied to it his trunk key. So he has clothes, it seems, somewhere; but when a man has put every rag he has in the world into his trunk, in what pocket shall he put his key? A knotty question, which the fellow seems to have solved completely.

But the most amazing problem of political economy I ever tried to solve is how to nerve a naked vagabond up to almost superhuman exertions, day after day, in a land where starvation is impossible. The boga's task used to be to push his huge champán against a violent current upstream, from Mompós to Honda—a month's dire task of twelve hours' dreadful labor every day, except two or three accustomed stops, where neither promises, threats, blaspheming, nor pistols could start him a particle; but you may as well inquire why a man will be a poet, a naturalist, or a bookmaker, with the certainty of hard labor and bad pay, as a boga. Boga nascitur.

The truth seems to be that our boga is a great sensualist. He has his finery and embroidered shirts, and he must have his dances and drinking frolics. We may suppose him, then, to arrive home with an amount of money that the upland Indian never has seen; but his old debts, and one or two benders, make short work with it. Then he resorts to borrowing till that resource is exhausted, and again he must get a champán; but I must forewarn my readers that the borrowing part of the business will not go far, for the credit system is not well understood in low latitudes. So the river craft is based on the vice and improvidence of its victims. I see many analogies between bogas, the deckhands of the Mississippi, and common sailors.

Generally, in all parts of the Magdalena, one bank is steep and the other shallow. The champán chooses the latter, and, when it changes to the other side of the river, we must cross it. All the men on the toldo jump down forward, and each one takes his paddle—canalete. Then we have an intermission of the noise till they are again at their poles. Some of them stand in the proa all the time, and push there. These occasionally exchange the pole for the hook—gancha—and thus, at times, manage to pass a small turn of steep bank, and save crossing the river twice, which is always effected with a great loss of ground.

One of the greatest trials of life used to be to manage the bogas in ascending from Mompós to Honda. It is almost impossible to hurry them; sometimes they desert, sometimes rebel. The laws now give you even less control of them than formerly; and, unless the navigation of the Magdalena is specially protected, it is quite likely that it may be impeded, delayed, and rendered more costly by the change. The tendency of the ultrarepublicanism now springing up is to protect the vagabond, but this must soon reach its limit.

We always ate while the boat was going, and, as the kitchen was nothing but a frame filled with earth in the popa, with tulpas, our meals could not, even had we wished it, been simultaneous with those of the bogas. In fact, we preferred taking their mealtime for a little ramble on shore. In one of these rambles with Dordelli I came upon two men at work, a really strange sight in this land.

With the most shocking substitute for axes they had cut
down a large tree, hewn it four-square, and were now
cutting a deep groove on the upper side, like a trough.
They showed me a similar but deeper groove on the under
side, and told me that when these two grooves met in the
middle they would have two planks—a hard way of making lumber. I think they were to make part of a champán.
This was the only instance of men at work that I saw between Cartagena and Bogotá, except one man making a
fishnet at a town on the Magdalena.

We were gone longer than we expected, and found
the company all waiting for us. We had left them under
the impression that they were going up to a house to buy
provisions, which they did not. They were little satisfied
with our delay, as the bogas had been fighting while they
were waiting, and it was feared that they would go no
farther for some hours. However, in a little while they
prayed again, and were in as good starting order as ever.
After this they contrived their midday halt generally on
an island, or in shallow water, where they would wade
ashore to eat, leaving us in the boat.

But of nothing can I complain so much as of the
Jamaica Negro, Richard, who was our steward. He
seemed determined to carry economy to the utmost. He
had now turned cook, though I imagine any one of our
number would have shown more science in the matter.
Nothing was to be had. Frequently the whole meal for
eight of us was a single fowl and hard crackers. Nay, he
even complained that the "gentlemen used too much
sugar in their coffee" (milk we had none in all the voyage),
and undertook the task of sweetening it for us. As for fruit
or other luxuries, there was none to be had. Save a green
pineapple that I saw at one of our stopping places, I saw
neither fruit nor fruit tree after leaving San Pablo. And
here we were, almost without resources, and with no
remedy but to advance.

Once again we all went ashore in hopes of buying
something to eat. After passing through a skirting of wood,
we came to a platanal or plantain field. We proceeded half

a mile through the platanal, and came to a house or hut where lounged and sat two or three half-naked lazy mortals. Here I saw, for the first time, the cacao tree which yields chocolate. The first thing that strikes the beholder is the strange way that the fruit is stuck against the side of the tree or the larger limbs, projecting horizontally, as if stuck endwise on a peg. The fruit is six or seven inches long, and three or four in diameter. It is ribbed like a melon, but never opens. It is knocked off when it appears to the eye to be ripe; two or three, perhaps, from a tree, are as many as will be ripe at the same time. Children carry them in their hands to a central heap, that grows from day to day, till enough is collected to make a batch.

Then come the man, his wife, all the boys and girls, all the babies and dogs. The effective force surrounds the pile. Two of them draw their machetes, and begin opening the fruit. They apply the word mazorca equally to an ear of Indian corn or a fruit of cacao, only the granos of one are on the outside and those of the other within. The man gives the mazorca three cuts lengthwise, not so deep as to injure the precious seeds within, and tosses it over to the softer sex and smaller fry. They tear it open with their claws, and find within the thick fleshy rind a central cavity, from the center of which rose a column with the seeds attached; but when ripe, the whole is reduced to a pulp, in which the large seeds are packed so compactly that they alone, if thrown in loosely, would be more than sufficient to fill the entire cavity. These they separate a little from the pulp, and throw them into a tray, upon a skin, or on some plantain leaves. The pulp is as agreeable in taste as any fruit we have, but, as it is difficult to get a spoonful from a fruit that contains a pint of seeds, it is not worth the trouble of eating. They often suck it off the seeds as they get them out. If the seeds are to be loaded on a mule, they are put into a guambía, a bag made of network. As the meshes are large enough to let potatoes through, it requires some management to fill it with seeds of cacao. First you put in pieces of plantain leaf, and upon them the quantity of cacao they will hold. Pieces of leaf are added to the edges of the first, overlapping freely, till, when it is full, the whole guambía appears lined with leaf. Arrived home, they are put into a trough—canoa—and left to ferment till the seed is freed from what appears to be an aril or false covering. Then it is spread on a skin in the dooryard to dry.

It is prepared by grinding on a warm, flat stone, by the application of another stone, held, like a rolling pin, in both hands, but not rolled. The stone has under it a place to put coals, and it is heated to about 120°. Maize is always ground on this stone. The cacao is first ground alone, and then with a coarse sugar, to which dried bread is sometimes added, for a cheap article for the poor. This kind I have sometimes eaten in bulk. Cho-co-lá-te is made into tablas, or cakes, of from an ounce to an ounce and a half, the quantity to which two ounces of water are to be added for a cup. They are boiled together, generally in a small brass jar—olleta—and, before pouring out, as much of it is reduced to foam as possible by making a grass stem, on which portions of the roots are left, to revolve rapidly, as in beating eggs.

The cacao loves the tierra caliente. Its price varies exceedingly, being often dearer than in New York, and sometimes ten cents per pound, or less. It is never so cheap as to be an unprofitable crop. It is generally sold in the seed, and ground by the family that use it.

In all these days we saw but one town. It was Buena-vista, near the mouth of the Río Negro, that rises below and west of the great plain of Bogotá. On Friday the river became more tortuous and rapid. On our left, on the west bank of the river, and not very far from Honda, we saw a mountain range of the boldest description. High on the summit were enormous perpendicular precipices, seen in clear profile against the sky. Rarely can we place our-selves in a situation to get a profile view of a single preci-pice, but the top of a distant mountain ridge so set off looks more like cloud than rock.

At last, on Saturday morning, I was called from my hammock and asked to decide whether I would submit to another day's imprisonment or walk to Honda. It did not take me long to decide. The two Hollanders were of the same mind, and we hastily closed our seventeen days' voyage with a cup of chocolate and a hard, dry cracker, and leaped ashore.

We struck off directly from the river through a variegated country, over an old mule road. Soon we found high hills between us and the river. Monkeys were climbing over the trees, and various flowers covered the ground. A little grasslike plant here first met my eye, that I have found everywhere since. It is noticeable in having its upper leaves (bracts) white at the base. It is the Dichromena ciliata.

We had walked some miles before we came to any of the few houses that are found on the road. Then we entered a pasture through an open gate with a roof on the top. I was surprised at this, but I learned, from further observations, that all gates here have roofs. Doors, gates, and bars all have the name of puerta. A pair of bars is puerta de trancos, and a gate puerta de golpe. It is often very inconvenient to the traveler not to know some such phrases, which, being perhaps local, are not to be found in dictionaries or phrase books. These last I have found very deficient for Granadan use, being generally composed for the longitude of Madrid.

We began to wonder, after going six or eight miles, whether it might not be possible that we had made some false turn, and were getting into the interior, when a roaring drew us a little to the right, and there was the river, rushing and tumbling over the rocks, so that we wondered how the poor champán was ever to get past this point, called Quita-palanca.

We reached the foot of the rapids unexpectedly. We found there a small collection of cottages, a good-sized rough storehouse, and a magnificently planned government structure, either in ruins or unfinished. It bore the inscription of BODEGA DE BOGOTÁ on the arch over the door.

Near the bodega, under a large tree, I saw the sections

of an immense sugar boiler. They were six or eight in number, and were destined for Cuni, two days' journey in the mountain. To carry one of them there would be a task comparable only with that of transporting one of Hannibal's elephants or a piece of Napoleon's artillery over the Alps. But all the region through which they have been brought is a fine sugar country, and here the concern has been lying for years like a stranded whale. Some transportation transactions that begin here are to be compared with the movement of a small army. One piece was so heavy that the cargueros (as human beasts of burden are called) are said to have eaten a cow a day. The heaviest load ever carried to Bogotá by a single carguero is said to have been carried by a woman. It is given at 216 pounds; but there is always an uncertainty about translating weights.

The carguero, like the boga, has a more laborious calling than any known in the United States, and the philosophy of his attachment to it is even more difficult than that of the boga. He is a native of a higher, colder clime, and of a more industrious race. Nor is he always a poor man. Colonel Santamaria tells me he was once riding a sillero or saddleman, who, from a summit, pointed out a farm of his on which he had a tenant. They are of Indian blood, mixed or unmixed, and go naked from the waist upward, and from the middle of the thigh downward. The weight is supported by two straps across the chest. I am told the carguero's wife meets him on the last day of his journey, brings him food, and takes his load.

I met them once as I was coming down from Bogotá, stringing along the road for hours, with boxes of all imaginable shapes, and found here at the bodega the fountain from which the stream flowed. It was the machinery of some kind of a factory.

After hallooing "Paso!" and "Pasero!"—ferry and ferryman—till we were tired, we started out a dilatory ferryman, who took us across to a large sandy beach. He is obliged to carry the neighbors gratis, and pay the prov-

ince something for the privilege of charging a half dime
and extorting a dime when he can from all others. This
pasaje is an item of provincial revenue that ought to be
centralized, as they say, for it is drawn from the pockets
of inhabitants of other provinces rather than of their own.
This particular ferry is the worse off, as it is on no traveled
road, so that the Hondeños are almost the only ones that
cross, and they cross gratis.

The road descends by a pavement to a very old stone
bridge across a little dry ravine, and immediately after
enters the ancient city of Honda. Here once united two
currents of trade, flowing toward Spain from the lofty
cities of Bogotá and Quito. The robbery of Indians, that
once enriched these cities, is over; their trade with Spain
is done. No trade from Quito seeks the Magdalena, and
the scanty exports and imports of Bogotá are beginning to
creep along the base of the mountain on the opposite side
of the river. No wonder, then, that ten steps in the old city
show it to be decayed. Many a rich old house is reduced
to a roofless ruin, hedging in tall weeds with walls of thick,
rough masonry. Honda is all stone and tile, so that never
had an obsolete old place harder work to tumble down,
and it would not have succeeded without the respectable
aid of a few earthquakes.

The richest specimen of earthquake architecture I
ever saw is the bridge over the Gualí, a noisy river that
runs right through the middle of the town.

So anxious are the provincial solons to consummate
the utter ruin of Honda, that they have imposed a peaje of
a dime on each tercio of merchandise that passes the
bridge, while on the other side is an unobstructed portage
from the smooth water above the rapids to that below.
Altogether, I should like dearly to pack up this victorious
rival of the tower of Pisa in a box, and send it to New York;
but they can not spare it, for the rapid Gualí is never
fordable, and I fear it will be a long time ere another
bridge will span it.

The heart of the town, just south of the bridge, is a

dense mass of stone houses and crooked, rough-paved streets, crowded in between a hill and two rivers—a perfect petrifaction.

To me the chief attraction of Honda is because it is the residence of two as excellent gentlemen as ever a traveler would wish to meet with in a strange land. I allude to Mr. J. H. Jenney, of Boston, and Mr. Treffrey, an Englishman, who has lived a long time in New Granada, and is married to a native of the country. To both these gentlemen I am indebted for almost everything it was possible for me to need or for them to bestow. The presence of such men in a foreign land is a source of national pride, too often mortified by the unworthy representatives of the Anglo-Saxon race dispersed over the world. I had no letters to either, and, at my first visit, Mr. Jenney was from home. I directed my steps to Mr. Treffrey, and was welcomed with a cordiality that put me entirely at my ease. He took me to breakfast with him, hunted up Mr. Jenney's keys, and at once installed me solitary master of the best house in Honda, as I should judge.

To relieve me of the care of housekeeping, he showed me a place where I could take my meals. A traveler here would call Mr. Jenney's house my posada, and the place where I ate, my fonda. It would be hard to translate these words by hotel and eating house, but they are the nearest approximations we have here. The fonda would not have been considered entirely unexceptionable by northern moralists, inasmuch as the lady hostess had a few illegitimate children playing about the house; but travelers must get over their scruples, or manage them as best they may.

I found the house spacious and exceedingly comfortable, though far inferior to what the society of its master and the hospitality of his table afterward made it. It had a date palm growing in the narrow patio, or court, and reaching up nearly as high as the roof. All the rooms were in the second story, and communicated by means of a gallery—corredor—running around the court. Balconies overhung the narrow streets, and gave an opportunity of seeing what was going on in town.

I went to the fonda four times a day; early and late for chocolate and sweetmeats—dulce—and at about ten and four for my meals. These were generally beef, with yuca and plantains. Fish are very plenty here, for you will see, of a morning, men and boys with three or four huge ones, as much as they can carry, balanced over their shoulder on a stick, or propped up by another stick leaning against a wall. They labor under the demerit of being cheap, and our fondista would not feel that she is giving her guests their money's worth if she set fish before them. There is a smaller species, however, possessing the same merit as the round clam (quahog, Bostonicé) has in New York—it is dearer. I preferred the larger kind. They are frequently dried, and I have met them in the market of Bogotá.

In the market I saw a curious mineral for sale, which I at first took to be marble. It was of a dirty reddish-white color, and with a grain like sandstone, and was broken in pieces. I inquired its use, and learned that it was salt. Most of the salt is from Cipaquirá. They take water from a salt spring, and dissolve impure rock salt in it till the water is saturated. It then settles and is decanted into earthen jars over a furnace. These are supplied with brine till they are full of a mass of conglomerated salt. The jars are then broken, and the mass within—moya—broken into pieces of a good size for loading on the backs of mules. No cover is used to protect this load from the rain, which, however, does not greatly diminish the huge compact masses. Nearly all salt springs and mines are national property, and the salt is made by contract, and sold by the government at prices fixed by law. This monopoly has many enemies, and the government would gladly abolish it, but their revenues are already too scanty. I saw, in another place, some moyas made in smaller jars; these I knew to be contraband, made secretly, without paying the excise duty.

At night Mr. Treffrey sent four men down for my baggage. It made me ache to see my heavy trunks mounted on a man's back for a two-mile porterage. I paid two of them a dime each; the other two demanded a dime and a quarter. All agreed that the difference was just, though they did not deny that the weight was equal. Soon after they arrived a collector came in for peaje for two bales of merchandise. I had two bales of paper for drying plants: it was not merchandise, and they let it pass.

Honda is a forwarding town rather than mercantile. One industry, however, is carried on here, that is fast growing in New Granada—cigar-making. It is but recently that the free cultivation of tobacco has been permitted. Tobacco culture used to be limited to two places: Ambalema, a town above Honda, on the same side of the river, the richest town in the province of Mariquita, and Palmira, in the Cauca. Each cultivator took out a license to raise so many plants, and if he exceeded the number a heavy fine followed. No peasant dared raise any for his own use. I cannot see how the multiplication of cigars or the reduction of price can benefit the world, but the abrogation of this monopoly has certainly given a great impulse to industry in this region. The abolition was begun by Mosquera, but accomplished by President López, his successor.

The next day was Sabbath, but I had not yet learned that he who would go to mass must go early, so I have always found the churches closed. It was rather a busy day, for it seemed as if all the population were bent on a public swim. The little river has its congregation when it has any water. The Magdalena is much frequented just where the rapids begin, and again at the mouth of the Gualí. The Gualí itself, between the bridge and the Magdalena, was the resort of a few quiet ones, but the liveliest scenes were in the rapid current just above the bridge. There were full-grown men and large boys stark naked, young girls in the same state, and women of all ages with their bodies more or less covered with a blue skirt.

The better bred of these would come down under an umbrella to shade them from the sun, a servant following with a skirt, a sheet, and a totuma. The bather would throw the sheet over her, and emerge from it in the skirt. Next the body is covered with soap, and the hair filled; this is then converted into lather. Then follows a pouring of water from the totuma for a long time without intermission. If any children are to be washed, now is the time to take them in hand. After this, they plunge into the stream, if they choose, and thus pass the time they have to spend in the water. Again they envelop themselves in the sheet, which now serves for a towel as well as a dressing room, and at length they emerge from it nearly dressed. The servant rinses the skirt in the river, wrings it, and puts it and the other wet clothes into a tray, which she carries home on her head. Thus the lady has secured a good swim in the open river without any violation of decorum. But it would not be fair to the reader to leave him to imagine that all these details are the result of one day's observation. It would be difficult to find the hour in all the week in which some of these scenes are not going on.

I called on Señor Tanco one evening. I found no place to knock, neither at the portón, at the foot of the stairs, nor yet at the head of them. Señor Tanco told me the custom was to advance till the visitor meets someone. I found a little monkey chained to the top of the stairs, that manifested, as usual, a lively desire to bite me. Within I found the family, partly in the balcony, and the rest near the windows. I was much pleased with my call.

I experienced a material kindness at Señor Tanco's hand on the eve of leaving Honda. I had found a young chap at the Bodega de Bogotá who would take my cargas and myself to Guaduas, where he lived. The bargain was struck, but it remained to be seen whether, in all Honda, I could borrow or hire a saddle. I was about giving up in despair, when Señor Tanco came forward to my relief with the spontaneous offer of his saddle, which I gladly accepted.

The start was to be an early one, and the men were all engaged who were to carry my baggage to the upper ferry, and Gregorio, the peon, had engaged the ferryman

to be at his post at daybreak. I then bought some chocolate
and bread for my breakfast. They have a convenient
pouch or pocket to sling over the shoulder, called a carriel.
Some have locks to them; some are highly ornamented.
As a substitute for this useful article, I now bought a little
bag, here called a mochila, and elsewhere a guambía.

I had some terrible ideas of the mountain road to
Bogotá, and of passive submission to the fantasies of my
mule. This last thing has been wrongly represented. You
should select the path for your mule just as you would for
your horse at home; but, at home or abroad, when you
come to a difficulty in your path, you must, after ordering
your animal to pass it, let him do so in his own way, without pulling at the bit. The doctrine, as ordinarily stated,
endangered my neck unnecessarily. The mountain mule
possesses no miraculous instinct that will lead him to
encounter a less difficulty now, to save him from a greater
one farther ahead.

Guaduas contains one of the two houses of correction
—casas de reclusión—of New Granada. They have three
orders of penitentiaries, according to the nature of crimes
—forced labors, presidio, and the house of correction.
Where the law would condemn a man to either of the
two former, a woman or youth is sent to the house of correction for a longer period, so that the proportion of boys
and females here is large to that of men. Through the
kindness of General Acosta, jefe político pro tem., who
alone had power to grant admission to visitors, I was
conducted all over the establishment. It was an extinct
Franciscan convent, founded in 1606. These buildings
make excellent prisons without any alteration. All public
buildings, with scarce an exception, were originally built
for convents, or have been seized on by the monks.

I found the inmates making cigars and cigar boxes,
and sawing out boards for these by hand. The discipline
seemed excellent. The matron appeared to be well fitted
for her task. To one of her punishments I ventured to
object, as being hardest on the most sensitive or least

depraved. It was shutting them up in the public coffin, in which corpses are taken to the grave, and then taken out to be buried.

There are some criminals here whose cases would be great novelties in a criminal calendar. One was pointed out to me who conspired with a priest. She killed a man for whom she was housekeeper; and the priest testified to having married her to him in private before his death. She hoped to inherit his property, and share it with the priest.

Another woman and her daughter were there for a series of horrid cruelties practiced on unfortunate persons of their own sex that fell into their power. It seemed to be without motive, something like the case of a woman in New Orleans of whom I have read. This mother and daughter left one of their mutilated victims at the door of the hospital when they supposed she could never speak again. I think, too, that after their imprisonment a skeleton was discovered walled up in their house.

Guaduas was the residence of the father of the best-known writer of New Granada, Colonel Joaquín Acosta, as he is known on his title pages, although he was a general when he died. He has done much for the geography and history of his country, especially while minister at Paris. There he collected and translated into Spanish numerous memoirs of Boussingault, and abridged and republished the only scientific periodical ever published in New Granada, the *Semanario*. He put in the church at Guaduas the only town clock that I know of that has two hands in all the country. Part of his valuable library has become national property. His widow, an English lady, still resides here. The immense estate of his father is divided, I am told, between his family and his half-brother, General Acosta.

General Acosta is said to be a man of immense wealth. It is a pity that he has arrived now at the evening of life without ever marrying. Such a circumstance is far more common here than it ought to be. He is one of the most hospitable men in all the land. "Many persons," says

Steuart, "are in the habit of partaking of General Acosta's hospitalities, and then of abusing him afterward," an example which he accordingly imitates; I cannot.

I ate at his table one of the most characteristically Granadan dinners I ever saw. Among other articles too numerous and strange for me to enumerate, was one called bollo, which I took to be a white, tender, insipid root. It proved to be a preparation of maize, wrapped in the husks of the same and boiled.

It could not have been a favorable time for a botanist when I was at Guaduas, being just at the close of the dry season. In one excursion I went out on the north side of the river that runs through the place, intending to cross it far above, and come down a road that ran along its south bank. When I had gone up as far as I wished, I found a place where a hut had once stood, and the little path by which its occupants had brought water from the brook. Here I was within less than two rods of the road; but I had not taken my machete. After nearly an hour fruitlessly spent in trying to penetrate the thicket, I found night was coming on, and I gave myself up for foiled, and made an immense circuit over a horrid tract of rough grassy hills, and thus reached town.

In connection with Guaduas I must notice the gua-dua itself, the most indispensable plant of all New Granada after the plantain, the cane, and maize. It might be called the lumber tree, for it supplies all our fencing except walls of brick, rammed earth, and, rarely, of stone, and also the woodwork of most houses, and whatever is made of boards at the North. It is an enormous grass, like the bamboo of the Eastern tropics, growing, however, to a less height, only thirty or forty feet. The slender foliage is of inconceivable beauty, comparing with that of other trees as ostrich feathers do with goose quills. The stem is about six inches in diameter, with joints about twenty inches apart. The thickness of the wood is nearly an inch.

When poles or slats are wanted, the stem is split into four, six, or eight parts. For boards for the top of a coarse table, bench, or bedstead, it is opened and flattened out, splitting almost at every inch of width, but not coming entirely apart. For a dish, candle case, grease pot, or extemporaneous vessel for carrying drink to a company of hunters or laborers, it is cut off just below the partitions. Such a receptacle is called a tarro. Tarros of double capacity are made for bringing the domestic supply of water for a family, by taking a piece two joints long, with a septum at each end and one in the middle. A hole is made in the upper and middle septa, and if they be used for carrying molasses, a bung can be put in, or an orange used for a stopper. Bottles of a single joint are used for holding castor oil, etc. In short, the uses of the guadua are innumerable.

One night Mr. Gooding's little daughters showed me a luminous coleopterous insect about an inch long, called here cocuyo. It was a snap bug of the size and form of the largest known at home as the Elater ocellata, which closely resembles it except in the luminous faculty. They had three of them prisoners in "houses" made by splitting a piece of cane and cutting a cavity in it for each one, so that the walls of their cell serve them for food. They shine continuously, except when at rest, with a light no brighter than the instantaneous flash of the best of ours. But their light is of two distinct and beautiful colors, red and a yellowish green. I do not know if this depends on sex. It is generally believed that you can call the cocuyo to you by whistling, but the experiments I witnessed in the Cauca were adverse to this conclusion. I think it is Elater noctiluca.

I passed a Sabbath at Guaduas. At early dawn the plaza in front of the church was nearly filled with country people of all shades, from Indian and Negro to white, with all imaginable productions of all altitudes. A Sunday market is a great annoyance to any decent family. It is so particularly to Mr. Haldane of Palmar, whose very name is suggestive of stiff Scotch Presbyterianism. He applied to Archbishop Mosquera to suppress the Sunday market at

Guaduas, but he told him that it was the best day for a
market, as these poor peasants could not spare two days
to come to town, and Sunday being a holiday, they were
bound to hear mass on it. There being two priests here,
they have two masses, and the market people may take
charge of each other's goods in turn during the mass. The
archbishop laughed at the scruples of the good Scot, and
applied to him the sobriquet of "Bishop of Guaduas."

I attended here the first mass I heard in New Granada, having always before gone too late. A little daughter
of Mr. Gooding went with me. She left her hat at home,
and put on her shoulders a black shawl, which, on entering the church, she put on her head, and sat down flat on
the floor. I felt a pang to see the amiable, intelligent child
assimilated with the masses around her in dress and posture. The men never sit on the floor. If there be benches,
men alone sit on them; and, if not, they stand; the women
never stand. There are times when all must kneel, or be
counted impious; at these times the bells peal, and the
buyers and sellers in the market all uncover, at least. A
Protestant who remains covered is liable to have things
thrown at him, but would be protected by law. No resident Protestant has ever attempted to resist these req-
uisitions of superstition, as far as I have learned. A traveler like myself, can generally escape compliance without
inconvenience; but I hold that they have a right to insist
on our uncovering in church, though in the rare cases that
a lady wears a European bonnet—gorra—it is rather inconvenient.

Before describing the mass I will premise that the
church, like almost all the others I have seen here, besides
a gorgeous or gaudy altar at the end, had others of inferior
splendor extending all along down the sides, looking not
unlike a row of highly ornamented mantelpieces. Peculiar
merit is ascribed to some of these side altars. Over each
was generally an image, sometimes a picture, covered by
one or two curtains that roll up at the top by pulling a
string. All the images are painted to the life, and dressed

often absurdly, and the pictures often have jewels or finery stuck upon them, to the great injury of the few that are of merit. One form of the crucifixion disgusts the stranger particularly. You get the impression that it was painted absolutely nude, and that some person, shocked at the indecency, has sewed on a piece of muslin. I have no doubt, however, that, on removing the real muslin, painted drapery would be found under it.

Another feature of Guaduas remains to be noticed. It is the fountain in the plaza. It is a structure resembling a monument, and is surrounded with a wall about three feet high. In the front and ends of the monument are the mouths of iron tubes, from which issue streams of clear water, brought from the neighboring hill in an open, drainlike aqueduct, called an acequia. The fountain itself is called a pila; the same word is applied to a baptismal font.

The water girls come here with a large earthen jar— múcura—slung so as to rest on their hips, and a long tube in their hand. The múcura is placed on the low wall, one end of the long reed—often terminating in a cow's horn— applied to the mouth of one of the iron tubes, and thus the stream conducted to the múcura. When a múcura is nearly full, a struggle often occurs between two expectants, each desirous to fit her horn to the spout as soon as the other leaves it.

On reaching the house the múcura is emptied into the tinaja, which is a much larger jar with a wide mouth. Each house has a sort of arch of burned bricks, built generally in the corridor, with holes to receive two or three tinajas. This is called a tinajera. The tinajera might sustain the same relation to the family circle here, if anything does, that the sacred hearth does at the North.

## V

# The Plain of Bogotá

Our party from Guaduas consisted of the two musicians, who had also been waiting in Guaduas in order not to change too suddenly their temperature and altitude, and two persons who had arrived in a subsequent boat the night before. These were a Bogotano, a printer by the name of Martínez, and a boy from Caracas named Páez, traveling under the protection of Martínez. Altogether we had eleven beasts, furnished by the enterprising Negress Francisca—la negra Francisca, as they always call her. She meant to count us off into three parties, each with less than five beasts, and, consequently, each obliged to pay for a peon as an extra beast. She would send with us three peons, and we would pay for fourteen beasts. We resisted. I sent back the peon that was putting my trunks in their encerados, saying that I should engage another set of mules and peon, and travel by myself. She gave in, and sent two peons, and received pay for but eleven beasts. She had great difficulty in counting the money. I had to pay extra for my saddle, which was, at last, a bad one. I have lost the minute I made of the prices; but I once paid $12.80 for three beasts and peon (four) from Bogotá to Guaduas, and $6.40 from Guaduas to the bodega below Honda. These were high prices.

We started at nine, having already breakfasted. At the Alto del Trigo I gave my horse into the charge of Nepomuceno, the little peon of little Páez, and walked down the long hill to Cuni. Three women fearlessly waded across the brook at Cuni while I was about picking my way across on some stones. They entered the first house; I followed them, and saw there the most perfect specimen of a venta that I have ever seen. You would have called the room I entered, the tienda, a miniature grocery, but it was less and more. How they live on their slender sales I cannot guess; but in this instance they had managed to get up almost a casa claustrada, a perfect house. Most ventas consist of but a single room except the tienda, with perhaps a little cooking house in the rear. At Cuni there is a small place where you may ride into the patio, and there is food that could be sold for horses, but gentlemen rarely buy, even when stopping overnight.

As I was determined to wait here till the company overtook me, I set myself to watch the women. They called for a cuartillo of ajiaco. A cuartillo is not a measure; no measures of capacity are ever used in New Granada, and very rarely any other weight than the carga of from two hundred to two hundred and fifty of our pounds—a mule load. A cuartillo is a fourth of a dime, and is the smallest of our silver coin. Some other passers at this time showed me the only copper Granadan coin I have ever seen. Practically the cuartillo is subdivided into cuartos, but you must lay out your whole cuartillo at the same tienda. Most loaves of bread and tablas of cheap chocolate are made to sell at a cuarto. A half cuartillo is a mitad, a medio is a coin worth half a dime, and a real is exactly a dime. It is legally divided into ten centimos, but they are never used.

I may as well say what remains to be said on coins now. The legal meaning of the word peso is ten dimes, but the word is always used for eight dimes. The traveler must never doubt on that point, but he is very apt to on being told once only. If, after a *verbal* agreement, legal pesos of ten dimes are demanded, resist the demand; it is an attempt to cheat that they never would try on an experienced traveler. Dollars are always denominated pesos fuertes, duros, or fuertes, except at auctions and in law documents. A patacón is a coin of eight reals, or a transverse section of green plaintain fried hard. An onza is a gold coin sold at about sixteen dollars. They have a piece a little heavier than our double eagle, called a condor.

Well, numismatics have kept us till the poor women's ajiaco is hot, and brought in and set in a wooden ring nailed to the counter to hold the round-bottomed totuma steady. It is a broth or stew, containing pieces of potato or plantain, and perhaps, if the seller be generous, a mouthful or two of meat. If you had any confidence in the cook, the composition would not be bad to take. There was a single spoon, of totuma or wood, in the dish, with which each one took a mouthful in her turn, till, too soon, alas! the totuma was empty. There had been in it only a moderate allowance for one, and perhaps it was a case where the richer of the three was dividing her little all with her neighbors.

We followed up the Río Negro, crossed Guama bridge, passed Guayabal and Mauve. It was now dark, and we would gladly have found our baggage halted, but they had passed on with a diligence as yet inexplicable. We now entered on the Salitre, a patch of road that is sometimes so bad as to cost half a day to pass what we unconsciously crossed after dark. At last we arrived at a venta filled with a noisy crowd, and there we found all our trunks piled up under the eaves in a heap. It consisted of a single room besides the tienda. Within, one or two tallow candles, in a rude wooden chandelier, shed a dim light upon a dense mass of men and women. I made my way through it to where two or three were sitting at a table playing a sort of cards unknown to Hoyle in number, name, or form. Cups, cudgels, golds, and swords—espadas —were the four suits, and I believe the number of cards was forty.

But there was music too, vocal and instrumental, and, I believe, dancing. The principal musical instrument was the tiple, a diminutive of the bandola, which is itself a reduction of the common guitar. The length of this imple- ment of torment is a little more than a foot, and I do not think the strings are ever shortened by stopping them, as in the guitar and violin. This banjo, jr., is easily played, when once in tune, by drawing your fingers across it in any manner, only keeping time. It costs only two or three dimes, and the number that infest the land, not only in the tiendas, but by the roadside, is dreadful. The tiple was accompanied by an alfandoque, a small joint of guadua, with numerous pegs across the cavity within. It contains some pebbles or grains of maize. In a word, it is the most stupendous rattlebox ever clutched by grown-up baby. The word alfandoque also applies to a composition of sugar, full of cavities, so that it crumbles in the mouth like the candy they call kisses; but alfandoque is in the size of biscuits.

The eagerness of our peons to press on was now explained. The traveler must guard against passing near night a place where there is a holiday or merrymaking, if his baggage is in the rear. Some unforeseen accident will inevitably happen to beast or peon, and you will sleep without your baggage.

## VI

## POSADA AT BOGOTÁ

The reader surely can have no wish to know the precise names of those who for sixteen dollars per calendar month gave me shelter, food, and attendance, and all the other thousand comforts and annoyances incident to family life in Bogotá. That city has no hotel, and but one boarding-house, and, as that is an English one and has few inmates that do not speak English almost entirely, the very words "board" and "boardinghouse" have scarcely an equivalent in the popular language. Perhaps, like the English word "self-government," these too may be yet transferred to the language to which the idea is now foreign.

The normal way of living here is to hire a house or a "habitation," and either eat at a fonda, have your meals sent in to you from a fonda, or hire a cook. This last implies either that you also go to market and have your provisions stolen at home, or send your cook to market to steal your money. The last is preferable, if the cook be not insatiable; but an alternation of evils is always better than the long continuance of the same, so you should at least make a part of your purchases. It is not wise to turn off a servant for peculation, for you may get in his place one who has been long out of employment, and who, consequently, has some months' back stealing to do. It would not be imprudent to take a servant into your service who has just been discharged for theft, for of all thieves an unsuspected one is the worst. In a word, any inquiry into the morals of your servants is simply ridiculous; you may rest assured that they have none.

From all these perplexities I was saved by a letter of introduction from Mr. Gooding to Don Fulano de Tal. This I delivered in person to la Señora Tomasa, his wife. La Señora Tomasa is said to be the fattest woman in

Bogotá, where obesity is not common. She is chiefly characterized by a head of black hair that always looks like a rat's nest, but there is no part of her whole person that is not in keeping with it. The worst of her is external; but a man with a strong mind and a strong stomach makes little account of externals. I followed Mr. Gooding's advice, and became at once her guest.

She showed me the house, which was a casa claustrada of one story, with a second patio behind the first, built only on two sides, and a third behind that, which has only a shed on one side. The front is equal to about three house-fronts in a northern city. It fronts the west, and the zaguán is in the northwest corner. It is paved with stones of the size of a double fist. The door from the zaguán to the patio is very large, and is opened only to let in horses. It has a little door cut in it, and, as you pass, you must raise your foot and lower your head. This last I often forgot to do till I had received a blow.

The front was occupied by the sala, with its portraits of Mary and Joseph, and a nice image closet that contained a Dolores or la Dolorosa; that is, a Mary, with a dagger in her heart, her hands spread out, with a cloth lying across them, and her upturned eyes red with weeping. Some stuffed birds; two sofas, of chintz; a strange ottoman, that looked like the middle section of a trough, with flaring sides, and the matting on the floor completed the furniture. Carpets are not to be expected in ordinary houses here. But I forget an important and rather uncommon article—a good mantel clock.

The adjoining bedroom was devoted to the riding establishment of Don Fulano, his gun, his blunderbuss, and other precious articles. The windows of the parlor and this room opened to the street. The south side of the patio was occupied with a little dining room, having no window, and a little room with an unglazed window, where three servants slept. The east side had one large room with a door and window, which became my quarters. Next was a passage to the second court, closed with

a leathern door by day and stout wooden ones at night.
North of this was the family sleeping room, which extended into the corner so as to leave no room for a window. On
the north side were two little rooms appropriated to Don
Pastor, the landlord, who occasionally came to town and
spent a night. All these windows were furnished with a
reja, and with doors to them, and most of them, also, with
glazed sash on hinges. Glass is almost a necessary to the
rich here, but unknown to me in all other places in New
Granada.

The first patio was paved, but had several plum
trees, cherished objects with Don Fulano, and some pots
of flowers. Its corredor had a matting on the northern half,
as this was more trodden by visitors and less used by
servants than the rest. The second patio had an unpaved
garden, with a fig tree, a papaya, more plums, and a
minute apple tree half-dead with cold. By way of annuals,
there were potatoes and other esculents. The west side of
this patio was occupied with my little study, an open corredor, and a dirty pantry. A few steps led down to a still
dirtier kitchen, to a little space containing an oven, in
which there never has been a fire, and to the door of the
third patio. This is all paved, has a shed and manger on
the south side, with a door opening on a back street or
vacant lot.

This place, designed to accommodate more horses
than the house could hold of guests, was entirely in the
occupation of a dog of the Newfoundland breed and
feminine gender, whose offspring were held by the señora
at high prices, as they were difficult to raise at lower
altitudes. These would do well but for the supposed nightly
visits of the bats, who are said to keep them poor by
sucking their blood. No one doubts these vampire stories,
but some confirmation of them would be desirable.

While I was looking at these things, a servant girl had
placed on the parlor table a little cup of chocolate, a slice
of cake, and a saucer of sweetmeats. This was my dinner
that day, as frequently happens on a journey. This over, I

sallied out to meet my baggage, which, fortunately, was just entering town at the close of twilight. We proceeded to the little Plaza of San Victorino, and had halted for an instant, when I heard an English voice ask, "Is there an American here?" It was Mr. John A. Bennet, our excellent consul, who had learned that he had a countryman coming in the party. And I have never found him less prompt or less friendly to any stranger, even though he come, as I did, without any letters to him.

Thus I settled myself in the family of Don Fulano de Tal. A little cot bed gave me a warmer embrace than my cold couch at El Botello. I awoke from it, and waited in the morning to see whether I was to eat in the house. While meditating on this, Ignacia, an Indian girl of seventeen years, and a little over five feet in stature, came into my room and spread a cloth on my table. What else she put on I cannot say, only first there was something that they called sopa, because it resembled soup in being eaten with a spoon. I can offer no conjecture as to the ingredients. Another dish was the ajiaco that we saw at Cuni; it contained potato, fluid a little thickened with something, and traces of meat. Another dish contained what comparative anatomy would call chicken, but the palate would conjecture might be lizard. But it is colored yellow. This is one of the inventions of Spanish cookery. It is often done with arnotto, called achiote or bija. Some time afterward I objected to this addition, which only served to prevent the eye from judging of the real condition of things. La señora named it cover-dirt (tapa-mugre), and banished it from her kitchen. My breakfast ended in chocolate.

My dinner seemed but a repetition of my breakfast, except that it ended in sweetmeats instead of chocolate. As to what occupied the butter plate, I ventured to suggest that if the butter were on one plate by itself, and the other ingredients on another, I could perhaps make a mixture more in accordance with my own palate. The good lady tried to improve on my suggestion, but with indifferent success. So minute were the particles, and so intimate their dissemination through the butyraceous gangue, that it seemed as easy for the Ethiopian to change his skin. The result was, that though Bogotá furnishes a dozen kinds of good bread, I soon forgot the use of butter.

All bread is made in small loaves of sixteen for a dime (a cuarto each). None is made in families, as far as I ever knew, nor have I yet seen a bakery. I suspect those that make it sell but a dollar's worth or so per day. There is little consumption for the article, as it is beyond the reach of the poor.

Only the last session at the table afforded unmingled pleasure. I cannot call it a meal. It was but a single cup of chocolate, with a piece of bread or cake, a saucer of dulce —sweetmeats—and a silver goblet of cold water.

After a day or two I asked permission to come to the family table, which was acceded to with much satisfaction, but my little tea continued to be in my own room. The change of table gave my landlady a better opportunity to study my tastes, which she did with the diligence that I afterward gave to those of an armadillo. She spared no pains to gratify my palate. I am sorry she succeeded no better; but, while my pet starved to death, hers has survived. And, if variety would have sufficed, none could have excelled her; and my dishes were almost as exclusively mine as when I ate alone. Never was hostess more indefatigable, nor guest more uncomplaining in his sufferings. Suffice it that the experiments lasted the two months of my stay. I dare not undertake to tell you of all the strange things I ate and attempted in this time. One of their dishes was blood thickened, seasoned, etc. This I would not eat.

One day I wanted to see the señora, and she was in the kitchen. So I went in. Of course, the kitchen has no floor. A floor would be useless—nay, impossible. As well might you carpet a foundry. Second, it has no chimney. A chimney would not be impossible—there are several in Bogotá, but of what use are they? Smoke consists of creosote, acetic acid, and carbon. The last is perfectly inert, the first a valuable antiseptic, and the other an important condiment, and no harm can arise from an admixture of the three as in bacon. A portion of the roof is raised, so as to permit the egress of smoke and steam without admitting rain.

Most ordinary cookery is done in a sort of forge, having a series of little fireplaces over which ollas can be placed. These are coarse earthen pots, often unglazed, and of various shapes and sizes. The olleta of cast brass, in which chocolate is made, resembles a quart pitcher in size and shape.

And now what is doing here? Petronila is busy at the grinding stone bruising wet maize to dough. The Indian corn here never enters a water mill, nor does it enter largely into Granadan cookery. La señora is seated on a low stool; before her is a jar—tinajón—as large as the oil jars in the *Forty Thieves*, each of which was capable of concealing a man in its capacious abdomen. It is mounted on three stones—tulpas—so that a fire can be put under it where it is and when she chooses. Here you see the convenience of dispensing with those troublesome contrivances, floors and chimneys. On her right hand is a tray of Petronila's freshly ground dough, and a dish of peas (alverjas) or chick-peas (garbanzas—Cicer Arietinum). On her left is a tray containing part of the mortal remains of a pig, cut in pieces of about an ounce each, bone extra, and a pile of the green leaves of an Indian-shot plant—a Canna, called achira. It may be Canna Indica, and its leaves are used here, like those of other Marantate plants, for wrapping up things.

She takes half a leaf, puts in it a spoonful of dough, a spoonful of peas, and a piece of pork, folds the whole up, and deposits it in the tinajón. This she repeats till the ingredients are exhausted. Water is then put in. All Saturday night these little green packages of miscellany are boiling over a slow fire, and on Sunday morning la señora's tienda is thronged with purchasers of tamales. Imagine a tamale now on your plate. You open it with fork or fingers, and you see what irresistibly strikes you as an accidental juxtaposition, not mixture, of heterogeneous matters, like the contents of a turkey's crop disclosed by the carving knife. It is hard to overcome prejudice, but I have learned to eat tamales with relish, and have even perpetrated the pun, "No está mal, it is not bad." No es tamal would mean it is not a tamal.

But I have said nothing of Don Fulano; indeed, there is little to say. He is the reverse of his wife, a dry little Quiteño, rather neat, and as friendly as a man can be. He was a helpmeet for la señora in the arduous task of pleasing her guest. Señor de Tal had but one weakness; after church, at which he was quite constant, he must go to the cockfight every Sunday. He never lost large sums, for he could not afford to bet high. His only income was derived from his salary as shopkeeper in a small dry goods store. A sprightly little boy, of very inoffensive, affectionate manners, was all their family.

Not to use terms for dress before defining them, I may as well here describe an ordinary peasant dress throughout; nor is the task a long one. The camisa begins a few inches below the chin, and extends as far below the waist. It has an inch or two of sleeve, and a sort of collar, cape, or ruffle falling down from the upper edge—arandela. This is often embroidered with red or blue, but the garment, when clean, is white. The enaguas extends from the waist to a proper distance from the ground. As this may be the only other garment, an accidental loss of it might discompose even the least reserved of the wearers of it; so it is divided into two flaps by openings at the sides, and each one is secured to the body by a separate string, that of the forward lobe being tied behind, and the other in front; so the whole person, or enough of it, is scientifically covered, but the two garments do not overlap much. Add to the dress indoors a woolen shawl—the mantellina—which, like the enaguas, should be always blue or black, and a man's palm-leaf hat, and you have the peasant Granadina in sufficient dress for street or church. In warmer climates, a thinner shawl or large handkerchief—pañolón—is substituted for the mantellina.

A girl named Petronila formerly made her appearance every morning, with her múcura and long tube, bringing water. I am sorry to say that, when a regiment stationed in Bogotá left for the south, she disappeared. These bodies of troops are said to be followed by more women than there are men in them.

While here I paid the common matriculation fee to a residence—an attack of the diarrhea. The exciting cause was a brief dip in the icy waters of the Fucha, a mile or so south of the city, where others bathe almost by the hour with impunity. I am sorry that I must believe that the attack was prolonged by the interference of my medical advisers in my plan of treatment.

My disease involved a variety of privations besides that of locomotion, and impressed me with the idea that my motherly hostess had not the talent that we often find in kind ladies of her age. She fed me at first on sagú— arrowroot (hence, perhaps, our word sago), of which New Granada cultivates all it uses, and no more. If I found this insipid, the chicken broth that succeeded it was not much less so, for the Andine cooks have an innate faculty of destroying the natural flavor of all meats. Turkeys are here reduced, by their process, to a viand as unpalatable as the rest.

One other little circumstance occurs to me: from some cause, I had occasion to spit frequently, and laid down a paper on the floor for a spittoon. La señora sent in a mat as a substitute for the paper; and the Indian girl, after putting it just where I wished, spat on the floor beside it, and went out. Indeed, I had no other reason for using the mat than to keep myself from learning nasty tricks, for there was no way of saving my floors from my visitors, nor even from la señora herself, although, for a wonder, I never saw her or any of her family smoke. The servants, I presume, smoked, but it is contrary to etiquette

for a servant to smoke in the presence of superiors, or for a
soldier to do so on duty. I never should have changed my
boarding place but for circumstances that connected me
with a companion for traveling. He was a cachaco: the
word indicates such young men as wear coats, and might
include all English words from buck and dandy to gentleman. The cachaco in question, whom I will call Don Pepe
(Pepe means José María), was an LL.D., a graduate of the
Holy Ghost College of Señor Lorenzo Lleras (since Secretary for Foreign Affairs).

We commenced our life in common with three thievish servants, who professed to take charge of some horses
said to be kept in some pasture near the city for us, but we
soon succeeded in getting the two best off our hands. As
for the other, Bentura (Buenaventura), nobody would
have him, so we kept him.

We took rooms in a large casa baja, opposite the
fonda of Doña Paz. She rented this house to let to guests,
and she took us in hopes that we should frequent her table
also. This did not suit Don Pepe, who alleged a want of
neatness in her dining room, indicative of still more in her
kitchen. Of our rooms we could not complain. Besides a
small bedroom, with a cowhide bed for Don Pepe and a
cot bed for me, who am too much of a Sybarite to sleep well
on the soft side of a dry hide, we had a huge parlor, with
three sofas, three tables, two chairs, and two looking
glasses, all of which might have been sold for between five
and ten dollars in Chatham Square.

But now came a vermilion edict from Doña Paz that
all who occupied her rooms must patronize her fonda
exclusively. But we had found at another fonda a table
more to my satisfaction than I have elsewhere found
among the Spanish race. I explained to La Señora Margarita the necessity we should be under of leaving her table
or finding new rooms. She assured me that she had no
rooms fit for us; but she showed me an inner pantry, or
storeroom, that, besides communicating with the pantry,
had a door opening into the sala, and another that opened

upon what once was the corredor of a back patio. A portion of this corredor had been transformed into a snug little bedroom, at the expense of great ingenuity and very little money. I at once insisted on having the two rooms, and that night our two servants carried our trastos—effects, including monturas, trunks, atillos, and petacas—on their shoulders to the large room. The pantry door was locked, the sala door unlocked, and both keys delivered to me. The rooms were entirely transformed; for La Señora Margarita had set about it herself, and worked, she assured me, "like a demonio."

Don Pepe slept, as before, in a stylish cowhide bed in the large room with the baggage and servants; and as all the light came through glass doors from my room, of which they shut the blinds every night, they all slept as late as they chose, undisturbed by daylight. I was equally suited with my little room, that just held the indispensable cot bed, bought expressly for me, a table, and a chair, with space on the walls to hang my maps. Here I was at the top of fortune's wheel, and I expect nothing equal to it, or at all to be compared to it, in all my exile. I paid here, as before, sixteen dollars per calendar month.

I did have one cause of complaint on the first night. My pillow felt too much like a well-stuffed ragbag. La señora would have it righted as soon as mentioned; so we ripped it open, and behold! as much cotton, in solid wads, just as it came off the seed, as could possibly be got in. We picked loose a third of it, and filled the pillow nicely, and the lady probably jotted down in her notebook that los Ingleses are very particular about soft pillows.

La señora was an Ibagueña—a native of Ibagué— quite a handsome matron, perhaps more prepossessing than any other that I have seen here; nor were my expectations disappointed, for she was a nice lady, excepting, perhaps, a violence of temper, which I never knew excited without cause, though occasionally it went beyond bounds. When she raged, it was like a sea or like a lioness —she never fretted. She kept a tienda and a fonda, both of superior order, and sold no chicha, and more brandy than rum. Her husband, who was a major on half pay or pension, appeared to be a confidential boarder, and her best friend rather than her liege lord. I do not know what his business was, but it may have been gambling. They had three fine little daughters, the oldest of whom went to a boarding school a few blocks off, but occasionally came home of a Sunday morning. The second went to the same school as a day scholar. A strong-willed little boy, who had a great passion for riding a horse around the corredor, and a babe in charge of a wet nurse, completed the family record.

The house, which they rented of a friar, was a casa baja claustrada—a one-story house, with the rooms opening on the patio or court. It stood on the corner, and was much larger than usual. The corner room opened on both streets, but had nothing to do with the house, although it appeared to be a part of it, while the tienda, which appeared to belong to the next house, as seen externally, had its only inner door opening into a spacious refectory, where at first our meals were served with those of chance comers who paid by the meal. At my instance, we removed to the family table in a separate dining room. The husband had a room that served him for bedroom and office, far removed from the two rooms that served as dormitories for the lady, the children, and the nurse. Another room served for several female servants, including the shoptender—cajera —while of other rooms I knew no destination. A fellow boarder, a physician in poor health, a relative of Margarita, occupied still another room in the house. Back of the house was a large patio, divided in two by a high brick wall. One half was paved, and the other may have once been a garden, of which a fig tree and a papaya seemed to be the only remains. In a shed at the back side was an oven, with a peephole made in the side.

Such were the premises where I found more physical comfort than in any other Granadan family. Our meals were two a day, at about nine and two. The latter nearly always included a dish called puchero, made of boiled beef, potatoes, and cabbage, not unlike a common boiled dish at the North. It was preceded by a soup, often with vermicelli, of which I seldom tasted. A delicious dish here was the terminal bud of the palm, but it seems almost a crime to destroy a stately tree for so insignificant a treat. It is eaten with butter, and commonly called palmiche. It is a little curious that, among all the strange Spanish dishes I found, the olla podrida never made its appearance. As to ask for it would be to commit myself to eating of it, I waited till it should come, but it never did.

We had a good supply of fruits, bought once a week at the market. On Friday, and sometimes Saturday, the last course was fruit just from market. An immense dish of strawberries, with sugar and milk; the curuba, before mentioned; a fruit tasting very much like a cucumber, and therefore called pepino; and bananas; such were the ordinary table fruits.

The Granadinos do not understand eggs. They make them into a omelet, unpalatable to us, called tortilla; they fry them, but, in eating them, they break a hole in the center of the yolk, and put in a good quantity of salt, and after all it seems as if they may have been fried in water. They offer you also what they call warm eggs—huevos tibios—which are eggs boiled in the shell; if they would offer you a bit of nice butter at the same time, you would relish them all the better. As for custard, pie, tart, and pudding, I believe these words have no equivalent in Spanish. I have once seen a thing that had the same anatomical structure as a pie, and bore the name of pastilla, but it was an outrage on the palate.

# VII

## BOGOTÁ AND THE BOGOTANOS

The very first impression that Bogotá makes is on the soles of the feet, and that is by no means an agreeable one. You feel that it is making a beast of you by compelling you to contend with packmules for passage along the cobblestone pavement. There are no brick sidewalks, and few of flat stone. These are but two feet wide, and are highly prized by the mules; a string of them never fail to take possession of them when they come in their way.

Look at the houses. None are more than two stories; most are but one. They are whitewashed, but not white. They have a plenty of front, a large, ugly portal, and a few small grated windows, from which the female inhabitants seem to be constantly looking out like prisoners.

The poor live on the ground floors of the two-story houses, in tenements of one room, with no access to court or yard. It may seem incredible, but they have none of the outbuildings or domestic conveniences thought necessary elsewhere. There are no sewers—no drainage—and the ground floors are generally damp; hence the second floors are occupied by the rich, and so extremes meet. But here we come to a horse with his head in a door and his heels out in the middle of the street. We must make the circuit of them; every passer has done so for half an hour past. I never knew a horse, mule, or ass to kick in this country, though I am assured that they do.

The plan of the city was, in the main, laid out by nature. The streets generally bear the names of battlefields or provinces. The barrios—wards—take their names from their parish churches.

I called on the day after my arrival at the house of a merchant there with a friend. We entered the zaguán of a casa baja, and advanced to the inner door, on which he struck one or two blows with the palm of his hand. A brief dialogue ensued with a servant who came to a door on the other side of the patio. It was "Quién?" "Yo." "Adelante" —"Who?" "I." "Forward." We pushed open the coarse, heavy square door. It resisted our push because of a stone hung to a peg over the door by a leather thong. The stone rises as the door opens, and its weight shuts the door as we release it. "Que entran por dentro" is the invitation to walk in. The sala is high and spacious, the floor is matted, and two or three cheap sofas extend along the sides of the room. Instinctively you look around for books or papers, but you see neither. The windows are high, and are furnished with glazed sashes, that open inward with hinges. The walls, of unburnt brick—adobe—or of tapias, are two feet through. In the thickness of the wall is a step as high as a chair, by means of which you can mount and seat yourself in the jamb of the window. Two persons thus seated and two more standing make a snug party. All windows are protected with a reja or grate, and no reliance is placed on the sash for protection.

The lady of the house came in, and we learned that the gentleman we wished to see was not in town. She ordered a servant to bring fire—candela. It was a brand from the kitchen, or else a coal in a massive silver spoon, and with it she handed round cigars. I declined, saying that I do not know how to smoke—No sé fumar.

She and my friend went to smoking. She was of about the middle age, rather coarsely dressed, as I should say, and seemed uninteresting, rather from the want of intelligence than from the lack of the elements of physical beauty. Her black-eyed daughter, whom I afterward saw rather by accident, as she was engaged with other company when I called, was scarce able to converse about things, and I cared little to converse about persons, so that, in spite of personal attractions, I tired of her as I would of a moving, speaking image.

But how can we expect conversational powers without reading? The young lady is, in fact, almost a prisoner.

Her sole enjoyment and employment seems to be to seat herself in the window, and exchange salutations with those who pass. Should I ask her to take a walk with me, it could be little less than an insult. She can never go out but with her parents and brothers. In fact, she scarce ever enters the street except to go to church. Her school was a prison to her, her house is a prison, and what does she lose if she betake herself to a nunnery, as a prison from which she shall go no more out? In fact, the nunnery receives no prisoners without a respectable dowry, and perhaps it secures her as much happiness as she might find in the married state.

I did not see the young lady smoke, but I presume she does. Many assert that it is not disreputable for ladies to smoke; but it is said that many smoke secretly, but not openly, so that there must be some discredit about it. As for the practice of smoking with the lighted end of the cigar in the mouth, which prevails in the tierra caliente among the women, I have never seen it here. It probably is economical of tobacco, as none of the smoke wastes its sweetness on the outer air till it has deposited a part of its narcotic principle on the mucous membrane. Cigarillos, made by wrapping tobacco in paper, are rarely used; the ladies smoke unmitigated cigars.

There are in Bogotá many that know what hunger and scanty fare mean. Among them are a large proportion of females, occupying a position more like that of the grisettes of Paris, only the latter far excel the guarichas of Bogotá in intelligence, wealth, comforts, attractiveness, and in morals.

The guarichas furnish an ample supply of wet nurses at a very reasonable price, only that when they have gained the affections of their charge they abuse their advantage, as the heartless of that class are apt to do. Their own children are no obstacle, for, if they live, they can put them into the foundling wheel as soon as a good offer for their services occurs.

I called on my washerwoman one day. She lives in a

tenement on the ground floor of a casa alta. Cold as is the
weather in Bogotá, the door is open to admit light, for she
has no glass. To prevent the intrusion of prying eyes, a
screen—mampara—is placed before the door. It is too
high for a five-foot Indian to look over, and placed just so
that we can run round it. The little room looks like a
prison cell, only it has no grated window, nor loophole,
nor breathing hole, except the open door. Within is an
inner cell, smaller than the outer, with no door, and all its
light and air comes from the outer door. A table, as large
and as high as an ottoman, a low stool, the seat of which is
made of two equal surfaces descending to the center like
a trough, two or three little earthen dishes, the poyo or
immovable seat built around the walls, pieces of rawhide
or mat for beds, and the mampara, are all her furniture.
The washtub? It is the river. The ironing apparatus?
Another woman does the ironing.

Where is her door leading into the patio? She has
none, and can have none. A fine house would it be if any
guaricha that chose to rent this miserable tenement could
come into the patio. But what can she do? Where can she
go? for modern improvements are not dreamed of, and
sewerage there is none. She has no rights outside these two
little holes, except in the streets, vacant lots, and by the
riverside. Blame not, then, the poor peasant women by
the riverside; they keep the laws of decorum as far as is in
their power; and when you are sickened at the sight of
filth in the street in a city 314 years old, washed by two
rivers, and placed on a sidehill to make drainage as easy
as possible, let it be a motive to urge upon the gobierno of
the province some such radical measures as health and
decency demand.

The number of families living in this way exceed,
perhaps, the number of well-living families in Bogotá. The
ground floor is often regarded as not so healthy as the first
floor, so each house has but one respectable family that has
access to the patios. The front room of these lairs, excavated, so to speak, in the foundations of the best houses (the

vice-president's among the rest), are often used as shops by shoemakers, tailors, saddlers, etc., some of whose implements even occupy part of the street, to the inconvenience of every passerby. Here you see a gamecock anchored to a peg by a string that has a segment of cow's horn, of the size of a napkin ring, forming a sort of swivel link in the middle, that the prisoner may not twist his cord up into knots. The bird is out here at board; his owner might not wish such an ornament in his own patio.

Bogotá has a daily market in the Plaza of San Francisco. It is, however, small, and resorted to mainly to supply accidental deficiencies and unforeseen wants. The great market day of Bogotá is Friday, though the market really opens on Thursday in the principal plaza. On Friday the whole square is covered with sellers and their merchandise. They invade the steps of the Altozano, but the platform above is left free. The square is paved with cobblestone, except two diagonal walks of flat stone, which are so arranged in some places as to form troughs to save the rainwater to moisten the thirsty sole of some passer at night. One of them, near the northwest corner, almost deserves a place on the map of the city; and there are others in the city that I could avoid even now by my distant recollections of repeated disasters. A person who designs stopping in Bogotá should bring his lantern and a good pair of India-rubber shoes.

But I was speaking of the market. Wednesday is the market day of Facatavitá. Many things sold or unsold there are transferred to the Plaza of Bogotá on Thursday. Here there is a stream of sirup, panela, yellowish loaf sugar, fruits, etc., flowing toward Bogotá, along the great macadamized road, in bullcarts, and on the backs of men and beasts. Here an unfortunate descendant of the warlike Panches, that climbed up the steep height on Tuesday night, sat all day on Wednesday in the market of Facatativá, is taking his weary way, with his unsold backload, twenty-eight miles more, and tomorrow he hopes to sell his load and start home.

I went to market once for string, and, as I had had
no other opportunity of making practical experiments, I
made the most of this. The first time the price asked was
more than I had been told to give. I accordingly went off
without making my purchase, after having offered what I
had been told was proper. One of the girls took the balls
of string, and followed me all over the market, where I
must have spent more than half an hour. It was some time
before I discovered her, and she was not aware of my
discovery. She seemed to wait for me to apply to another
for the same article, but I did not, and at length left to go
home. Still the poor indiacita followed me some rods
beyond the plaza, when, finding me really going, she
offered her balls at the usual price, and received her pay.

Overcharging strangers from richer nations is a fault
of the mean and wicked everywhere. It vexes the traveler,
who now submits, and now resists with more benefit to his
successors than to himself; but I think, on the whole, there
is far less of it in New Granada than might reasonably be
expected; and if the market people could only be made to
husband their gains, one could not help loving them. But
the tiendas where chicha is sold witness a great many sad
scenes at the close of a market, and some of a disgusting
character. Many reach home without a cuartillo of all
their sales.

## VIII

## Churches and Convents

Bogotá is preeminently the city of churches. With a population of 29,649, it has little short of 30 churches, while Paris, with its million of souls, has but about 50. Of the numerous churches there I have visited between 20 and 25, a feat that I doubt whether any other visitor has ever accomplished. But fear not that I will give the results of all this labor in detail.

There are no new churches here; I know not their dates, but judge that most, if not all of them, were built before the beginning of the last century. I wish to take you to a church that never has been a part of a convent. And now it occurs to me for the first time that all these churches without convents must be small churches, and comparatively poor ones; so I must take the largest of them, Las Nieves. The façade, like all the others, is decidedly homely, as I count homeliness, though admirers of the Gothic may not agree with me. In the belfry are the bells, tier above tier, fewer and smaller successively, till at the apex is one of the size of a magnificent cowbell. They are not hung as ours are, but a string is tied to the tongue of each, and they are pulled without the intervention of any machinery. Of course, the largest are small, for they have been brought from Honda by mule or by carguero. There is no tolling, no solemn peals, but a rang-a-tang-tang on all occasions, and as in all the city there must be over one hundred of them (Steuart says one thousand), they can make considerable noise.

All along down the sides are altars, with their camarines and saints. It is quite desirable that there should be five at least. One of these is, in this instance, in a capilla, that projects out beyond the walls on the left-hand side. This particular chapel is remarkable for being used as a storeroom for the twelve apostles, which are here all left to shiver in coarse shirts—all except the beloved disciple, who, in a very dilapidated robe, leans on the bosom of his Master in robes equally superannuated.

Directly over the door as we enter is the organ loft. There are two pairs of bellows outside of the organ; it takes a stout man to blow them. Each is loaded with a heavy stone, and the man alternately lifts up the upper valve of each. The music is horrible. I may as well get through this at once by saying that in all New Granada I have heard but one good or even decent singer, an Italian monk. Even he had never studied music. On extra occasions secular singers are hired as at a ball, but they are poor at that, and, but for the performers of the military band, poor indeed would be the music on the most urgent occasion. Rarely is it better than none.

Often there are no seats in the church. In Bogotá there are generally a series, placed end to end, running down from the high altar to near the door on each side of the central line; so the occupants of the seats sit facing each other, six or eight feet apart. The seats are occupied by men only; all females sit flat on the floor, or on a pellón carried by a servant. The pellón is a rug, like the finest that we lay at our doors for a mat, and is used for a bed, on the saddle, and for a seat in church. As the floor abounds in fleas, and creatures still more unclean are carried away from there—as all women spit on it, and as, in the uniformity of mantillas and sayas, it is difficult to find a friend or judge of a stranger, a crowded church is a disagreeable place for a lady. The men who do not get seats stand. No woman stands or sits on a bench, and no man sits on the floor. Only when they kneel are they all on a level. Now comes the signal for all to kneel; the little bell at the altar—the bells in the tower—the merriest strains of music, all mark the elevation of the hostia as the crisis of the mass. The women rise and the men sink, and all are together on their knees.

We enter the Church of San Francisco. I first visited

it, I believe, on Saint Francis' day. Never was decoration so elaborate; and the church itself was meant to be rich; the walls are covered with carvings, and almost the whole interior of the church is gilded with ancient heavy red gold. The crowd was enormous, and the ceremonies, as usual, stupid. A great many new figures and pictures were brought out. The explanations of many of them were written with chalk or soap on looking glasses; and the number of these aids to reflection that are found among altar ornaments in New Granada is wonderful, but the most of them are cracked or otherwise damaged. I take one of these figures as an example. It was cut out of paste-board, and painted, and set up on edge. The looking glass below said, "Saint Francis, in order to convince a heretic prince, shows the hostia to an ass, which immediately kneels." I saw the church lighted up at night with more candles then I ever before saw in one room. The monks were climbing like ants in little galleries high up the wall, now hugging a saint for support, now climbing in or out of portholes. They were lighting candles wherever they could reach. Now down comes a blazing candle; take care of your shaven crowns below!

I went into the convent; it was the first I ever visited. You do not meet so good treatment here as with the Augustinians, but the pictures will pay a visit. They are usually covered with large screens hanging by hinges from the top; on this day these were all drawn up. The pictures are a series, illustrating the life of Saint Francis. I am not sure now whether it begins before or after his birth. They are large, say five feet by six, but of no artistic merit. The most interesting one to me is Saint Francis preaching to the fishes. His audience are thrusting their faces out of the water, not "with ears erect" indeed, but with their large eyes staring out of their heads, and their mouths agape with a wonderful expression of credulity. A stork near the saint's feet is poised demurely on one leg, one eye fastened on the preacher, while the opposite one may be stealthily estimating the weight of some beloved object in the audience. I confess it reminds me of some things which I have seen at church before.

All these pictures are in the corredor of the principal patio. There are several other patios, some of them gardens that are absolutely uncultivated. I made some vain attempts to see the library. I fear they were ashamed to show it. I got, however, a glimpse of the kitchen and its productions. The room is spacious enough for a hotel kitchen, but of the fare I should be a poor judge. My taste certainly differs from that of the sleek brethren. Monasticism is not dead yet; some of the monks are quite young. I made them several calls, but got very little more insight into their life than at first.

A bird's-eye view of Bogotá would surprise you with the number of churches and the size of the convents. Many of the convents have already been taken from the Church, and converted to some purpose more useful to the descendants of those whose money built them, such as schools, hospitals, etc., but the space occupied by the remainder is enormous, and they are said to own about half the real estate of Bogotá.

The number of monks and nuns cannot be great, for, in the 32 Granadan convents there are but 697 persons, exclusive of 469 servants and 97 pupils. All of these could find space enough in a single convent of this city. Jolly times they must have had of it till Archbishop Mosquera took away the nuns' horses, abolished their theaters, forbade their masquerading in male attire, and allowed even to the aged and infirm but *two* servants each. Even now their sufferings cannot be excessive, for in Santa Inés there are 73 servants and but 46 other inmates. Nuns are never suffered to leave their convents, nor have I ever heard of any recent charges of their violating their vows.

## IX

### EXCURSIONS

Bogotá, being situated at the western foot of a mountain range, is half surrounded with mountain and half with plain. My visits have chiefly been to the mountains. I will take these up in the order of the points visited, beginning at the north. I take first, then, the expedition of December 1, 1852—the longest, the most disagreeable and unprofitable of them all. I wished to see a páramo—a region too cold for cultivation. I set out very early in the morning, mounted on a fine horse, kindly lent me by our minister, Mr. King, and accompanied by Dr. Hoyos and Señor Triana, of the Chorographic Commission.

On the left is a hacienda, to which, at a later period, I walked with Mr. Green, to see something of a political festival to celebrate the accession of the Liberals to power on the famous 7th of March, 1849. We stayed but a short time, and left before the affair was fully under way, as our worthy representative soon tired of the affair. We saw some dancing worth notice. In a small room near the entrance there was a fiddle or clarinet playing, in anticipation of the military band yet to arrive. Two or three females, not of the highest class, were present, and ten times as many of their peers of the other sex. Two of them stood up to waltz. In two minutes a second man stepped in and took the place of the first, without breaking the time. A third and a fourth succeeded, till, the girl becoming tired, her place was supplied by another in the same way. How long the waltz lasted uninterrupted I cannot say, as we came off. If the musicians had relieved each other in the same way, there is no saying when the time would have varied or the step ceased. In nothing is the Granadino more indefatigable than in dancing, either by night, or, as in this instance, by day.

We were mounted on horses unused to climbing. On our way up we were overtaken by a loaded bull from Bogotá. We were amused to see how little he made of climbing where our fine animals were put to their utmost. For the very worst of roads they are surer of foot than a mule, but cannot supersede them on any other. Mules are quicker, and will, I think, carry a much heavier load. A mule costs much more than a horse. They are surer of foot, but I suspect they cannot endure more. The fact is, that the mule will not let you abuse him as a horse will. A horse, to escape the lash or the spur, will exert himself till he will never see another day of health; but when the mule can do no more without injury to his constitution, he is as conscientious as a politician; urge him as you will, he will do no violence to that sacred trust. Hence mules are a semi-barbarous institution, as cargueros are a barbarous one; and as cargueros have successfully opposed the opening of mule roads in some instances, so the Spanish institution of mules has opposed itself to wheel roads, and in one instance, in the mother country, even to the opening of a railroad when completed!

We rise higher, and vegetation is ever changing. Here I noticed for the first time a peculiar and beautiful shrub of the Tiliate order, the Vallea stipularis, with its copious pink blossoms and pretty leaves, larger and thinner than shrubs at this altitude often indulge in, not unlike those of the poplar. A still more beautiful Ericate shrub, the Befaria resinosa, bears here the name of pega-pega, from its sticky blossoms, an inch long, growing in dense clusters, of a rich rose color of all shades, from the deepest to the most delicate. Here only did I find them with so little varnish as to be readily detached from the paper in drying.

At length we ceased to ascend. At the top we found a hilly country rather than a plain, and on a distant hill saw a tree. We descended to a hacienda, consisting of three mud cottages. The largest was in the form of two sides of a square, and had three habitable but very small rooms, apparently for the occupancy of one man, not very nice, but, judging from his chapel, particularly pious.

The other houses were at a little distance, and were a house for a dependent, and a kitchen. From the gentleman's bedroom a bellpull extends to the other house, a contrivance almost unknown in this country—the first bell I have seen, in fact, large or small, except those in churches. We left our horses in one of the vacant rooms, and sallied out for plants. We were soon driven in by a storm, for the páramo had got angry, as they say here.

We were kept wet and cold a long time at the house, while they were preparing some chocolate for us at the kitchen, on the strength of a friendship between the proprietor and Dr. Hoyos. I walked up and down two of the rooms to gain heat. It was actually hailing without, the nearest approximation to snow ever ventured on here.

I have not yet spoken of my zamarras. Don Fulano thought it not respectable for me to ride out without zamarras, so he lent me his. They are a sort of overalls, or imperfect pantaloons of hide—I should judge, in this instance, of bull's hide. Certain it is that, once in them, I was as helpless as a modern knight in ancient armor. It took two to extract me from them and encase me in them; to mount, I had to climb on a bench; and when I dismounted, it seemed as if the saddle was sticking to me. It was months before I repeated the experiment, and then with a more pliable pair. Zamarras are exhibited in the figures of the orejón, the carguero and babe, and the vaquero. In the last they are of the skin of the tigre, called jaguar in other Spanish countries, which I suppose to be the Felis discolor, the most formidable animal of the New World, but fortunately rather rare, and cowardly.

Once fairly stuck upon my horse, I had time to look again at the weather. The ground was white with hail, but now it neither hailed nor rained. *Facilis descensus* was not written on the side of a wet mountain. Before the rain the descent would have been difficult, now it was absolutely dangerous. Both my friends' horses fell with them during the trip, but we escaped unhurt. In some places, after again reaching the plain, we found five inches of hail! In a fit of absence of mind, it seemed natural enough to me. I forgot that today is here reckoned the first day of summer, or, as we would call it, of the dry season. The terms seem equally inapplicable today. This crop of hail-stones is counted a blessing, and is eagerly treasured up for ice creams.

Indeed, the plain had been visited by no ordinary storm. Roads were turned into rivers. Encumbered as were our hands, to say nothing of my zamarras, it was no easy task to pick our way. However, we reached home, before dinner of necessity, but near night, not very richly rewarded for our journey except by the good we derived from each other's company.

One day I wished to bathe. The most attentive friend I had in Bogotá, who could never do too much for me, conducted me here (the Río Arzobispo). We were to start at ten, but he was occupied till twelve. In fact, it is almost impossible to set out at a fixed time here. We proceeded along the alameda till we came to the convent of San Diego, when we began obliquely to ascend the foot of the mountain. We soon struck the aqueduct that supplies our part of Bogotá. It is a sort of drain a foot wide, with the water six inches deep. Most of the way it is covered, but not so as to protect it from surface wash.

It had recently rained, and the water at the pila was of a rich brown color, but where it entered the head of the aqueduct through a small strainer it was perfectly clear. I did not like very well to know that the dirt I drink had been so recently incorporated with my chocolate.

We followed the acequia to its origin, and the river upward from this point. Soon the climbing became arduous, and at two (our dinner hour at home) we stood together at a fine fall of twenty feet into a pretty little basin. I began to make preparations for a bath, but my guide and physician assured me that the water was too cold and I too warm.

The barrier before us seemed insuperable. We passed it, however, at the risk of our necks, to another fall and basin very similar to the lower, and just above it. We came near being imprisoned here by a shower making absolutely impassable the dangerous path we had climbed.

High above us on the cliff was a man throwing down sticks and roots for fuel. They fell to a spot near the path by which we had been coming up here, but before we had passed the place where his projectiles struck, he had completed his load, descended with an unbroken neck, drawn his ropes out from a hiding place where we had seen them, bound the fagots on his shoulders, and gone to sell them.

Our descent was not so easy. We could not tell why we came there, as, though the lower falls yielded us a large number of plants, and some very rare ones, a Vaccinium among the rest, there was nothing new that we wanted after passing the first point where our bones were in danger. Farther down was an Aroid plant in flower that I must have. We could not reach it. We looked about for a stick to pull it down with. Absurd idea! every stick big enough to strike a mule with has long since been carried to town and sold for fuel. But I must have it; so I mounted Dr. Pacho on my shoulders, as he was the lighter and I the stronger. He could barely reach it, but after several good pulls down came it, he, and I in a heap together. Farther on, we passed the proper place without even discussing the proposition of bathing, as night was now approaching. I returned loaded with rare plants.

On the banks of the river, below where we first came upon it, was the smallest human habitation I ever have seen or expect ever to see. It was so small that I could not have lain straight in it except diagonally, and its breadth and height were less than the length. I have seen poorer houses, however, for it was tight, and had a door that would fasten, and was fastened; it was a house, and not a hovel. But a house is not always a home. I know not, indeed, that there is really a home except among the northern races of Europe. I know of no word nearer to it than casa—house—in Spanish, and have not once found it a loved place, as home is with us, in all my wanderings. The perennial absence of fires for warmth may have something to do with it. In this respect our poorest cabin stands as far above the richest residences in Bogotá as they excel the little kennel against the eaves of which I was leaning, looking over the ridgepole as some sad thoughts passed through my mind.

The next visit in geographical order was Montser-rate, the chapel-crowned peak that hangs over the north end of the city. Señor Triana, the young conservador and botanist, was here my companion. The time of day he selected was before breakfast, and being, perhaps, the most prompt man in New Granada, he called for me at daylight. I went at once, to the astonishment of the ser-vants, and to the great scandal of my hosts when they found that I had gone out without my chocolate. I carried with me, however, the materials necessary for that bever-age, and a small tin pail in which to boil it.

We threaded our way through the city to the point where a dotted line along the San Francisco leaves the city, and runs up to the quinta. This dotted line is a path along the bank, with a range of miserable huts, like the Negro quarters on a southern plantation, extending along the north side for some distance. We soon turned out of this toward the north, and then rose so high as to overlook the little patch of fruit trees, enclosed by high walls, that, with the house within, was once a magnificent present from the Liberator to Pepe Paris, a worthy patriot since dead, who erected the statue of Bolívar that adorns the plaza.

Soon from steep walking we came to climbing. Here the various paths became contracted into one that went up in zigzags. It was amazingly worn, being sunk into the earth in some places to the depth of many feet by the travel of three centuries upon the same spot. Had it been a road of daily use for business, it would not have surprised me; but that a road, traveled only for pleasure or devotion (often for both at once), should have become so deeply worn in the steep face of a mountain, seemed incredible. Some of these cuts—here called callejones—look like deep ditches worn into the ground by the action of water, so that you cannot see out as you pass them.

As we rose, the plain opened out beneath us, and the city displayed itself as in a map. It is anything but a beautiful sight, for you see but little except tiled roofs, and the ugly towers of churches, that look all the uglier when you look down upon them instead of seeing them from below.

Now we come to several little niches, called eremitas —hermitages. They have nothing in them but a little cross in each. The larger ones might shelter a couple of persons from the weather, and here, possibly, other objects than Our Lady may be worshiped sometimes.

At a distance of ten or twelve miles, the Chapel of Our Lady of Montserrate appears to be about two-thirds the way up the hill, while from the city beneath it seems perched on the highest pinnacle. Neither view is correct; there is land adjoining the chapel fifty or one hundred feet higher, but the higher tops seen over it from the distant plain are much farther off. The altitude of the church is little more than eighteen hundred feet above the city. Observers differ as to whether it is more or less than two miles above the sea. The thermometer stands here from 49 to 52 degrees.

Arrived at the top, we found a group of buildings, consisting of a church and residences for priest and sacristan, the last of whom resides there with a disgusting family and a pack of very noisy dogs. The key, I was told, had been carried down to the city that morning by a boy. It was a lie, no doubt. Two sides of the pile could be seen from the plain, and these were beautifully whitewashed. All around, outdoors, were the remains of fires, and other evidences of field feasts. Of the brands of our predecessors we made a reluctant fire to boil some water, brought from a spring a little below, for our chocolate. After all, it cost more than it was worth in precious time, for, though the air was rather keen, we had provided against it by extra dress.

While this was doing, we went up to a platform with a parapet around it, and looked off. The prospect here well repays the toil. First, there is the city beneath your feet. You could see the houses and all their courts, the rivers with their few bridges, the convents and men in the plaza dwarfed to insects. Beyond lies the plain, covered in spots with water, which has been increasing ever since the rains began. Then there are hills rising like islands, and the irregular coastline of the rim of the basin. But beyond, my eye caught an object which is never seen without interest. It was a peak and a long plain at its base. Both are covered with perpetual snow. They are the Peak of Tolima and the Páramo of Ruiz. They lie ninety miles, air line, to the west, five days' journey beyond the Magdalena. The clouds soon shut out the sight, and I have never seen it since.

I dare not trust myself to speak of the plants that I found here. Some I saw on the before-mentioned trips, and some even in ascending to the plain of Bogotá. Most of the plants I speak of at this altitude are scraggy shrubs, with small stiff leaves. Few, indeed, are as high as my head, and I know not that there was an annual herb among the whole.

Here, too, I saw the characteristic plant of the páramos—the frailejón. They have yellow composite flowers, like elecampane, and trunks like gigantic mullein stalks, in some places six feet high and four inches in diameter, and without branches. The frailejón yields a stiff kind of turpentine, that is brought to market in a sort of bottle, made by folding the leaves of the plant. These leaves are eight or ten inches long, tomentose and white like those of the mullein. They serve sometimes to save the traveler from death by cold when he is caught in the páramo by night or storm, without any refuge from the cold except by burying himself in these leaves. Fire is not thought of. There is no fuel.

The only other plant I shall mention is the chusquea, a grass that might be regarded almost as a climber. Its hard woody stem is brought in bundles into Bogotá, to be used in the construction of the roofs and sides of cheap houses. It is the Chusquea scandens.

We entered the buildings attached to the church. They seemed a convent on a small scale, uninhabited, indeed, but in good order. Not so the kitchen. It seems to be the daily and nightly habitation of a large family, human and canine. The former seemed to care very little for us, but the latter manifested a great interest in our legs, but evidently were afraid of the consequences of yielding to their impulses. In the church there is said to be a miracle-working copy of a miracle-working picture of Our Lady of Montserrate in Spain; but this could work nothing for heretics, of course, nor for Liberales, who, in fact, are little better.

The kitchen faces the north, and from the parapet there the ground descends rapidly to the garden and the spring, in a little amphitheater scooped in the mountain. We passed round west and north of this. On a little plot of grass near the kitchen the family were spreading out a large supply of priestly vestments—albas, casullas, capas pluviales, ornamentos, parmentos, cíngulos, estolas, frontales, etc., etc., etc.

We walked along to the north, nearly to the head of the Archbishop River. First we rose a hill higher than the top of the church. Then descending, we walked a long way on the top of the ridge, having on our right a gentle descent, and again beyond higher mountains, nearly twice as high in reality as the place where we are. On our left was almost a precipice extending to the plain beneath. All this distance we met scarce a plant that grew on the plain beneath, or on the mountain's base.

Southward of the church the ground descends gradually for some distance. I was shown a spot here where it is affirmed that the ground is warm. I think the word ought to be used with some qualification, for I doubt whether a thermometer buried there would ever rise to 60 degrees before the final conflagration. Imagination works wonders—indeed it works most of the wonders that I have yet examined here.

I saw growing here a gentian, a veritable *Gentiana*, five inches high, sometimes blue, and sometimes entirely white. And another familiar genus, the *Lupinus*, I found represented by a huge plant as high as my head, near the church; but I am forgetting my promise a little while back. Well, I will just mention one more, which closely resembles our common houseleek or live-forever. I suppose it to be *Sedum bicolor*.

A little southward of the "warm ground" the land descends rapidly toward a huge gulf, the Boquerón, through which rushes the San Francisco River, with a road creeping along its side. We descended to a peak, called the Macaw's Bill, which looks up the basin of the San Francisco, a space of moderately hilly country, dotted with cottages and small fields cleared of bushes.

But I must not dismiss it so. From the head of the Boquerón, which might easily be spanned by a suspension bridge one thousand feet above the river, the ground rises in every direction. The west side of this amphitheater is the wall through which the San Francisco breaks at the Boquerón, and on the two sides of which once stood the chapels of Montserrate and Guadalupe. The first we have just left; the other, which stood at a greater elevation, is a pile of ruins that we have yet to visit. The eastern border of this habitable slope is the páramo of Choachí. We might make the circuit of all this slope, occupied perhaps by fifty wood-selling families in huts and hovels, by traveling about twenty miles, without descending at any time to a spot as low as where we now stand. Our track would be nearly a circle.

All the space within it seems at first to be a forest, into which settlers have moved for the first time only a month ago, and have just cleared spots large enough to build on. But it would need but a single tree to dispel the illusion.

In all that space there is not perhaps a trunk three inches in diameter, or a bough twenty feet above the ground. All is bushes—stunted, gnarled shrubs, that make a walk there a terrible monotony. We know no English name for any useful plant that will grow there, except potatoes and barley. Not even these are cultivated, and how and why people live there is an inexplicable mystery.

## X

# THE PRISON, THE HOSPITAL, THE GRAVE

My kind friend Dr. Pacho, who showed me where to swim, but not when to swim, proposed one day, as I was recovering from a sickness, that we should make a short excursion the next day. Though still somewhat weak, I consented.

I breakfasted early, and we were soon above the city, at a place called Agua Nueva. We came to the foundations of a church on a shoulder of the hill. The origin is said to be in the fact that, when the fane above was ruined by an earthquake, its sacred image was thrown down here, many hundred feet below, but that the next night it returned to the ruins above. They then attempted to rebuild the chapel down here, but the design fell through, and the poor image was at length compelled to content itself with quarters in the Church of San Juan de Dios in the city below, from whence it has not since tried to escape.

Up went the tortuous ascent, but in many places the path was sunk into deep callejones. We still ascended till we could see over Montserrate—could see the horizon beyond—nay, even look down on the plain as it stretched off to the north of it. We came at length to the ruins of the upper church, in its day more splendid than that of Montserrate. This is the chapel of Our Lady of Guadalupe.

From this point my friend, who never lost an opportunity of getting into trouble, suggested a descent toward the northeast, from which we could reach the city by passing through the Boquerón. A task remained; it was to pass the Boquerón without wetting my feet, as at this time, when I was not acclimated, such a course would have inevitably brought on a relapse. The wild magnificence of the scene is unsurpassed by anything I recollect. For more than a mile the walls were too steep to scale, and the bottom too narrow for a wagon road.

Through this narrow gorge much of the supplies of Bogotá pass on the shoulders of men and women and the backs of oxen. Wood, charcoal, wheat, fowls, turpentine of frailejón in bottles made of leaves, and even plantains from the warmer regions beyond the mountains, come pouring down at all hours of the day, and particularly early Friday morning.

Narrowly escaping a complete ducking in my efforts to save my feet, I had crossed and recrossed the stream till but one more crossing remained at the outlet of the Boquerón. Here a new obstacle met me. To pass where the road did was clearly impossible; above was unscalable rock. Below was a narrow path close beside the water, where a group of bathing girls held possession. The whiteness of their skin showed them of no plebeian caste; indeed, I learned they were headed by a schoolmistress. How these naiads lived in the freezing current, where I dared not dip my foot, was to me a mystery; but there they were. I must get round them as best I could. I did so, and at length below passed the stream, and gained the mouth of the Boquerón. Now came the rain. It rains every afternoon in the middle of the rainy season, but I was slow to find it out, and my kind friends generally managed to be caught in it.

We took refuge in a venta. Passing through a little tienda, where market people are apt to leave too much money and take too much chicha, we entered a desolate, empty sala, and seated ourselves on the cold poyo of adobe—a brick bench running around the room. Here we watched to see it rain. Across the patio were two other mean mud huts. The posts of the corredor were of the rough, curious stems of tree ferns—palo bobo.

I saw here a stupendous earthworm—yes, an angleworm, almost big enough to "bob for whale" with. But there is no need of hyperbole; it was about two-thirds of an inch in diameter, and eight or ten inches long.

About three the rain ceased, and the doctor, finding I had had as much exercise and fasting as was good for a convalescent, agreed with me that it might be time to get home to our dinners.

I made a somewhat similar expedition a few days after, only I left the height of Guadalupe at my left. As I was going up a steep pitch, I met a sight which I shall not soon forget. It was a young girl, apparently fifteen, but doubtless older. She had on her back a large load of wood, but was descending the steep road with a quick, elastic step; in her right hand was the long staff they always carry, and on her left arm her babe, unconsciously drawing its nourishment from the living fountain. Ah, woman, how varied but universal are thy wrongs!

On the very banks of the Fucha stands the magazine, under a guard of soldiers. It is a solitary building, with a piazza, surrounded by a high wall, part of which has been carried away by the floods. The soldiers were asleep, and I had entered the enclosure before I knew it was guarded. In the piazza hung a soldier's babe in a hammock, and near stood their guns. Their cooking was done by building a fire in the piazza against the walls of the magazine. We found the mother of the babe near the desolate concern.

A little way from here I saw a body of troops washing clothes in the river within a line of sentinels. They had a few women engaged with them. The fewness surprised me, for when an army is on march there are more women than men. I have been repeatedly assured of this, and that the commanders expedite their march, and aid them across the rivers with the greatest attention. Soldiers here are smaller than other people. I am not tall, but I can look over the heads of a long line of troops, and see the top of every cap. I was first struck with the diminutive stature of the natives in a dense crowd in a church. It was new to me, who had been so often buried in crowds, to find my head projecting over the upper surface of one. I have sometimes been mortified by the rowdy conduct of the offscouring of the States in Spanish countries; but when I see such troops, I do not wonder they are tempted to pitch into them, just for a little fun. One of the officers I saw was of unmixed African blood.

The theory of rural cemeteries is not understood in New Granada. Romantic situations are not sought, and great extent is not desired. It may be desirable that some monuments be perpetuated, but the bones themselves are not a sacred deposit, so it matters not how full the ground may be while there is room on the surface. Hence the Granadan cemetery or panteón is condensed, and most of the bodies are placed in the ovenlike bóvedas. The wall of the Cemetery of Bogotá is made up of bóvedas. These "narrow houses" are placed side by side, in three or four tiers, extending around the vast ellipse, except that the space opposite the entrance is occupied by a chapel, without which a cemetery is not complete. The roof that covers the bóvedas extends over a walk before them, where the visitor is protected from the weather, as he contemplates paintings and inscriptions, on tinplate, in watercolors or oil, or chiseled in marble, and beautiful rose-colored fine sandstone that would never bear frost. Many remain as they were left when the aperture was closed on the inhabitant, and the name and date were written in the fresh mortar with a stick.

A series of masses were going on, with the humane intention of rescuing the deceased from an unpleasant situation, in which some of them must now have been for long months. While the chapel was full of worshipers, another group were going from grave to grave, with one or two priests, singing a little, and sprinkling a little water on each grave. The price of a bóveda is eight dollars, which gives a right for ten years, when the bones are drawn forth without further expense to either the purses or the feelings of the survivors. A grave in the ground is cheaper, and the body is left till the ground is wanted again. A perpetual right in the ground can be secured, but not in a bóveda.

I had left the ground, when I met a bier on the shoulders of four men, who were walking at a brisk pace, and shaking from side to side a body of which I could see the clasped hands and naked face. The body was that of an aged female, dressed in white flannel. Arrived at the grave, it was full of water. Here was a pause; some were for thrusting the body down into the water, others for dipping it out; but some men who were digging an adjoining grave gave it up to the necessities of the case, and awkwardly, and with offensive exposure of the person, the body was laid in it. Then a boy caught up a huge lump of mud and pitched it down. It struck the body with a sullen sound, made the whole corpse quiver, tore aside part of the clothes, and disclosed the face and one little hand of a babe a few months old that had been concealed there! I was horrified, but stood my ground. Clod after clod fell on their naked faces, until, little by little, the shocking scene passed from view.

The burial place of the poor is down in the damp plain west of the city. The Bogotanos hoped I should not see it, for it is truly a horrible place. The fence leading to it was of wood—sticks tied to poles with thongs of rawhide; but the fence of the cemetery was of tapias and tile. Within were bones scattered over the ground, and even a skull or two, and that unclean bird, the gallinazo or chulo (Vultur Jota), nearly allied to our turkey buzzard, was perched on the wall, desiring to defile his beak with the flesh of Christians, which I hope he could not reach, though he could smell it. This creature usually finds its upper limit before reaching the height of this plain, but Bogotá seems to be an exception, as it is warm considering its altitude. We see large numbers of them walking over the waste places, seeking food, or opening out their sooty wings on a roof, where their peculiar position leads people to say that they are praying in cross, as they do at La Tercera. The king of the vultures, rey de los gallinazos—Vultur papa, the vulture pope—is a different bird, and not gregarious, like the gallinazo. When he comes to their feast, they, either from respect, or possibly from mere prudence, leave the whole to him till his majesty pleases to eat no

more. On the whole, I do not think the gallinazo, though
a graceless loafer, is so uncleanly as our turkey buzzard—
Vultur aura—whose every feather disgusts, and when he
has gorged so that he cannot escape, is not ashamed to
spew out his obscene repast on his captor.

Halfway up to the ledge above the city, near a brick-
kiln, where they burn their bricks with brush smaller than
hazel bushes, is a place where they bury suicides, and
sometimes, it is said, malefactors. They are buried like
beasts, and their memory perishes with them. Still, the
good woman, whose rancho stands near the spot, dares
not venture outdoors at night, as if the miserable walls
that cannot keep out the air could protect her from ghosts.
I will add, now that my theme has taken so grave a turn,
that the use of coffins is a new and growing practice here,
but as yet they are very expensive. The poor are carried to
their last resort by four prisoners from the presidio, attended by soldiers with loaded muskets. The introduction of
bóvedas would, I think, be a benefit to our own cemeteries.

From the grave to the doctor is to go back but a single
step, and yet I mean no disrespect to the profession, or to
Dr. Merizalde, to make it and him the subject of my next
remarks. A more estimable or modest man I do not know
than this pious and venerable physician. His library is to
me the most interesting private library I have seen in this
country, and it is worthy of a more extended notice than I
can give of it. It contains many very rare books, some of
which have here been reposing for two centuries, while the
other copies of them have been exposed to various casual-
ties in Europe—have been flooded over and lost among the
offspring of a prolific press, or worn out by too much use.
To such dangers a book is no longer exposed when it has
found a refuge here; and I know of no more promising a
field for a hunter of rare books than in the old libraries of
New Granada.

Dr. Merizalde is the principal physician of the hospital. I met him there once at the early hour which he
devotes to this labor of love. The good old man had quite

a number of students in his train, and went from bed to bed with the tenderness of a father. I was surprised at the number of patients I saw with a cake in their hand, but at length I noticed on the doctor's arm a blue cotton handkerchief, tied at the four corners, that must have held near a peck at first, from which they had been dexterously transferred to the beds of patients without attracting any notice.

The hospital is an old convent of the Hospital Brethren of St. John-of-God—San Juan de Dios. The hospital is not in good order; the rooms are old, the bricks of the floor are traversed by several crevices in each, that form so many secure depositories of dirt, some of which may perhaps date from the last century. Everything seemed to have been badly contrived, and needed a thorough reform. This would require funds which there is no probability of their soon receiving. The kitchen was dirty and inefficient, without any large vessels for wholesale cookery, or any labor-saving arrangements. It seemed as if the cooking for each separate patient may have been carried on independently of the others, and everything looked more as if the whole affair was there only temporarily. So, too, of the dispensatory: it was in the most shocking condition, and never can be any better without a radical reform. It gives the impression, too, that the medicines themselves must be the worst of their kind, when everything about them bears evidence of so much neglect.

As to the diseases, they cannot be the same here as with us. There is little or no consumption; I do not recollect of even a single case. Dysentery reigns prime minister in the court of death. I tried in vain to get at the statistics of the matter, but there were none at hand, and can only express an opinion that about one-third of the deaths, if not one-half, are ultimately from this disease. I was surprised at the small number of insane patients. Dismal indeed is their condition, and I think few recoveries could occur here. Syphilitic patients are not admitted. Many that apply from other diseases must be refused; and Dr.

Merizalde assured me that, were the hospital empty and opened for this disease alone, it would be filled in a day!

Of course, the old monastery is not without its pictures illustrative of the life of its patron saint. Here we see two devils tossing him back and forth to each other. I saw the hanging scene described by Steuart, but our recollections differ widely; instead of a monk hanging a heretic, it seemed rather to me that the devil was strangling a man either with a rope or his tail, and that the saint delivers the victim. It is not very important which is right, only I would put this most charitable construction on the matter; but if I am wrong, so much the worse for the devil.

Speaking of pictures, I saw one that, I confess, surprised me a little, hanging at the door of the church at a great fiesta. Pictures are frequently loaned on such occasions, and any face, male or female, is at once received as a saint. The one in question, however, was not in a shape to give much scope to charity; it was the priest Abelard making love to Heloise. I mentioned the matter at home, and a guest present showed that she was better posted in that old love affair than was creditable to her, in my opinion.

I cannot say that I think the medical school or the faculty stand very high in general. Probably one half of the population never pay a fee—dying is cheaper. Dr. Cheyne, a Scotch gentleman who married here long since, and one or two natives who have studied in Paris, are the only ones on whom I could venture to rely. Fortunately, I never stood in need of them. The people here are said to be very averse to large fees. Out of cities a man cannot live by practice, so it seems to me, as there is not a tenth of the whole population that ever receive any medical assistance from the day of their birth till their death, both inclusive.

There are four or five apothecaries' shops here. They appear as good as need be; not as showy as our best, but really in good condition and well served. I knew best that of Dr. Lombana. If a prescription were written with the weights here used, I would have no fear but that it would be properly put up. The safest way would be to write the prescription in granos of seventy-seven hundreths of a grain, a useful fact to remember, if we could only be sure of it. But the diversity of languages on earth is hardly more perplexing than the diversity of weights and measures, and here they are little sure of them, for their own have been changed so often. Now the legal standard is that of the French. It ought to be universal.

You are struck with the medicines here as being the same as at home. There are no druggists here. Even the ipecacuanha, if not the sarsarparilla, are brought from Europe or the United States. The pharmacopœia is the old Spanish one, but most of the medical books read here are French. Indeed, a man who reads no other language than Spanish ought never to pass for an educated physician.

From the hospital it is natural to go to the prison. I would wish to be excused from this task; but as the jefe político offered to accompany me in person, and as a prison is always a proper place to tell the truth of, I could not excuse myself. The provincial prison is in the same block with the Halls of Congress, and distant not two hundred feet from the chair of the President of the Senate. The entrance is on the street that runs down from the south side of the square. A guard of soldiers is always at the door. The prison within is very small and dirty at least, if not excessively so. It has not a whole patio to itself, but only a part of one, built in by a high brick wall, with a corredor running round two sides only. Here I saw still some debtors, though on recent notes there is now no liability to prison. One room was used as a chapel, having a meanly furnished altar, but at the same time it served as dormitory. This building is the nightly resort of a detachment of presidarios, that are employed during the day as scavengers, and in the burial of the poor, etc., always under the watch of soldiers.

The prisons can hardly be alleged as a reproach to the government. True, they are horrible, with the single exception of the Casa de Reclusión at Guaduas, but the authorities cannot remedy the matter, though they would. The government is poor. It cannot maintain suitable officers, nor can it furnish new buildings; and with crowded rooms and low salaries, not Howard himself, were he alive, could keep a prison from being what that of Bogotá emphatically is—a nuisance.

## XI

# THE VALLEY OF THE ORINOCO

I had seen plantains and oranges descending to Bogotá by the steep roads that lead from the páramos. They do not grow there. Beyond there must be a warmer place, and I wished to see it. They told me I must go to Ubaque. To Ubaque I resolved to go.

In all my previous expeditions I wore boots. I now introduced my foot to a new *chaussure*, the alpargate or alpargata. Imagine a mat made of braided string of the exact size of the sole of the foot. The braid is first coiled in the proper shape, and then sewed by a long needle passing through the whole width from side to side. A woven cap is sewed on at the toe, although the very tip is left open, so that the extremity of the great toe is visible. At the heel a strap is fastened, so as to come up behind, and be held in place by a showy woven string that ties in front of the ankle. It is worn slipper-fashion, and to the practiced eye looks strange, with the leg of the pantaloons in such close proximity.

The alpargate is the best possible defense for the foot in walking. It yields to the motions of the foot, lets it take hold of the ground, and does not heat it. Were I ever to walk for my life, I should, if possible, walk in alpargatas. The price in Bogotá is fifteen cents a pair, but in the Cauca they are both dearer and poorer. Still, I cannot do without them. It is a significant circumstance, too, that I often find no pair large enough. I am not in the habit of looking much at feet, but all testimony goes to the point that this is a land of beautiful feet, and that, I suppose, means small feet. If so, the best proof that I can allege is to say that I never yet found one alpargate too large for me, although I can wear most gentlemen's slippers that I have had occasion to try.

The Orinoco and Amazon drain nearly one half of New Granada, but of its 2,243,730 souls in the census of 1851, only 51,072 are ascribed to this region, besides that of some cold lands usually supposed to be drained into the Magdalena. Of these, 28,873 are in the cantones of San Martín and Cáqueza, in the province of Bogotá—the empire province, that extends from the Magdalena to the Orinoco; 18,523 to the province of Casanare, and 3676 to the vast territories of San Martín and Mocoa, between which the law has not marked out the limits.

And in all this vast space there are but seven post offices. Here, then, we have a future world, the very edge of which only is occupied with a few civilized Indians. Cáqueza, a good day's journey from Bogotá (twenty-five miles), is as far in as people often penetrate. All this side is sparse settlement; all beyond is effectively wilderness.

While pausing as if for a plunge, let us take a survey of a party just emerging from the depths beneath us, who have been stopping to adjust their dress to the climate on which they are entering. The principal figure, which a casual observer might regard as a heap of something carelessly laid on a mule, would, after unwrapping it like a mummy, be found to have for its nucleus a respectable and somewhat elegant lady of Bogotá, though not at present in a condition for athletic exercises. Hence she has been condemned to make this expedition in a sillón —a conveyance by no means so secure, except when a lady is clumsy, as the Turkish, or even the European.

Her feet are on the contrary side from that which they occupy when she uses the sidesaddle. The sillón is richly ornamented with red morocco and silver, and is so cushioned as to be quite easy to the rider when going at the pace of an ox, but not probably as comfortable to the beast as a saddle. Behind follows her husband, bearing her firstborn in his arms.

I proceeded south to Choachí. This is a tolerable village, standing on a level spot on the sidehill, but a mile or more from the roaring stream that flowed along the base. Both sides of this river are thickly settled with Indians. I have not seen so much cultivation in all this country, and the scene delighted me inexpressibly. The district of Choachí contains 4691 inhabitants; Ubaque, a little farther on, 3399; while on the other side of the stream, the district of Fómeque contains 6645. The amount of white blood in all this multitude is quite small.

The land here has been kept in the hands of the Indians by a benevolent provision of the law, restraining them from selling except according to certain provisions; but, with the advancing ideas of liberty, it is seen that it is undemocratic to restrain thus a man's liberty. The matter is now with the provincial legislatures, and in some provinces these reserves—resguardas—can be sold only at auction, and in others, any man that can persuade one of these thoughtless aborigines to sell to him can buy at any price, however small. It grieves me to hear that large numbers have sold. Among the most diligent buyers of resguardas is the cura of Choachí, who is now the owner of land that once was occupied by a score of families.

I was talking with one of his flock, and mischievously asked what kind of a mistress the priest kept, and the simpleton, without any apparent surprise at the question, told me that she was very pretty. And yet, I think, it is of this place that they tell me of a cute trick at the confessional. An Indian was going to confess, and his unlawful companion accompanied him as far as a certain cross, where he desired her to await his return. So our priest, who disliked concubinage, as it diminished his marriage fees, asks him,

"Are you married?"

"No, señor."

"Do you live with a woman?"

"I have lived with one, señor, but I have left her as far back as the cross."

Now by The Cross the priest understood their festival of 3rd May, which had elapsed so long that he thought proper to let bygones be bygones, and José got off with quite a light penance. The matter being squared up to mutual satisfaction, he returned to "the cross," rejoined his companion, and they went home.

Choachí is by no means a pretty place. The houses are all of one story, and thatched; and if any of them are casas claustradas, still they appear more like four huts placed corner to corner than a regular house. The plaza is small, and I think I would much prefer to reside on the opposite slope. Still, the vicinity of the thermal spring, and other causes, make it something of a watering place.

## XII

## GOVERNMENT AND EDUCATION

Congress meets as soon as the festivities of Christmas and New Year are over. The plan of the ceremonies is nearly based on our own. I had the pleasure of witnessing the opening on one occasion. The heads of departments (ministros), who have a voice in the House, have seats there, and were present. The message was ready printed, and, at the proper time, when each house had chosen its president, and the message had been read, copies of it were distributed to the members. One little peculiarity of their ceremonies is to place the military of the capital (generally some hundreds of troops) at the disposal of the presidents of the two houses.

The halls are one enormous room, nearly divided into two by a partition. The western end, farthest from the front, is for the Senate. A gallery runs round the whole except the western end, and the space not under the gallery is railed off for the use of the members. Speaking places (tribunos), like pulpits, are provided, but not used except in set speeches. The north gallery, the east, and the east half of the south is open to all, and also the space beneath, so that the Chamber of Representatives is surrounded on three sides by the spectators. But the south of the Senate is reserved, and over the President's chair there is no gallery, so that the Senate is exposed to observation only on the north side. Ladies with tickets, foreign ministers, and some officials have access to the reserved gallery, which extends a little way into the House of Representatives.

The spectators are called the barra. Their conduct is outrageous, often disturbing the proceedings with cries and insults against some of the members, and always with impunity. It would be a happy thing for the nation if a new capital could be selected west of Cipaquirá or Muzo, where there could not be a large city. If that is impossible, the English system must be resorted to of admitting to the House only by ticket. I saw little of Congress, for the very reason that it was disagreeable—perhaps it is undemocratic to avow it—to mingle with such a rabble. One member, I was told, could not speak without being taunted with a petty theft he had once been charged with.

I may as well speak here of the constitution. That of 1843 was so long a document that I never had a chance to read it; it is, in fact, a treatise on politics. For changes, it was requisite that one Congress should pass them, and that another, chosen certain months after their publication, should confirm them. Congress made an entirely new constitution in 1851, and, I believe, a very good one. It was not before 1853 that it could be sanctioned. That Congress made so many changes in it that it might be called an entirely new one; but they voted that it was the old one, and that it was constitutionally adopted. No man, as I know, in the whole nation disputed its validity, and most hailed it as the advent of "the true republic"—a thing that seems to all of them like a millennium, always at hand, but, alas! never yet seen.

The crowning defect of the Constitution of 1853 is that the executive is too weak. It has no veto. An objected bill has but to pass both houses a second time. The patronage of the executive is very limited, and no power is left it that could have been taken from it.

The next most fatal defect is that the two houses of congress are not a sufficient check upon each other. Six persons are voted for on the same ballot for congress. The highest six are elected: the first is senador; the second and third, diputados; the fourth, senador suplente; fifth and sixth, diputados suplentes. All hold their office for but one year. If the two houses disagree on a bill, they meet together as one, and the majority carries everything. Here is no element of stability. The most astounding changes are ventured on with little hesitation, and everything can be as easily reversed next year. Three times has the entire system of weights and measures been changed; that of the French has now been adopted for the second time. Important changes in the number of provinces are made continually; new ones are erected, and then again suppressed. Each new whim of the nation will carry in a congress that scorns to look to its predecessors for wisdom. Though there is a party called Conservador, the conservative spirit is entirely unknown in all the nation, so I have no hopes of any stability under the new Constitution of 1853.

The highest story of the great house in which Congress meets has the Treasury offices at the northern end. The Ministro de Hacienda, its head, Señor José María Plata, is a good man, but he has a terrible task. The treasury is in a state of perennial bankruptcy—all the effect of bad legislation and revolutions. The last remedy of this was *descentralización*. It was a happy idea of assigning to the provinces a small part of the revenues and a large part of the expenses for them to manage just as they could. This measure was called for because the nation is opposed to all indirect taxation, and direct taxation by national officers is nearly impossible in such a country.

Of indirect taxes the first important one abolished was the alcabala, or a percentage on all sales. The last was the monopoly of tobacco. Those now remaining are salt, spirits, stamps, peaje or toll, and customs. Spirits, and peaje, and the old ecclesiastical taxes of tithes and first-fruits, have been passed over to the provinces; most of them have abolished the excise on spirits and ecclesiastical taxes.

Señor Plata has been in correspondence with me on coinage. We find that the silver real is a little heavier than the new dime, while the gold condor is somewhat lighter than the double eagle. He at length decided to recommend the slight changes necessary to make our coins identical. The silver is now identical with that of France, and is a tender for all sums. Consequently, the gold is bought and sold at varying prices.

The Secretary of Finance (Hacienda) has the charge of the whole matter of mails. A priori, I should expect this to be the worst managed post of the whole administration. To my admiration, it is the best. It is far more wisely adapted to their condition than ours is to us, and is not susceptible of any radical improvement. Despite barbarism and barbarous roads, there are comparatively few irregularities, and the losses very few, and all borne by government. The department not only supports itself, but yields a revenue.

Most of the mails are weekly each way; the rest are twenty-six a year. The offices are few, not over one hundred and fifty. The mode of conveyance is left at the option of the contractor, but in many places the mail must always be carried on men's shoulders. On better roads, mules carry cubical trunks, called balijas. They are covered with tanned leather. Cargas are not to exceed two hundred and twenty pounds. Correristas may not carry things to traffic in, and their bundles are searched to prevent it. The Indian is born a commercial traveler, for within a few hours of him many things may vary 50 or 100 per cent in price. Hence this needful precaution.

The hours of arrival and leaving every office are fixed by decree, and each postmaster—Administrador de Correos—must state the hour on the waybill, and actually see him off. Their regulations to secure suitable correristas are different from ours. Theirs permit a Negro to carry the mail, but would take it from a drunken man, and imprison him. Ours are satisfied if he is a white man, and it matters less if he be drunk or sober. Indeed, I doubt if nine-tenths of their carriers would not be prohibited by the laws of our glorious Union from serving in that capacity, and yet, incomprehensibly enough (I am ashamed to admit it), their department is served far better than ours.

When I came up the Magdalena there were two steamboat companies on the river. In the Santa Marta Company the nation has an interest, but it was too poor to buy one in the other. A system of canoes and bogas for mails is provided on the river independent of both, but when the Santa Marta boats overtake a mail, they must take it in. The others, in self-defense, are obliged to refuse to do so. We left one behind us so in Barranquilla, but it afterward passed us as easily when we were in the champán. The nation has the power to require all boats to take a mail at a fixed price, or even gratis, if it chooses. It would do a real service to the country should it require fixed starting days for at least one weekly steamer each way, and forbid any irregular steamer from starting just in advance of the packets. The uncertainty of meeting boats is a great obstacle to travel here.

One important peculiarity of the mail system here is what are called encomiendas. We have no bank notes, and if we remit, it must be in coin. Gold dust, emeralds, sample cards, etc., are sent in this way, and once, I believe, I saw even a saddletree thus mailed. I once sent a horse by mail —a live horse! Its head was securely tied to the tail of the mail horse at the beginning and end of the journey; I know not which horse carried the balijas the most. I had a ruana once sent by encomienda from Bogotá to Cartago. It is supposed to have left Bogotá at 2 P.M. of Wednesday by mule, and Ibagué at 10 A.M. of Saturday by a human carrier—carguero—and to have arrived at Cartago at 6 P.M. of Tuesday. Travelers rarely pass this space in less than a fortnight.

The identical coin committed to encomienda is paid out. Bills of exchange, drafts, etc., are unknown. No fear of loss is entertained. Not one mail robbery per year occurs. A peon, wretchedly poor, carries it through a wilderness where it is 126 hours from office to office (Popayán to Pasto); an Indian takes it 125 hours' journey to the next office (Pasto to Mocoa); both know that their heavy load is mostly money, but they neither think of robbing or being robbed. Never mind; they are barbarians, and their very color would be a legal bar in our happier land to their being placed in such temptations. We ought to send them missionaries to Christianize them.

The rates of postage are high, and that is more ex-

cusable in a country where so few write letters. A letter
from one place to another in the same province pays ten
cents per half-ounce; beyond the bounds of the province
it is fifteen. Books under four ounces, newspapers, seeds,
and grafts go free. The rates for encomiendas vary according to value and distance.

One word of advice as to foreign mails. There is
nominally a mail connection at Panama between the
United States and New Granada, and you can pay
through. Do no such thing, unless you wish to lose both
money and letter, as I have done. To get letters to New
Granada, get them on board some ship that will touch at
a Granadan port, and let them be mailed there. To get
them from here, arrange with some consul. That model of
a consul, Mr. Sánchez, of Cartagena, is full of good works
of this kind toward entire strangers. I have been under
similar obligations to an unknown consul at Panama; but
trust not the United States mail at Panama unless in the
last extremity. I would sooner trust the cook of a schooner
bound to Santa Marta, Sabanilla, or Cartagena.

Among other favors due to the governor was an intro-
troduction to the Colegio de la Merced. It is in the extinct
and spacious convent of the Capuchins, at the beginning
of the alameda, just north of the Plaza de San Victorino.
I knocked at the door, and it was opened by the porteress,
who usually sits on the floor of the locutory sewing. She
informed me that the order was not sufficient for my admission, but that it must be taken to a gentleman who is
authorized to admit. I begged, however, to see the direc-
tress, and she conducted me to the locutory.

The room is divided lengthwise by a fence, and the
door by which pupils entered to see their visitors was the
other side of it. It was much too low to separate lovers, and
too high by far for the convenience of mammas that call to
see their daughters. The directora entered, however, by
the door from the hall. I begged her to excuse informalities,
and admit me without delaying me, and she cheerfully
did so.

I have often wished to get a fair insight into the colegios for boys, and have never got farther than the public halls. I despair ever seeing anything of the internal life and domestic arrangements of these institutions. Here I was taken by surprise; I was shown everything. I was asked into every room—parlors, halls, dormitory, teachers' apartments, chapel, bathroom, refectory, garden, and kitchen.

An interesting sight it was. Not a room but had some curious peculiarity, but all arranged with the best intentions. The whole was neat, but nothing elegant. Drawing and needlework were taught to excess, but vocal music not at all. Their rigid discipline allows no girl to go into the streets, and allows access to parents with some difficulty. The pupils were at their drawing lessons. They appeared cheerful and pretty. I volunteered some suggestions, among which were to get the garden cultivated, to fix the chimney in the kitchen so that it could be used, to pray less, and sing some. All of this, and my sincere commendations of the school, were very kindly received by the lady whose politeness and cordiality made this one of my most delightful calls in the country.

The Colegio del Rosario is just two hundred years old, having been founded in 1653 by Archbishop Torres. It is in the third block north of the cathedral. I entered it from the house of the vice-director, on the north side of the block. Here I saw a very old library, with few or no new books, some very old portraits, and one or two halls. Students were walking to and fro in the corridors repeating aloud the lessons they were to recite. They were an intelligent body of students, but very young. I heard a class reciting English to a teacher who could barely speak it a little. It was "as good as a play" to hear them make mistakes, and especially to hear him correct them. Ours is a terribly hard language for them to articulate.

I visited repeatedly the Colegio Militar. It is in the second block south of the plaza, with the entrance on the east side. The school appears in a highly creditable condition as to mathematics, and some examinations that I witnessed there are worthy of all praise. The library is modern, and good for its extent, which is not great.

I visited two common schools, one of each sex. That for girls is the poorest girls' school I have seen, while that for boys was not much better, poorer than any other girls' school, but about equal to the average of boys' schools. The pedagogic profession is not respectable in New Granada. It would be well to require from candidates for certain offices that they shall have taught an entire year in the same common school. Should this be required before gaining a doctor's degree, for instance, quite a different class of talent would be called into these schools.

In the southeast corner of the city, or just out of it, is one establishment, however, that does credit to Granadan perseverance and talent. It is the pottery of Don Nicolás Leiva. To understand the difficulties he has contended with, you must know something of native character, and especially its aversion to steady labor. In entire provinces you cannot find one man who has ever wrought faithfully all the working days of an entire month; and yet this pottery would do credit to the United States. Among the uncommon articles made here are porcelain mortars and pestles, and those Venetian shades that exhibit soft and delicate figures by transmitted light. In one of these Señor Leiva had achieved a very good likeness of himself. I am under particular obligations to the attentive and persevering proprietor.

The glass enterprise had a much more natural termination. Of all bipeds, perhaps the most unmanageable is the glassblower. To succeed here, a glass manufactory would need special laws, giving the director all power short of life or death for the space of ten years after the enlistment of the operative. But so limited is the demand for glass, that it would be better not attempt to make it here again for a few hundred years to come.

The cotton factory and the paper mill, the quinine works and the foundry, have all failed. I attribute most of

the failures to the same cause—the want of suitable opera-
tives. Even now vast quantities of rags—a perfect mine of
them—are to be seen on the borders of the San Francisco.
The quinine works manufactured only the crude alkaloid,
which the European manufacturers are said to have finally
decided not to buy, lest it should ruin some parts of their
own business; so the San Francisco, as it hurries down
from the Boquerón, can find nothing to do but turn two
common gristmills, which, though they never grind maize,
would not, in the North, be thought suitable for wheat.

The key to all this is a want of education in the
masses. They are tolerant of hunger; of comforts they
know nothing, and desire none. Their morals can sink no
lower, and their religion can raise them no higher. Their
beau ideal is to escape hunger, to keep dry from the rain,
and to be free from labor and care. They pay no taxes,
beg when they can, and earn nothing except in case of
extreme emergency, but in such case they will submit to
anything. Once they had the hospicio fitted up as a work-
house, but such a thing can only be kept up so long as
some man shall make it his hobby; it is all run down, and
is become a beggars' nest. Even prostitution would not be
likely to be a gainful course, wars have carried off so many
of the one sex, and the low masses of the other are so
abject. Poor Bogotá!

## XIII

# The Falls of Tequendama

Two months had my trunks rested quietly in Bogotá, while their owner became acclimated, and learned something of the ways of the Andine world. I now determined to visit the two most stupendous works of nature in this region, the Falls (Salto) of Tequendama and the Bridge of Pandi. Most visitors at the falls spend only an hour there. They ride there from Bogotá, and return the same day; or leave Bogotá in the afternoon, spend an uncomfortable night in the village of Soacha, or are guests at the hacienda of Canoas, take a picnic breakfast at the falls, and then return. This last is generally a good plan, but I wished to spend more time there, and therefore availed myself of the permission of Señor Manuel Umaña to make the hacienda of Tequendama my home for a few days.

Now came the inevitable trouble of the Andine traveler—to find cattle. I was not aware that a good carriage road ran to the very head of the falls, and that a return coal cart might be found in which my trunks could be deposited without that careful packing and equalizing necessary in mule travel. After I had lost one day in trying to find mules, the kind Señora Tomasa engaged two carga mules, a saddle horse, and a peon from Soacha. They came, of course, later than promised, and, after taking leave of my disinterestedly kind friends, I was soon alone on the vast sabana, leaving my cargas and peon to follow.

Two months' daily rain had made less difference than I had expected. The color had improved, but was not as beautiful as our spring spreads over fields long covered with snow. The road was a carriage road, but not so remarkably good as that toward Honda. As I journeyed south, the hills were never far distant on my left. A mile or two south of the city, a young gentleman, whom I had never seen before, overtook me on the road, and continued some way past his destination to a substantial bridge across the Fucha, when he took a polite leave and returned.

Three hours' easy riding brought me to Soacha, famous for the bones of carnivorous elephants once exhumed here. It is a small, scattered village, in a district of 2918 inhabitants. My mules were owned here, and I stopped a moment and paid for them. Leaving Soacha, I found myself on an arm of the plain, having on my right two ridges of hill. Between them, rising mist marked the falls. Disregarding this, I had still to pursue my way to the south, till, after a mile or two, I entered the great gate of the plantation, and took a course more consonant with my wishes.

Several small plows were scratching up the rich black soil, and some men were laying a stone wall, substantial enough for the foundation of a house. Before me was the mansion, now deserted of the family; and hid in a hollow by its side were a sawmill, the houses of some dependent families, and a quinine factory.

The director, M. Louis Godin, an intelligent French chemist, was domiciled, I was told, with a countrywoman of mine. I found her of pure African blood, and a very favorable specimen of her race. She bore in youth the name of Joanna Jackson, and thirteen years ago had a mother living in Haverstraw, to whom she said she would gladly send a hundred or two of dollars if she knew she was living. She said that when she left the people were talking of voting for General Jackson and Mr. Van Buren, but she conjectures the general must be dead by this time. In the interim she has been over Ireland, England, Germany, and Russia, as a servant, and is now a lady in New Granada, and has her white servant. Of the two persons who can make quinine on a large scale in New Granada, she is one.

At length my baggage arrived, and the large parlor of the mansion was thrown open to its reception. The patio of the house is very large, and the buildings are of but one story on three sides, while there is a second story in front, nearly all of which is occupied by the sala or parlor. The room contained four sofas, a dozen chairs, and three tables. A comfortable mat bed was thrown on the floor, in a corner, and, after taking a child's toy mug full of chocolate, with bread and sweetmeats for my dinner, I was left to repose.

At length we are upon the brink of an immense chasm, and we will pause to describe it. The fall is not a clear fall. The water falls smoothly for twenty-seven feet eight inches, and here, striking on a ledge, the sheet is dashed almost into foam, and accomplishes the remainder of its journey more like spray hurled downward by irregular violence than a fluid under the influence of gravitation. Its irregular and constantly varying outline reminds us of a column of smoke or steam, but as this motion is violent and angular, while that is slow and graceful, a comparison between them can only be justified for want of a better. Cones of spray here and there seem to shoot out suddenly in advance of a falling mass, but are soon overtaken and absorbed by the body from which they sprung. These cones must be masses of water not yet broken up, that are carried by their momentum out of the body of spray that falls more slowly. Here the resistance of the air breaks them up into drops, and they are lost in the mass to which they are now assimilated. A rainbow hangs over the falls when the position of the sun permits. It is varying every instant. Of the depth you can judge nothing. It does not look much, if any, deeper than Niagara, but it is almost exactly three times as deep.

Tequendama is one of the richest localities of plants that I have ever seen. The woods are damp, while most land at this altitude is dry. On four of the five days I have spent here, I have literally loaded myself with rich specimens. For some I have had to reach far over the abyss, in a position in which caution is instinctive.

## XIV

### BALLS AND BULLS

I like to start early in the week. The Soacha mule owner
had promised to have beasts ready. We agreed on the
price. I was abundantly satisfied with six dimes per beast
from Bogotá to Tequendama, and unfortunately told the
owner so. He demanded eight dimes from there to Fusagasugá. As I thought it reasonable, he added that he must
count the peon as a beast, making thirty-two dimes instead
of twenty-four. To this I assented, and he feared his
generosity would be his ruin; so, when I sent for the beasts,
instead of sending them, he sent word he must have ten
dimes. He made me lose a day, but he, in turn, lost his
bargain. I returned no answer, and when, the day after,
he sent his peon and mules, another was loading my baggage for the trip.

Traveling south, I have had all the time at my left
that chain of the Andes at the foot of which lies Bogotá.
At Cibaté I parted company with a priest—a fine, pleasant
fellow—who had been settled at Pandi, but was now without charge. He invited me here to take some refreshment
with him, to which I was not inclined. He was quite
inquisitive about the United States, and wished to know
if it would be long before the immigrant Catholics would
be so far able to outvote the Protestants as to establish
their religion by law.

At Fusagasugá I found the church in full blast with
explosive rockets, whirligigs, and other fireworks letting
off outside, for it was the eve of some saint. I rode past all
this, and in the bosom of an English family, entire strangers to me, I found satisfaction enough in one hour to
repay me for the day's ride.

By daylight, the plain, instead of paradisiac alluvium,
proved to be diluvium, or drift of rather a diabolic kind,

for it was thickly strewn, in some places almost paved, with huge stones. Nor was it horizontal, but descended rapidly toward the River Fusagasugá, which lay at the foot of a ridge of the mountain, and ran west. The plain lay between this ridge and the one next interior or southeast of it, and might itself be considered as one of the many spurs sent down by the latter ridge, all terminating at the base of the former.

Fusagasugá is an ugly-looking town, lying at the upper end of the plain, adjoining the mountain, as all Spanish towns generally are. With one exception, there are no houses but mud cottages. I cannot solve the politico-economic problem of the existence of the town, as there are not visitors enough to aid it essentially, and there is not industry enough to support it. These puzzles are driving me to the conclusion that the Granadino earns little and spends little, and, rather than work, will endure the ills of poverty. Nearly every house in Fusagasugá is a tienda, a regular tavern minus lodging-rooms. The rooms are two, besides, perhaps, a kitchen in the rear. One is the store, in which the customers are admitted only just within the door; the other a parlor, scantily furnished. The floors are mostly of earth.

I spent most of the holidays at Fusagasugá, but saw little to interest me in the village. I absented myself from the pleasant family long enough to see a part of three balls, held in the parlors of friends. They were solemn affairs, both the dancing and the sitting still. The ladies sat by themselves, and, with the children, filled nearly all the seats. The music was from two clarinets and a tamborine, for the "Brighton of Bogotá" cannot boast a fiddler. Very little beauty was present, and a decided amount of ugliness. The morals of the place are said to be in so happy a state that there is not a female in the place whose character is such as to exclude her from these reunions, to which neither invitations nor partners are requisite.

One of the balls had a supper of hot roast meat and turkey, with quantities of pies seasoned with garlic, and dishes flavored with lime juice and capsicum. The ladies ate first. One gentleman, in helping the ladies, helped himself also. He had in his hand a double joint of turkey. When a piece was nearly cut off, he would offer it to a lady, who would take it in her fingers. When his own piece was nearly off, for want of another hand, he took it in his teeth, and then went on with grave impartiality to help the next. A lady wanted drink. A gentleman held a cup to her lips, and, as she drank, made the noise nurses make when inviting babes to drink. In all this there was a vein of humor, in strong contrast with the general solemnity of the performances.

The Christmas ball was at its height when the church bells rattled out the time for cock mass. All parties went to church reenforced by the ascetic part of community, so as to make a respectable congregation. The same musicians went into the choir with their clarinets and tamborines, and gave us the same or similar tunes. The priest had in his lap a doll or image of a boy, which a large number crowded round to kiss. Then came a procession as far as the church door and back to the altar. A long mass followed, and all parties, sleepy enough, went home and to bed.

Sabbath brought no intermission either to billiards or balls. I regretted not going on Sunday evening, just for a moment only, to see the cura officiating as "Ensign (patron) of the Ball," a fact of which he assured me himself afterward. This is also the marketday of Fusagasugá. Such an annoyance can never be understood by description. But if one could see, as I did, the ladylike daughters of my host patiently engaged for an hour, or even two, in a repulsive duty that could not be delegated to servants nor adjourned to another day, you would feel that the nuisance is beyond Christian endurance.

The mass and market occurred together, of course. I would not uncover at the elevation of the hostia, and generally was out of the market at that time, so as not to offend the faithful. Once, indeed, while I was with one of the ladies in market, we were caught by a procession which came out of the church and went round the square. I did not remove my hat. Fortunately, no fanatic who would dare interfere saw me. Many are in favor of prohibiting all processions out of church.

Christmas is the season of bullfights at Fusagasugá, an amusement forbidden at Bogotá, on account of the sacrifice of human life with which it is frequently attended there. They were busy enclosing the square in front of the church with a pole fence on Sunday. I had determined to witness this sport, notwithstanding the cruelty of it. Both the sport and the cruelty I found were entirely imaginary. After one or two irresolute pushes at his tormentors, who invariably dodge him, he often becomes so obstinately quiet that he will even let you throw firecrackers under his feet without deigning to respond, except by a look of sullen contempt. The toreador does not now bear the name matador, for he no longer kills, though he sometimes is killed, but always by accident. He bears no weapon, but often has his ruana in his hand, which he manages to throw over the bull's eyes, and then there is the fun of seeing him get it off without tearing it, perhaps. You will not fail to notice that the tips of the bull's horns have been sawed off.

I visited the cantonal prison in Fusagasugá with more indignation than any other I ever saw. We came to the door, and saw quite a number of men inside, who invited us to walk in, and we did. "Where is the alcaide?" asked my friend.

"He is out in the street, señor."

"And leaves you here without locking you in?"

"What would be the use of locking us in, where we can get out when we please? We could dig through the walls, or break the rods of the window; and the fence between the yard in the rear and the woods beyond would not stop a hog."

"Why, then, do you not escape?"

"It is against the law, señor."

"Evidently this is wrong," said I to my friend. "A man who can be kept in this mud shell ought to be at large on parole. It is a cruel mockery to shut a man up by law in a room, and leave the doors open."

Most of these men had been charged with the theft of a quantity of cinchona bark. Had they been guilty, they would have run away.

The festivals still continued: the 28th of December is the Innocents' day, or the commemoration of the children slaughtered by Herod. Persons take the liberty of acting in some respects like children in honor of the day, particularly in what we would call April-fooling. When a person is victimized, he is told to consider himself an Innocent— "téngase por Inocente." The same idea runs through some satirical poetry. One, for instance, devotes a stanza to our friend López. In English and Spanish it might run thus:

> El que por ser Presidente
> Creyó así gozar del mando,
> Y es juguete de algun bando
> Téngase por Inocente.

> Let him who thought the land to rule
> When he became a President,
> But finds himself a party's tool,
> Regard himself an Innocent.

I shall not to describe the grotesque masquerades that held possession of the streets by day and partially at night. The Yankees can beat them when they try; but the masquerade ball of the evening did not deserve the name. A man who had sewed some bands of white on the seams of his clothes, or a lady who had dressed her hair in calico, was considered to be in masquerade.

Street gambling of various kinds, by the light of flaring tallow candles, helped to add to the liveliness of the nights. Most of these games appear peculiar. A favorite game was called lotería. I could look over the heads of all the company that surrounded the little table, where each of a definite number of players had staked his cuartillo, and had a card with a series of pictures on it. The pictures were in different order on every card. The same pictures, on blocks, were in the dealer's bag. He puts in his hand and draws out one, and calls out, in a loud, drawling tone, "Chulo chupando tripo"—"Gallinazo eating entrail." Each player lays a grain of maize on his copy of that interesting picture. The dealer lays down the block and draws another, always using several words in proclaiming it. At length a lucky fellow cries out "Lotería!" He has four grains in a row. The dealer ascertains that the four corresponding blocks have been drawn, gives him all the cuartillos except one, and makes up a new game.

I cannot think the remark of a traveler (Duane) correct, that the Bogotanos come to these places to gamble because they are ashamed to do it in Bogotá. I fear it cannot be denied to be a national vice, too common to excite shame. They come here to enjoy themselves, and gamble because they enjoy the occupation.

## XV

## To Pandi and Ibagué

I engaged, as guide and companion to Pandi, a hair-brained young fellow, an employee of the gobernación at Bogotá, as he tells me. He regretted not having gone in his military coat, to show me how the people would take him for a recruiting officer, and fly to the woods. He mounted himself on an animal that had two faults; he was both lazy and lame, if not even worn out—destroncado. My own beast, thanks to a fair friend, a much better judge of horseflesh than I, who kindly secured it for me, was as good as need be. We made an early start—that is, we were off before ten, and were soon on the edge of the inclined plane of Fusagasugá, where it is cut off by a large stream coming down from the hills.

Pandi is west of south of Fusagasugá, distant from twenty-five to thirty miles, over spurs of the left-hand mountain, while that on the other side of the Fusagasugá is uniform in its general direction, and with few projections. Each valley the road passes is sure to have a stream running to the right, where they unite with each other as they flow westward.

Each hill was lower than the preceding, and, thus descending, I reached Pandi at about eight at night, and found posada at the house of the alcalde. It is a tienda, with a third room adjoining the parlor. A miniature chicken and a very clean wooden spoon (no knife or fork) were set on for my dinner, and for my bed was placed an oxhide, afterward exchanged for a borrowed hammock. I asked for a chair to be put in the piazza, as this place is lower than Fusagasugá, and the night was warm. They had no chair, so they put out a bench ten feet long with no back to it.

Pandi has a church, but, at present, no cura. They

sent away their last for various reasons; among others, chasing one of his flock with a knife when he was drunk. The people of Pandi were once cursed with the present incumbent of Tibacui.

I spoke before of the eight national prisons of three kinds, and the thirty-one provincial prisons, which, however, contained (August 31, 1851) but forty-three prisoners. The system requires also 99 canton prisons and 756 district and hamlet prisons, making a total of 894 of these benevolent institutions for a population of 2,243,730, or a prison for every 2510 souls. That of Pandi occupies the two ends of the alcaldía. Of course, they never shut up a man in these cardhouses; it would be ridiculous. They lay down a hide for him to lie on, and put one leg in the stocks. This would seem no joke to an American who had not yet had his trial, especially if, with this slight impediment to his marketing and cooking, it was still to be done at his expense, or not at all. The treatment of different prisons is different. In Bogotá they feed the poor, but not sufficiently. The rules of the different provinces are different in this respect, nor can I, by any possibility, come at any general statement of them. I think in this province (for the canton of Fusagasugá was then in a province of Tequendama, since reunited with Bogotá) they give them water, and nothing more.

Beasts are not dear at Fusagasugá when the right persons look for them. I paid to Pandi, two days, sixty and eighty cents; to Bogotá, for a week's absence, $1.20; and to Ibagué, five-days' journey and back empty, $4.00 each. Ibagué lies on the western verge of the valley of the Magdalena, about seventy-five miles, air line, west of Fusagasugá. To reach it I must descend to within about seven hundred feet of sea level, and pass through the torrid zone. What sufferings I must endure from heat! What anacondas and boas, jaguars and pumas, I must kill or run away from! What perils from rattlesnakes, robbers, scorpions, centipedes, and other creatures of that ilk, I must encounter! I resolved to encounter all these perils on foot

—yes, absolutely on foot, contrary to the advice of every friend I could consult. All urged me to abandon the idea. I was to be seized by fever; killed by heat; used up by fatigue, and exterminated generally. We shall see.

I took an early start from Fusagasugá on Tuesday, 11th January, with two good baggage mules and a good peon. Said good peon failed to come in season, and my start was early only comparatively speaking; that is, I rose at four and left a little after ten. I had provided myself with bread and chocolate for five days, and a good-sized fowl— dear little Alice's purchase. Some meat was sent me, but it looked so green and smelled so strong that I sent it back, preferring to take my chance.

My first day's journey was on that inclined plain on the upper eastern end of which Fusagasugá stands. On my right I had the River Fusagasugá, and beyond, a chain of mountains almost without spurs. On my left was a stream formed by the union of all the streams I passed on my way to Pandi, all of which I then supposed flowed separately into the Fusagasugá. Beyond this, on the south, was a continual succession of spurs of the eastern branch of the Andes.

This plain is broken across in one place by a deep depression, from which you rise to La Puerta, the hacienda of Don Lucas Escobar. I had been before at his trapiche or sugar mill, one of the best in the land. I know of but three that go by water. That at Cuni may be better than this. Señor Escobar's rollers are of iron, horizontal, and three in number. They are turned by an overshot wheel, and the juice runs directly down into the kettles, where it is boiled by the waste cane—basajo.

All the cane is brought on the backs of mules, and the number of mules so employed is considerable, as the field is enormous. The chimney is built at a distance from the house, and is very tall. The horizontal flue dries the fuel. Don Lucas takes the *Correo de Ultramar*, published in Paris. It is so rare to find a man who takes a paper here that the fact is worth mentioning.

The house at La Puerta stands on a very pretty table of land, at the foot of which, toward the Fusagasugá, lie the cane fields and mill. It is not a pretty house, but rather a collection of huts. The plain on which it stands slopes to the west. It is very uniform in character, grassy, stony, and bosky. The whole day appeared like a walk for pleasure in a park, only the steady, gradual descent seemed too good to last—too much like the broad and easy road we are taught to shun.

My downward way had an unexpected termination, like many another. The path entered a clump of trees, and in a single rod I found myself almost surrounded by an abyss. I was on a point of land which had narrowed imperceptibly, till before me lay the Boquerón. This gorge appeared from Fusagasugá like a narrow plain between two hills, for the spot where I now stood seemed a part of it. Now it lay beneath me, a narrow, crooked chasm, just admitting a river to pass it.

I descended, crossed the united streams from the mountain spurs by a bridge of poles, and in a few rods farther came to the Suma Paz itself, and waited at the ferry for my mules. I suppose this ferry is two or three leagues below the natural bridge. The stream itself is not so mild as to merit the name of Perfect Peace, which it borrows from the awful mountain height in which it rises. Here, perhaps, is the only spot above its junction with the Fusagasugá where it would admit a boat. I found it here quite rapid, broad, and over my head. Just below, after receiving the stream I crossed, it unites with the Fusagasugá, and below the junction bears both names. It preserves rather the direction of the Fusagasugá, but the Suma Paz furnishes much the larger body of water. As a whole, the junction of these three rivers resembles Harper's Ferry, perhaps the most romantic spot in the United States.

A Granadan ferry is a serious event in a day's journey. The mules are to be unloaded and compelled to swim, and this is said to fatigue them very much. The baggage is to be placed in a canoe and ferried across; all is again to be adjusted to the backs of the beasts. The more beasts, of course, the worse the detention. Now it fortunately came just at night, and the reloading was but partial. The fare is generally so high as to be something of an object to the treasury, to which it falls. Here it was a half dime for each person and mule load.

We slept better for having the ferry behind us. There were two houses on the bank, and Roque selected the largest. My chicken and chocolate were placed on the fire as soon as the mules were put at ease, and I finished my dinner before dark. I had cut some candles into three pieces; one of these I now lighted, and read till I was sleepy, slung my hammock, and found myself more comfortable in it than I could have been in any bed in New York. Various hides were laid down on the earthen floor for the beds of the family and my peon. This is the bed of the Granadan peasant, and he sleeps on it in the clothes he wore in the day, and with no other devotions than crossing himself. Their practice of smoking in bed is very disagreeable to me.

I rose at daylight, my chocolate was made at once, and while the mules were loading I set out. As I intimated, I had to rise out of the gulf where I slept. This was pleasant enough for me, but a horrible thing for the poor mules.

At length I reached a point where I must take a last look at Fusagasugá. Beneath me lay the junctions of the three rivers, and the narrow channel by which they made their way to Magdalena. Beyond lay the sloping plain on which I journeyed yesterday, and at the farther end the mountains which formed the abutment to the plain of Bogotá. Far to the right I could just distinguish the walls of the basin from which the Suma Paz passes by its deep channel beneath the Bridge of Pandi.

On the left, the long, straight mountain that formed the right bank of the Fusagasugá, had assumed a singular aspect. It was naked of vegetation, and black, and almost as regular as the roof of a house; but it was divided into large irregular patches by means of vivid green of uniform width, and apparently consisting of grass without bushes. The rock was of a basaltic color, but I believe it is old red sandstone, judging at a distance.

I turned. My view was limited by other mountain spurs, but I could see that the mountain opposite here receded from the river, leaving space for a plain of great height and width, as green and apparently as perfect as any lawn. Beyond, all was shut in with hills, as was also all this side the river, except a little valley of palms and tree ferns.

In a corner of this valley was hidden a cottage at which I was to breakfast. Here I found two or three disgusting women; one making cigars with one hand, and holding a babe to the breast with the other. On the earth floor were two little girls about beginning to walk; one covered with dirt, the other with dirt and rags. Fortunately, I needed nothing from the house, and, after finishing my fowl with the aid of the two little monkeys, I went on my way.

A few ups and downs, and turns, opened to my view the broad, torrid valley of the Magdalena, varied by mountains, woods, meadows, and streams. I cannot attempt to describe it. I can only say it was "wondrous fair." To this lower level we were now to descend just as the day was waxing warm. Now came the test. The mula that bore my trunks acted as if she was possessed. All along she had been in the practice of running on ahead, and when she had gained enough she would lie down, putting the peon to the trouble of adjusting her carga each time. Now she raced on, and we had enough to do to keep up with her. The streams we passed were numerous, several compelling me to denude my feet to wade across. At every stream I lost ground. The heat was increasing. At length the beast slackened her pace, and I entered Melgar ahead of her.

Melgar is one of those market towns whose existence is a nut for politico-economists. Imagine, in the middle of an uncultivated plain, a large town of mud and thatch, with a church, chapel, and public square, without a trace of industry. I begin to believe the story of two cute chaps, who, shut up in a room together, swapped jackets back and forth till each had gained five dollars. I was desirous that Melgar should gain something by me, but I sought meat, eggs, and fruit in vain. I ate here an orange, but it was so poor I ate it only out of politeness.

My mule recovered her spirits in the pause at Melgar. She trotted on till she came to a large stream, running, as all the others run, toward the river on my right. She crossed the stream, and quietly lay down on her left side, just in the edge of the water. My Endlicher, a twenty-dollar book, and the dried plants of the last month, were the chief sufferers. It was a long time before we came to a suitable place to stop, but we arrived at 4 P.M. at a very clean house, where I removed the encerado from the trunk, and exposed the wet contents to the setting sun.

I had bought eight eggs for half a dime before reaching this house. I sent a quarter dime to another place, and the messenger returned with a totuma of milk, and the promise of a like quantity in the morning. I had sugar with me, and, much to the interest of the family, I made a custard in my smaller kettle, which I put in the next larger, filled with water. A bath in the stream, in which my trunks had been dipped above, consumed the rest of the day. I found my custard creditable to a chemist, and my hammock all that a hammock should be.

The master of this family has several peons in his employ, but himself goes without clothing from his hips upward. I remarked to him that he certainly bore one mark of a Christian, a broad cross of thick black hair along the mesian line and diaphragm.

We started late in the morning on account of a violent rain all night, which ceased about seven, but rendered a stream ahead impassable. Having made another custard and taken my chocolate, I set forward. Near the stream I stopped at a house, breakfasted on my custard, opened my trunks to dry their contents. The quick eye of a woman who stopped there discovered an unusual stock of desirables, and she came to me asking a present to remember me by. She was one of the last Granadinas that I would care to remember, or be remembered by, but I judged it best to comply, so I gave her a shell of an abundant species, which had lost its operculum, telling her that at home such a shell would be treasured up with much care. This is the first application for a present I have received.

The water fell slowly, and I gave four men three dimes to carry my cargas across. The current was so violent that I could not stand in it, but they carried everything across securely, and at dark I reached the banks of the Magdalena.

The road of this afternoon was diversified by winding round the bases of mountains. I passed the village of Fusagasugá Ferry, so called because the road down the Magdalena there crosses the Suma Paz. I kept on my course without stopping, Roque being half an hour behind. I had got twenty rods from the last house, when a body of men came running after me, calling to me to stop. I asked the reason, but received no answer till they came quite up to me, when a respectable-looking gentleman, feeling called upon to answer, said that they feared that I would lose my way. I replied that I had no fears on that head, and offered to go on, when they opened on me a volley of questions, which would have convinced me, had I doubted, that curiosity is the peculiarity of no sex or nation. In short, the object of this expedition was to solve a problem that perhaps had never occurred to any member of it before—where a stranger on foot could have come from or be going to all alone. I gratified them in this, together with my business, aims, and prospects.

I stopped for the night at a nice-looking house, where the peon had to destroy ten dollars' worth of cactus (Dunlap's estimation) to make the gateway wide enough for my cargas. The nice-looking house was occupied by two unmarried ladies and their babies. A hideous goitered servant had hers (I think its father must have been blind, but you may judge for yourself) slung in a hammock in the room where I slept, and she herself slept on the floor.

Here I found that my bread, sugar, and chocolate had been immersed in the stream we passed. I dined on bread and chocolate only, with a little sausage. My sleep was a little disturbed by two of the babies, which cried in turns, and, after an early chocolate, we repaired to the bank of the Magdalena.

The river here is about a broad as the Hudson at Albany, and much more rapid. The canoe could not take all my baggage at once, and the delay was so great that it was about ten when we left the ferry. After this delay I was not in a humor to be fooled with. We were to travel in good earnest, and, if the sun scorched or the rain poured, so much the worse.

And the sun did scorch. We were traveling south up the river, having it on our left, and before us a limitless prairie, intersected by a few small streams of milk-warm water. The road down to one of these was so narrow that the mula contrived to fasten her two trunks in the banks, so that to advance or recede was impossible. I turned back, and found that Roque had released her, leaving the load in the form of a rustic arch across the road. While reloading, the macho went on and hid himself. We were making up lost time, and the sun was doing its best to keep us warm, when we entered Espinal at about 1 or 2 P.M. This is one of the prettiest and neatest towns I have seen in New Granada, and its shops were of a superior order. But how came it posted here, upon the naked, parched, and shadeless plain?

Making no delay in Espinal, we went on our burning way. It was the 14th of January, and if all my friends managed to keep as warm as I that day, great must be the virtues of anthracite. In fact, I began to fear that I should kill or cripple my beasts; and at length, meeting cargas that had left Ibagué that morning, I judged the surest way of reaching my journey's end the next (Saturday) night was to relent a little.

The heat of this day reminds me to speak of my dress. I doubt if I could have performed the journey with any boots or shoes to be found in New York. The alpargata, which I have already described, cannot be surpassed in such service. My body was just covered with a single thickness of blue twilled cotton—the form of the dress almost exactly resembling the juvenile dress in which I gloried in my second year. To this was added nothing more than a belt and my hat. Except my hat, compass, knife, belt, and spectacles, the value of what I wore, when new, was $1.20.

I had begun my breakfast for today last night in good season. I had bought some eggs at noon when waiting for the water to fall, and at night beat them up with sugar. I found milk at the ferryman's after crossing this morning (a remarkable occurrence), and had just cooked my custard, when the peon was ready to start. I waited for the first good spot after I left Melgar, and breakfasted at 4 P.M. A large custard is not very nice after carrying all day tied on a mule's back under a vertical sun, but my appetite was good, and it passed for a late breakfast, but better than none. Late as it was, it was twenty-eight hours before dinner.

After breakfast I saw the first living snake I have met in this country, and as it is a good sign to kill the first snake seen every year, I did so. Before singing any pæans over my victory, I may as well give the dimensions of my foe. It was about six inches long, and a little thicker than a knitting needle; I put it into my spirit lamp to preserve it.

At dark I arrived at the River Coello. Here I found a tall man, naked except a handkerchief about his loins, standing on a stone in front of a house, talking with the proprietress. He offered to take my cargas across the stream on his shoulders. He appeared as nearly drunk as I ever saw a Granadino, and without answering him I went down to the river. He followed me, and as I saw there a good canoe, I let him pass. When the peon came up he found that there was no authorized ferryman. I explained to him that this did not forbid the owner of the boat passing us gratis, or, if no other way occurred, I would seize on the boat and ferry myself. But it was now night, and there was no denying that he and his mules were terribly tired, so we returned to the house.

Here I found a deaf and dumb girl, the first of this class I have met. I have before noticed the scarcity of lunatics; both of these classes will probably increase, the latter certainly, with increased cultivation of intellect. They were much surprised to hear of the education of the deaf and dumb.

Here I saw a sick babe, and I thought that those who are fond of a fling against the medical profession might read a lesson from the case. Among the lower people it appears as if the dangerous sickness of a child causes little anxiety, and its loss little grief; its burial is certainly a scene of rejoicing. It goes merrily to the grave with rites entirely peculiar, and bearing the name of a little angel.

I desired nothing after my four o'clock breakfast but chocolate and bread. Having repeated the same in the morning, as I could buy nothing here, I set forward with no breakfast in prospect till I reached Ibagué. A young man at the house, to save me from the crime of seizing on the boat, offered to ferry across my cargas for triple the price the law would allow a ferryman, and I permitted the peon to accede. I crossed in the boat, while Roque undertook to pass the horses below. He found it too deep, and I had to swim down and bring them across, with him clinging to the tail of the hindermost. He could not swim. So, after paying a triple ferriage across the river, I had to swim it twice.

I stopped at a venta, where I could get neither milk, bread, meat, nor fruits. Eggs and salt I refused, and pressed on. Here my peon begged permission to fall behind an hour or so and rest his beasts. I consented, added a thin coat to my scanty clothing, entered an arm of the plain between two stoneless mountains, and discovered Ibagué at 4 P.M., cooped up in a little elevated plain between two

spurs of the central cordillera of the Andes. The town lies
between the right bank of the Chiapala and the left bank
of the Combeima, which here unites with the Coello. The
Coello is here called the San Juan, and still above the
Toche.

The expenses of this trip are rather a curiosity:

| | |
|---|---|
| Two beasts and peon . . . . | $12.00 |
| Bread . . . . . . . . . . . . . . . . | 0.50 |
| Chocolate . . . . . . . . . . . . | 0.11 |
| Fowl . . . . . . . . . . . . . . . . . . | 0.20 |
| Ferriages of self and cargas | 0.85 |
| Candles. . . . . . . . . . . . . . . . | 0.05 |
| Eggs . . . . . . . . . . . . . . . . . . | 0.10 |
| Milk . . . . . . . . . . . . . . . . . . | 0.05 |
| Guarapo . . . . . . . . . . . . . . | 0.11 |
| Lodging and incidentals . . | 0.00 |
| Total | $13.97 |

Excluding what would come under the term of fare in the
United States, all that I could conveniently spend in four
days was $1.12, and none of this was at places where I
spent the nights. The peon paid the bill of the mules at the
stopping places, and provided for himself according to his
fancy. He is bound to pay his own ferriage; and if the
beasts are aided by the boats in swimming, he pays also
for that, but the owner of the cargas pays the ferriage of
them.

Although in these five days I saw no floor but earth,
and but few tables (those not spread, except with my
coarse utensils), no beds but dried hides, neither teacup,
tumbler, metal spoon, looking glass, newspaper, book, or
pamphlet, it was one of the most delightful trips I have
ever taken. When I found before me an ascent, I rejoiced.
It promised me prospects and coolness. When I came to a
descent, I rejoiced. It led to new trees and a purling brook.
When I came to a plain, I wished I had a horse, to fly
more quickly over it, but it would only have been to wait
the longer for the mules. Had I been taken lame or sick, a

horse could easily have been procured at any stage of the journey. And now I have proved my power of walking in the tropics, though I had been repeatedly assured I should find it impossible to walk.

I arrived in Ibagué on the afternoon of Saturday. Unluckily for the gentleman to whom I had a letter, I caught him in town, where he keeps in his house a dependent, a servant, and his little son, who attends school. He resides, with the rest of his family, in the country. Had his family been living in town, perhaps he would have been glad of company; had he been on his plantation, he would have escaped entirely. He could have kept me in his house, but it would have been only so much trouble and expense to be passed to the account of disinterested benevolence. Room in his house would have cost him nothing, had I sought my meals elsewhere, but that was not to be thought of; so he sent his son in different directions with little success. Ibagué has experienced two or three severe fires in as many years, and scarce a house has been rebuilt. In the midst of the search, an acquaintance passed the window. "Man," he called out, "do you know of a vacant house?" "No," he replied. "Will you have the goodness to look for one for my friend?" "Why not, man?" was his cheerful reply. By the time the weary beasts arrived, the task was accomplished, the eating place found, and all I had to do was to direct the unloading of my mules, and go to dinner about 8 P.M.

I fancied myself master of a large, deserted house. In a suite of three small rooms I found a bedstead of the usual construction—an oxhide stretched like a drumhead on a square frame. This was all the furniture of the three rooms. The middle one had a door, the others windows, differing from doors only in having a grating to prevent entrance when open. Here I put my baggage, and slung my hammock in the parlor. I retired, sole inhabitant as I supposed, leaving the doors open for Roque. In the night I heard a tramping and clanking like that of a German ghost dragging his chain. It was not a ghost, but a man who arrived from the country, and was making his way, jingling his spurs at every step, to an adjoining apartment.

Daylight showed that some rooms were used as a carpenter's shop, and others by the proprietress (who kept a grocery) for preparing chocolate, baking bread, etc. Two or three fat hogs passed from the front door to the back yard when it pleased their fancy; the midnight-comer's horse had the zaguán for his stable, with similar liberty of ingress and egress. The very hens flew out of the parlor windows when anything in the plaza invited them. All was liberty, except for a fighting cock who was tied to a stone in the patio.

Where I ate, several others also ate their solitary and sometimes scanty meal. They were young gentlemen, employed in offices in town. Of these chaotic meals I desire to retain no remembrance further than that they cost me exactly four dimes per day. Latterly there were added to our number two others, destined to be my fellow travelers all next week.

Sunday is market day in Ibagué; but the market is scantier than that of Fusagasugá, a town of half the size. Besides the market, the other institutions of the Sabbath are two masses, a cockpit, and billiard saloon.

The limits of authority are very vague here, but the priest seems to have no protection from the lowest. The priest of Ibagué preached a sermon on the Sabbath that the governor did not like. He wrote him a letter about it. About the 1st of January, 1852, the priest of Ambalema received eight dimes of a young woman whose child he baptized; the jefe político wrote to him to return the money. If a priest wishes to absent himself for four days, the governor ordains that he shall apply for leave to the alcalde of his parish. Thus the poor priest has three civil masters (four including the President), with an ecclesiastical head besides. The worst of it is, he receives contradictory orders, and is punished for disobedience of either.

Two interesting documents were read by the priest in the church at the Sabbath mass, both of which he kindly gave me. One was the *Allocutio* of Pius IX on the affairs of New Granada, censuring the action of the government under Mosquera as well as López, and pronouncing certain un-Christian laws null and void. The other was a circular enjoining faithfulness to religious duties during the approaching Lent.

The public schools of Ibagué are the provincial college, a boys' school, and a girls' school. I visited the latter on the third day of its session. It was the most pleasant sight I have seen in New Granada. The school had been burned out. It was now in a clean, new house. The girls were all seated on the floor in clean dresses, and as still and orderly as could be desired. Sewing and praying are two important branches in the female schools here. Fortunately, they were engaged in the former. Lately, theology has received a severe check in this province. The gobernación has banished from all the schools the catechism of Father Astete, the longest, dullest, and most orthodox of all the school catechisms. There are not less than three others in the schools, but these are forbidden every day but Saturday. Some in these schools learn to pray, but not to read.

The girls in this school were all young—none, perhaps, as old as twelve. All were learning to read, but scarcely any two had the same book. In one thing they all agreed; they were uninteresting to children, with perhaps one exception, a book written for the amusement of adults. A scandalous attack on the banished archbishop has been circulated by the government, and, it is said, used in schools as a reading book. I do not doubt it, nor that the still more impudent attack on the government by the Pope will be found in the same schools. Such of the Spanish narratives of the Tract Society as do not attack the religion of this country would do good service. One of them, "Theophilus and Sophia," was read with much interest in a school in Bogotá. There is here a great want of children's books, and an absolute destitution of school reading books.

Nor have they any good geography. In the colegio

here it is not permitted to study geography till after algebra and geometry. I have a good test question: Where is Patagonia? Those who know are not surprised at my ignorance, as it is in South America, of which they suppose me profoundly ignorant. But in general I get, even from educated men, the conjecture that it is somewhere in Europe. One of the most intelligent of my acquaintances was talking to me of our Fishery Question, and I was unable to convince him that a British squadron was not stationed in Greenland. At this moment he thinks me badly posted up in this matter.

Their arithmetics are a phenomenon for the psychologist to explain. I should not dare to write a critique on one of them, for it could not be regarded otherwise than as an exaggeration or a caricature. Their slates were all destroyed in the fire, and there are no others for sale nearer than Bogotá.

The teacher was a pleasant-looking woman, with two children, a clubfooted little boy of four or five, and a saucy girl of two. She has a husband, too (not a matter of course), secretary of the jefe político, I think with a salary of $192.

I attended an examination of the colegio provincial, but my efforts to get an idea of the ordinary routine were in vain. One feature I think objectionable; the province paid the board of some of the pupils, while others, too poor to pay tuition, were refused admission. The school edifices were much more spacious than necessary, but not in good order.

The duties of curate here are discharged by a vicar, with a nominal salary of $480, and an assistant, at $240. The vicar I found a pleasant man, anxious to render himself agreeable. I called on him on Sabbath afternoon to return a book that he had lent me. I found him dining al fresco. I had dined, but ate a piece of an ear of roasted maize and some sweetmeats. He then invited me to go with him to the cockfight. I did not consent, but went out with him. We were informed that the fight was over, and I went in with him. He was received as a boon companion, and immediately set himself to work to get up another fight for my gratification. This I thought was carrying politeness a little too far, but in vain were my protestations. I began to tremble for the result, for I would rather suffer anything than be the cause of so much cruelty to two noble birds like one that I saw dead at my feet. But the reverend father's exhortations did not appear to have as much effect as when in the pulpit in the morning, and, to my great relief, I escaped without witnessing a cockfight.

I was another time at the vicar's house, when he was called upon to administer the sacraments to a dying person. I begged permission to be present. "With pleasure," said he, "if you will only have the goodness, as a favor to me, to walk uncovered when I am carrying the Holiest." "Oh, as to that," I replied, throwing my hat in a chair, "do not be uneasy; the night is warm. I will leave my hat here." But neither proving too much nor conceding too much satisfies; so I had to take my hat, and enter a tienda till the Great Umbrella was at a sufficient distance. Then, Peter-like, I followed afar off, till I came to a crowd kneeling before a small house. As I entered I took off my hat, of course. The small room had been temporarily divided by a curtain. Behind it was a neat little chapel, with a bed in it. This conversion of half a dingy cabin into a beautiful niche of a chapel, with crucifixes, saints, candles, and flowers, had obviously been the result of attentions and loans from the neighbors. Here the priest was hard at his work. The confession and absolution were all over, and he was praying like a locomotive. You can easily tell when a priest is using Latin, which occurs only once or twice a year. He reads only about eighty words to the minute. But the moment he strikes into a much-used place, he gallops off at the rate of two hundred, or even more. After reeling off thus what would cost me an hour to utter, he opened a small metallic snuffbox, broke off a piece of a wafer, and put it into the patient's mouth. More rapid Latin. Then he took a bottle of oil; into this he dipped a silver wire, and, taking into his hand a piece of cotton, he applied the oil with one hand, and wiped it off with the other. He applied it to the ears, eyes, nose, mouth, thumbs, and toes. All this was done in the most expeditious manner, and with a nonchalance that implied that the poor fellow was used to dying. The moment that the dying man had received the consolations of religion, the good priest and his sacristan gathered up their traps and were off. That night the carpenter was busy making a queer-shaped box. It was a coffin for the dying, made, one would fancy, from a misunderstood description of those used at the North. One of those who were keeping the carpenter in good company and good spirits was the father of the dying. The cemetery of Ibagué was beautiful fifty years ago, but is now in disgusting disorder. It is finely situated on a point of the plain that overlooks the Combeima, but is overgrown with weeds and bushes, and the tombs are neglected and dilapidated. Here they laid that strange-shaped coffin next day, for the young man was dead. The priest did not come.

Ibagué is a peon town. Its foreign revenue has been chiefly from cargueros, who carried men across the Quindio Mountains, over a road too bad for mules. The road is now improved, so that, in the dry season, mules can pass quite comfortably; but there is now increased travel, and cargueros, servants, mail carriers (on foot), and chasquies are, perhaps, more in demand than ever. It bears the same relation to the Quindio that Independence does to the Rocky Mountains, except that it is impossible so to make arrangements as to avoid paying tribute to it. Ibagué is the fourth town in the province in population, and in wealth the fifth, sixth, or seventh.

In Ibagué fruit is attainable, and often cheap enough. I bought oranges at the rate of seventy-two for a dime. The plain is long, and the scattered cottages on it present a beautiful appearance, especially when the children are playing in the moonlight. Water is accessible; but we prefer quoting from *La Imprenta* of May, 1852: "The water comes to Ibagué from the sides of Tolima by a canal which passes through the principal street that crosses the town. At every square this canal has a deep opening, in which the incautious traveler, who does not understand geography, might breathe his last; but this is not the worst: the water carriers, and especially the female members of this profession, descend to the bottom of these wells for water, and, having performed such ablutions as suit their fancy, go their way. How clean must the water be when it comes upon the table?"

Another interesting chapter of Ibagué life is the niguas. Nigua is the Spanish for Pulex penetrans—the penetrating flea, jigger, chigger, or chigoe. This is a microscopic flea, about as large as the head or one joint of the leg of our well-known bosom companion. In like manner, she chooses her habitation in outhouses, houses where the cruel mop comes not, and the dire effects of water are unknown. There she hops about, like other damsels, seeking a settlement for life, till, by good fortune, she lights upon a human leg, or, still better, foot. She makes her way to a toe, and then her fortune is almost secured. She penetrates beneath the skin (not under the nail) by means that the miscroscope has not revealed to me. There she enjoys an unchanging and agreeable temperature. She is never destined to know what hunger is; her day of prosperity is come.

Prosperity in the nigua, as in the human race, works wonderful changes. The agile damsel of yesterday will be tomorrow a shocking obesity; so changed, in fact, that I absolutely failed to convince a naturalist friend of the identity. Place around the human waist a thousand yards of cotton sheeting between the skin and the flesh, and you would have an idea of the dislodged nigua that I have now beneath my microscope, with a white spherical body as large as a small pea, with head and arms of the original color and size, invisible to the naked eye. She is full of eggs, but it is past my conjecture where their father is. Every nigua that enters a toe becomes a mother in a few days, if left alone. They may be, like the leech, unisexual, or, as in the case of the soft-shelled turtles of southern rivers, the male may pass for another species.

The further history of the nigua, happily, I am unable to give from personal experience. The young are enterprising settlers, and soon remove to a suitable distance from their native spot, and, in their turn, find themselves blessed with a numerous family of daughters ready to obey the great organic law of nature.

Where there are niguas, a fortiori, there are fleas. To see both in perfection, I am recommended to visit the ancient town of Popayán. It is said that when you see a man who can catch fleas by instinct, you may be sure he is from Popayán. If you see him put his hand into his clothes and draw forth a backbiter from exactly between the shoulder blades, you may be sure he is a Popayanejo. You draw the same inference from his having lost a few toes, or even toenails. Popayán is the paradise of fleas. Turn an ungreased horse loose in a yard, and in half an hour he is frantic. In vain the inhabitants bathe two or three times a day; the plague knows no longer intermission than till their backs are dry. In going to bed at night, you mount a table, toss from you one article of dress after another, whip yourself thoroughly with your shirt, throw it in one direction, and rush for a high-hung hammock in the opposite. I tell the tale as it was told to me, for my desire to visit Popayán has much abated within a few days.

It is added that the niguas are, if possible, a more serious evil than the fleas there, even destroying life. The victim dies covered, or, rather, filled with one colony of niguas, from the extremities of the toes to the extremities of the fingers.

This is a long introduction to a very short story. One day that week I had three niguas taken from my toes, the next four, and the next five. As I needed my feet for another use on Monday, I was a little anxious at first, but I soon reduced the number to an average of less than two per day.

This was the first grand onset of the nigua, and some will call it a just penalty for the vulgarity of wearing alpargatas. Perhaps so, for I had but one nigua in all the time that I wore boots, while, in general, I have since had one or two a week. The last general attack was at Honda, and it was equal to the first, only that I had become able to extract them myself.

This is by no means a painful task, and there is a positive gratification in it. It is akin to the satisfaction of a good sneeze. The irritation of the presence of the insect occasions an itching, which is relieved at once as soon as the skillful operation is commenced. A pin, needle, or knife-point is used as a probe; an opening is made in the cuticle, and, by a skillful circular motion, the cutis is pressed away from the nigua on all sides, and then the whole body is extracted, without breaking, if possible. It is only in case of great personal neglect that limbs, and even lives, are lost. Numbers of lives have been lost so in hospitals. The old doctrine of applying the remedy to the instrument that inflicted the wound is not believed in here, but it would be efficacious; the nigua and the mop cannot coexist.

Ibagué is the capital of the province of Mariquita, not by virtue of size, commercial importance, or central position, but in consequence of its climate. With a good bed, this would be perfect. Humboldt says of it, *Nihil quietius, nihil muscosius, nihil amœnius.* I agree with him, save only that I found not a single moss in Ibagué. It is cooler than its altitude requires in consequence of its proximity to the Quindio range, and particularly to the perpetual snow of Tolima, to the cold páramo of Ruiz, and the Mesa de Hervéo.

I found the gobernación of the province in the house of the governor, a young man of unassuming appearance, who rejoices in the name of Uricoechea. He was unusually busy, making arrangements for a body of troops which went from Bogotá to Pasto in October, while the Republic of Ecuador expelled the Jesuits, and now, finding no further use for their services, were to be quartered a while in Ibagué.

The governor made me a present of a file of *La Imprenta*, now named *Voz de Tolima*, the government paper of the province, and the only one, I think, in the province. It is about the size of two folio leaves, and is published once a fortnight. Like all the papers of New Granada, northern readers would pronounce it insufferably dull, but to me it is full of interest. The cost to the government this year is $1626; and though at first I regarded the measure as foolish, I am well satisfied that it is a good one. It is divided into official and nonofficial parts. In the former I find the ordinances of the cámara, the decrees of the governor, law cases, and important decisions, circulars to the jefes políticos, and reports from them, examinations of schools, advertisements of runaway prisoners, and even the public documents of districts, when of sufficient interest. The nonofficial part contains everything else except news.

I passed the provincial prison many times a day, seldom without their calling to me from the windows, limosna—alms. At length I began to answer, "No tengo limones—I have no lemons or limes." At last, one day, I put some limes into my pocket, and when they assailed me with "limosna," I gave them to the fellow, saying, "Aquí teneis tus limoncitas—here are your limes." They gave me up. The prison was indeed a bad one.

I saw the cámara in session. It has a strong Conservador majority, while the gobernador is, of course, a Liberal. What I saw here teaches me not to translate the word *Conservador* by *Conservative*: there are no Conservatives in New Granada except fanatic Papists. All the rest deserve the name of Destructives, and might be classed into Red Republicans and Redder Republicans; and the Redder men may belong to either party, but, except the Gólgotas, the reddest I know of are the Conservadores of the province of Mariquita.

This assertion is too important in its general bearings to leave it unsupported with facts. I find in the *Imprenta* eight vetoes of Uricoechea in twenty-two days. In four cases the bill was passed over the veto, which can always be done by a majority of the one chamber, the most facile of all legislation except by an absolute monarchy, and worse even than that. I examined these eight cases, and in all I am confident that the gobernador (who seemed too young for his office) was right, and the cámara wrong. One of them deprived the jefes políticos, who are compelled to serve and to reside at the cabecera de cantón, of their salaries. They tried to change the name of the province to Marquetá, derived from the Marquetón Indians, who once resided there. Mariquita is a diminutive of Mary. The Supreme Court decided that a province could not change its name.

But my strongest facts relate to taxes. Direct taxes were unknown. They voted not only to introduce them, but to rely wholly on them at the first experiment. The excise on spirits was rented out for some years to come, at a good sum, to a man who had unfortunately introduced some ill-judged and costly apparatus that probably would not pay. From the monopoly the province suffered no other inconvenience but that vagabonds must work more or drink less. Well, the cámara ordered the contract to be rescinded without the contractor's assent, preferring to have cheaper rum and less revenue. But the new system, which was invented, not copied (for this is the way with all republics), would not work at all. Next year came another radical change. All direct taxes were repealed, and the whole revenues needed for two years, and for the indemnification of the spirit contractor, were to be raised at once from a tax on the exportation of tobacco. This threw all the burdens of the province on the largest town, Ambalema, the great tobacco mart of New Granada. The utmost they could hope to effect by this would be to drive away the tobacco trade to other provinces, and reduce the population of Ambalema from 9731 to less than 5000. But new difficulties beset them. At the lowest corner of the province, on the Magdalena, stands Nare. Under the new

order of things, no tobacco is exported, and Nare takes it
all. It seems that the Nareños, men, women, and children,
smoke more than their own weight of tobacco daily! The
last achievement of the Conservadores that has reached
me is a sumptuary law limiting Nare as to the amount of
tobacco it should consume, in order that some might be
left for exportation.

I wish I had done with this matter, but, as the hope
of all parties here seems to be the abolition of all indirect
taxes, I must tell my reader what a progressive tax is. Their
theory is philosophical. Taxes are to be paid out of income,
and he that has no income can pay no tax. No more can
he whose income shall be insufficient for his wants. Property is not taxed. A poll tax is feudalism, barbarism, and
slavery. A man needs a certain sum—say $100 a year—to
live on. He that has less than that can pay no tax. If his
income be between $100 and $400, he can spare 5 per cent
of it very well; should it be between $400 and $2000, he
can conveniently spare 15 per cent of it; and if it exceeded
$10,000 a year, he could easily spare half of it. This is
progressive taxation, only I have copied the figures of no
one scheme.

This scheme is designed, you see, for the special
protection of vagabonds. The thriftless and improvident
shall be exempt from all burdens to government. Nay,
were there but one citizen in the province of the wealth of
an English duke, they might exempt all incomes of less
than $100,000 a year from taxation, and make him alone
bear the expense of government. Such was the scheme
recommended by the editor in the *Voz de Tolima*, the
organ of a Conservador gobernación; and I saw a similar
one recommended by a gobernador of Bogotá—a Liberal.

But, insecure as the property of citizens must be under
this species of legislation, that of foreigners is not attacked
in this way. True, the province had the same constitutional
right to raise its revenue on the silver mines instead of the
tobacco, but they well knew that such a step would have
brought a British fleet before Cartagena, and therefore it
was not to be thought of.

Another consequence of this theory is, that vast amounts of property in the hands of the wealthy escape taxation. Broad leagues of land are held by wealthy families, waiting for another generation to buy and settle them. As they produce nothing, they are not subject to taxation. The addition of a horizontal tax of one cent an acre on land, and a poll tax of a dollar, would relieve all the embarrassments of the treasury, and the last would be a benefit to the taxed, but it would be an outrage on theory.

Ibagué is surrounded with beautiful scenery, whether you stand and look about you or take rides and walks. I do not often ride on my small excursions. I made a trip to Tolima, however, subject to the encumbrance of as uncomfortable a mule for a botanist as ever I saw. It was not, I am sorry to say, the Peak of Tolima that I visited, but only an Indian town a little way up the Combeima. This volcanic peak, that has thrown its pumice around Ibagué, is said to be only three leagues from it, but the way is so bad that a visit there costs five days. I had time to spare for such a trip, and it could not have been better employed; but the damage to my locomotive powers made me abandon all ideas of crystallized sulphur, rare plants, and volcanic action; so I only went up to the Indian town that does much to supply the market of Ibagué.

I followed the plain up a long way, and then descended to the lower grounds of the Combeima by a steep, zigzag, paved road. The agricultural spirit of the Indians has filled this valley with little properties and little cottages, and I gladly followed the river up to a ford that I was not willing to cross without necessity. What with rain, and mud, and the obstinacy of the mule, the trip did not pay.

I bathed in all these rivers, but the best place was found by going down the Combeima, and crossing by a frail footbridge, a little above its junction with the Coello, to that stream. They are of about equal size. The Chiapalo is much smaller, but warmer and nearer.

I do not like the Ibagueños. I have not found so unsociable a people in the whole country. Except the attentions that my letter of introduction compelled, and the official courtesies of the gobernador, neither of which were scanted at all, the only attentions I received were from the priest. I am sorry for this, for there seems nothing wanting to Ibagué but good society, or even the ordinary amount of Granadan hospitality and sociability.

In leaving, I had my first and last difficulty about a bill. My house rent was made $1.60 by charging to me all the vacant rooms that were accessible to me. I decided to pay only for what I had used. Not a symptom of accommodation did her ladyship show all the time my packing was going on, till it seemed to me that I should either leave without paying, or have some experience of the Granadan Code of Procedure, which I was not unwilling to try. Five minutes before starting, however, the terms were reduced to eight dimes. I gave her a dollar, for I thought the experiment was worth the balance. It was the most quiet quarrel I ever had, for not an unkind word was uttered in the whole of it.

## XVI

## THE BACK TRACK AND
## THE QUINDIO MOUNTAINS

I am on the back track this morning. I am on horseback, and entangled in with others, so that I am no longer the independent man that I was when on foot, and happy with only three bestias—two quadrupeds and a biped—I crossed the tierra caliente before. Our baggage is off some time since, under the charge of a thief, who has already been helping me transact some of my business. He employed a woman to do some washing for me. He assured me that the articles were all safely returned; but I missed a towel—my only crash towel.

Towels here are generally made of plain cotton cloth, and, though often embroidered with red, are not what our wet hands demand. This crash was a new article to her, and seemed cheap enough to be stolen, and dense enough to be highly desirable, so the affair was determined on. It so happened that we ate for a day or two at the house where the washerwoman harbored. Our horses were at the doors, all bills settled, and we ready to mount, when I had the washerwoman called in, and told her that I wanted my towel. It cost me great trouble to make her understand that it was not a nightshirt, a pocket-handker-chief, a ruana that I wanted. The word toalla is not used here, and she could not understand its equivalents. Then she went to her box, and drew forth article after article. She had got the box half emptied; I stood patiently looking on, till out came the towel; she seemed much pleased to find something that I would like, and gave it to me with an air of satisfaction that really looked like generosity. I felt like rewarding her with a dime or two, but refrained, and thanked her cordially, tied the towel round my waist, wished her good-day, sprung into the saddle, and was soon out of town.

The fine road through the streets of Mesa is at the cost of the nation. The province is not obliged to spend a dollar on it, but it might exact toll of all that pass over it. Every carga of molasses that enters Bogotá from here pays a toll at Puente Grande to the province of Bogotá. Briceño sees the impolicy and injustice of such impositions. He is extending this good road up to the plains of Bogotá. It is not intended for a wheel road, and, I fear, will, in some places, be too steep.

A detachment of the presidio is making the road. I saw one company near Tena, and another a little east of La Mesa. The troops that guard them are part of the regular army, and are under the command of the governor. The prisoners sleep in an ordinary cottage, and, by day and night, have no other wall around them than lead. They beg of the passers-by on every occasion. Señor Triana was contractor for furnishing the presidio with food and drink. They drink large quantities of guarapo. We drank the same at the table.

The hospital of the province and that of the presidio were one and the same. It is an ordinary cottage of two or three rooms and a kitchen. Things there could not well be worse. In the kitchen were no conveniences for cooking. The floors are infested with niguas, so that they destroy life. Half the cases here were large superficial ulcers. The governor is sure that they are not made on purpose, but I must doubt.

I was in the gobernación one day, when a man came in, who, addressing the secretary, Señor Guzmán, said,

"I am here, señor."

"Very well; where have you been?"

"I have been at work on the estate of Don Fulano."

"Will you continue there?"

"I shall for the present."

"Very well; come again this day two weeks."

The secretary had opened a book and made a record of the interview.

"Who was that?" I asked.

"It is a man condemned to a certain period of prison and another of surveillance—vigilancia. His imprisonment has expired, but he cannot pass certain bounds, and we must see him regularly, and know where he is and what he does."

"What trouble to you and him! We have not in the English language such a word even as surveillance. We use the French. Had he been at the North, he might perhaps have been let off on condition of never coming again where he is known."

The secretary stared. "And do you think a rogue does less damage where he is unknown?"

"No, I cannot say that; but then the evil that he does will not harm us."

"Ah! that indeed," and the good official shrugged his shoulders, as if to say, "That plan is good enough for heretics."

I went to the provincial prison to see a noted presidario of good family, Francisco Morales. He had entered into a plan with a doctor and a judge. They had poisoned a priest of Bogotá, held a coroner's inquest on his body, administered his estate, and robbed it. The robbery only could be proved, and Pancho Morales, as he is called, was condemned to the presidio. He has worried poor Briceño terribly. He asks whether any arrangement could be made at our best prisons to accommodate so refractory a fellow. He has not succeeded in getting a stroke of work out of him yet.

Once he commenced abusive and seditious declamations. A trumpeter was stationed by him, and commanded to blow every time he tried to speak. He chained him to a post, and has punished him to the last extent he dare, and now Pancho shams sickness. I wish I were his doctor a little while. I found him with his window toward the street stopped up (a great grievance), and a sentinel in sight of him continually. He was quite penitent, as he would have me think, and asked me for a Bible. Don Justo is fearing that he will make his escape.

One day I crossed the Apulo to see a volcán on the opposite slope, on the road to Anolaima. An immense descent brought me to the river, eight inches deep, and charged with black mud. A similar height was to be gained on the north bank. Here I found a scene of transcendent interest—a glacial motion of hot stones and earth. I took off my alpargatas, lest I should be betrayed to a place too hot to escape from. I could walk over most places. A pale smoke was issuing from some spots. The glow of fire is seen from some such places in the night. The slide was five or ten rods wide, and was advancing into a thicket of trees, overwhelming them at the rate of two or three feet a day. The sides of the fire-glacier, so to speak, were smooth, and grooved with the masses that had traveled down. The steepness was about that of steep carriage roads. I suppose the sliding is due to the spontaneous ignition of pyrites in the depths below, and the slow combustion of coal. Such phenomena are said to be more active in wet weather, which furnishes water to the pyrites.

When it shall have advanced a dozen or two rods more, it will reach a small pond that must have had some similar origin. It is not deep, for I waded in some way; but they tell me that there is a treasure in the center, in a large cauldron (funda), with another cauldron reversed over it. They cannot get off the cover. So said some peasant women living near, who urged me to take some refreshment with them, and were the more earnest when I told them that I had no money with me. The spot was not two miles air line from Mesa, but I found my trip a very fatiguing but interesting day's walk.

These phenomena are frequent, and I am coming to the conclusion that all the rough, irregular valleys west of the sabana, and, perhaps, on all the western slope of the Cordillera de Bogotá, are the work of similar decomposition. Signs of this must be sought by a man of more leisure than I have been.

I attended an examination of the public boys' school. The same faults I had noticed before were too plain here;

all was rote, and no thought. I picked out the smartest boy, and when he went to the blackboard, I handed to the gobernador the sum of "the hare and the greyhound." The hare starts eighty varas before the hound, and runs twenty varas a minute, while the hound runs twenty-five. Señor Briceño said no boy in school could do it. It passed from my hands to my neighbor's, and then the master asked for it. He left the examination in the hands of the committee, and bent all his energies on the sum. In ten minutes he had an answer, but it was wrong.

I attended a tertulia, or evening visit, in La Mesa. I hope I wrong no one in saying I thought it tedious and stupid. The ladies, who were pretty in the main, took possession of a corner of the room that just held them, and maintained it. The gentlemen formed a line, from one end of theirs to the other, through the middle of the room, but so that each person spoke only to his next neighbors. No general conversation went on, and none across the circle. A couple of ladies went out a few moments, and I exhorted the governor, who was apt for such encounters, to interpose his person in the vacancy, and break their phalanx for the evening. He attempted to do so, but the ladies, returning, claimed their places in such a manner that he had to yield. I attempted to engage a lady in conversation, when I found myself at one end of our line, but I could get nothing but commonplaces (the Spanish is poor in monosyllables), and gave up, in fear of being regarded as impudent or ill-mannered for conversing with a lady.

From Mesa I started for the Falls of Tequendama. We had in company Governor Briceño, and two young men who had never seen the salto. A servant and sumpter mule completed the train. We started late, of course. Briceño and I went on slowly to Tena, five or six miles, and then we waited for the rest hour after hour. They arrived about sunset, and we went on by the light of a full moon to pass the night at a hacienda. We lost our way, and had a horrible time. The road was hardly fit for quadrupeds, even by daylight. We began to feel the want of our dinner.

My horse fell down a bank. How he got out, or why I went not down, I could not see, for it was dark. At length we came to where a torrent tumbled over a pile of stones; whether it was in the road or out, we knew not, but we could not pass it. We turned back, and, after an hour more of dismal wanderings, we came to the hacienda of Zaragoza, and stopped there.

Our beasts were scarcely put up or turned loose when the owner came from Bogotá, and we got up quite a dinner, and by eleven we were taking a nap. This lasted till three, and then we were on our way, with a baquiano to guide us. He led us to and over the pile of stones—a perilous task in the dark, and thus on. Early in the morning we passed the ruins of San Antonio. It was a town of which the site had been carried off by a volcán or fire-slide. The whole face of the country had changed, and all we could see of the ruins was a bit of the corner of the church, half a mile, it is said, from where it was built. A rugged, naked valley occupies the place of the plain on which San Antonio stood.

A little farther on we paused to take something, I really cannot tell what. Then one of the laggers called out to the guide, "Baquiano, be spry now; a real if you will run." On we started; in ten rods we came to a house and a pretty girl, and the two worthies must stop and ask her some questions. We followed on with the guide up a long hill, and past some scattered houses, and an Indian settlement called Curzio. But our laggards came not, and we had no alternative but slowly to advance. Meanwhile, we asked repeatedly for a guide to the foot of the falls, but in vain; all assured us that no man could reach the spot. About nine we reached a point whence the falls were visible.

It was the middle of the afternoon when, returning from the head of the falls, we again reached this spot, and there we saw our two truant friends, who were now enjoying their first and last view of Tequendama. This glimpse of the upper part of the falls at a distance was all the reward they had for a ride of three days. When they left the pretty girl (how long they stopped they did not say), they mistook their road from that very spot. They did not discover their mistake till they were in sight of the sabana. Here they hired an Indian girl to guide them, and they had caught their first glimpse of the falls, and the last, perhaps, for their lives, just as it was time to return to Zaragoza, where we had left all our bedding, etc.

We stopped at the first cottage to do what we could to appease our hunger. I soon left them there, and started on foot, reviewing deliberately and carefully the scene of the catastrophe of San Antonio. At dark I was near Zaragoza, and, for the third time, threaded in darkness a trail through the woods that lay between the house and the little footpath that they called highway. Our kind host bade a servant wash my feet, and ordered dinner. Before it was ready the party arrived, two of them rather crestfallen. Their delays had spoiled the whole expedition, and they had reaped a corresponding part of its benefits. Don Justo had visited the salto repeatedly, and appreciates it as much as any Granadino I know.

Our host brought bitter complaints from Bogotá of sacrilegious laws. From the priests had been taken away the monopoly of marriage, and even the right to marry, as each marriage had to be acknowledged before the district judge. I tried to make him see that the judge did no more than give the certificate, which the priest gave before when he was a civil officer; but he insisted that it were better to leave their children to the consequences of legal illegitimacy than to receive a certificate of marriage from unconsecrated hands.

Presto! I am in Ibagué again. Was last chapter a dream? Was there a ghost in it? Yes, it must be; here I am, in my hammock, in a large sala in Ibagué. Four gentlemen are spread out, two on tables and two on the floor. The crying of a babe has awakened me, and a woman's voice, from the room where it is, calls Antonia! Antonia! Antonia appears to be a black girl sleeping just outside of her mistress's door, and sleeping to some purpose, if indeed, she be not dead.

Yes, it is even so. We are to start for the Quindio this morning, for, Sunday being market day, all our purchases and those of the peons are made, and we are to have an early start. An early start means to rise at dawn, or earlier, and get off at ten. We did not do so well as this, for we were finally off just about eleven.

The company consists of five gentlemen, two ladies, three children, four servant maids, eleven peons, twenty-five horses and mules, and one dog. Our train was a long one—the ladies on sidesaddles, the other girls astride, two little boys in a chair, one baby in a pine box, two vacant chairs for the ladies, one man with a box on his shoulders, two led horses, and an uncertain number of baggage mules. The gentlemen, of course, were mounted, except myself, who resolved to try the passage on foot. So we filed down the bluff to the banks of the Combeima, which we crossed on an ancient substantial bridge. Here, then, I stood at the very foot of the Quindio mountains, the middle range of the Andes. We ascended incessantly for some hours to and past Palmilla. This is not a village, but only a house or two. Then came a long farewell to cultivation, a long descent, and then, toward night, some land as varying as an ordinary road among, but not over, mountains. We had intended to sleep at El Moral, but we started too late.

A little before dark we reached Las Tapias. This consists of a house and kitchen, certainly not without occupants, but, in the confusion of peons and servants, I could not distinguish them. The baggage was behind. Only two mats, which came on a led horse, gave us a place to sit, without entering the dark, windowless cabin. We had nearly lost our hopes of our baggage when it arrived, and the girls set about getting dinner. The arrieros erected a tent over a huge pile of trunks and packages. These tents are generally erected in the center of the road, or, rather, the narrow road is in the center of the tent. The tent-poles are sought on the spot. The cloth of the tent is the property of the gentleman, who is the chief of our party by all consideration, as he is husband of one of the ladies. The other is an unmarried sister of his wife. I call him señor.

At ten a mat had been spread in the house, a table-cloth spread on it, and a comfortless, ill-prepared dinner was seasoned with cheerfulness, kindness, and hunger into a real feast. I had, however, one ground of complaint that none but the servants could remedy, and they would not. Besides paying my scot—escote—for the marketing, I had bought an extra supply of chocolate of my own; but the guarichas would always make me wait till the last for my chocolate, and then add water to it, so that, though I imbibed more fluid, I received no more nourishment. I found all contention on this point useless.

Supper over, an enormous almofrez was produced; out of it came a good bed, as large as a double bed ought to be, together with a mattress, hammocks, blankets, night-shirts, and dresses, an infinity of articles. Three hammocks were hung; a gentleman placed his bed under the three, at right angles with them, so that if any cord broke, he might be sure to share in the misfortune. The mattress was placed on a wide wooden bench made to sleep on, and the large bed occupied the place of our table on the floor.

I crossed the Coello on a covered bridge just above the mouth of the Tochecito, In the fork of the two rivers is a dry plain, covered thickly with large boulders, so as to be difficult to ride over. Here stands Toche.

I arrived about twelve, and my first idea was to supply the deficiencies of my breakfast. I called for bread, butter, chocolate, fruit, guarapo, and eggs, but could only obtain the latter, and at the rate of eight for a dime. I ordered four eggs boiled, and, by the time they were done, they had found two bits of dry bread. A board in a corner served for a table, the handle of a spoon for a spoon, a chair turned down for a seat. While eating, they assured me that the officers here used panela and water for choco-

late, and liked it. They could furnish me the same, and I
tried it.

Before two our party began to come in, but all the
beasts were not in till about three. It was decided that we
could not go on to Gallego; this gave us a dinner by day,
and afforded me an opportunity to observe the community in which we were to spend the night. Toche, I
think, was one house before the presidio was stationed
here. That has been enlarged, two others put up, and a
dozen little huts. The huts are for men on parole. They
are called francos, and are not, like the guardados, kept
all the time within shot. The franco that I met today was
a messenger that had been dispatched to Ibagué. It is
unwise for them to try to run away, but they often do.

At night the presidarios were marched down the
zigzag that we have to climb tomorrow. They were drawn
up in a line, the roll called, and their rations given them.
These are meal, or maize, or rice, and salt, and an im-
mensity of panela, a quarter of a pound per diem. Most of
the prisoners are on parole, and sleep in the huts; the
others are thrust into one of the houses, and kept under
guard. There are twenty-five soldiers, more or less. One
of them marched a prisoner up to us who wished to beg.
He had the additional merit of a large chain from his
waist to his ankle, showing him to be one of the worst of the
presidio. Even this did not avail him; we left him to the
mercy of the president, whose only pardons seem to have
been of prisoners who had risked their lives in the service
of cholera hospitals on the Isthmus.

Altogether, the prisoners are well treated here, and,
to a poor man, it is worse to wait his trial a week in Bogotá
or Ibagué than to serve a month here; and to any man, a
week here is better than to wait his trial a single night in
the prison (stocks) of Pandi.

We were here the guests of the warden, to whom all
the gentlemen of the party were personally known except
myself. He gave up to us his entire apartment, quartering
himself for the night abroad.

I stopped to see some presidarios work, and to talk

with the officer of the guard, when a new sight met my eyes; for the first time I saw one human being bearing another as a beast of burden. We were at the end of the labors of the presidio, and in advance were bad portions of road that the two ladies were thus to pass.

The sillero is not an extremely athletic man. He is nude from the waist up, and his pantaloons are rolled up at the bottom as far as possible, especially in muddy weather. A rude chair (silla) of guadua, with a piece of white cotton cloth put over to keep off such rain and sun as it may, is all the apparatus. This is secured to the sillero's body by two belts crossing over the chest, and another passing over the forehead. The rider must keep absolutely still. If the sillero slip or stumble, any motion, however slight, of the rider, will insure a fall. It is, therefore, much easier to ride asleep than awake, and far safer.

At two we reached Barcinal, the first house since leaving Toche, the sixth in seventy-two hours. Here was a family of Antioqueños, who supplied us with masamorra, made of cracked maize, boiled and eaten with milk. This is a favorite dish in that secluded province. I like the Antioqueños and the Antioqueñas, and I like their caps, but I think I should not like the too frequent recurrence of masamorra.

Between Barcinal and Toche there is no good place to pass the night, and yet they are more than a day's journey apart. The best remedy is a better road, and one could be made that would bring one through even in bad weather. Had we proceeded to Gallego the second night, we might have reached Barcinal on the following, and saved the martyrdom of Volcancito.

A steep, rough road led from Barcinal down to Boquía, on the banks of the Quindio. Boquía is the head of a district in the province of Cauca. It has some tolerable houses, a good posada, the beginnings of a church, a wheat mill that I saw in actual operation, and a covered bridge over a branch of the Quindio. Provisions might sometimes be bought here.

At Piedra de Moler, which signifies either grindstone

or millstone, is a ferry across the La Vieja, into which the Quindio empties some way above. Here we paid a peaje or tax of eighty cents each to the province of Cauca. It cannot be called toll, for it is not expended on the highways. With the exception of a little piece of territory that lies west of the Cauca, where a road that runs up and down the river may belong to the province, all the road in the province is national, but it is very rare for either nation or province to spend anything on it. I recollect in the space of nine months only the building of a single footbridge, and am sure I have seen no other labor or money expended on the highway.

This time we did not allow the ferry to delay us much. We stopped to see the beasts swim across—an interesting sight—went to the ferryman's house to eat some eggs and roasted plantains, and came on, leaving our baggage to follow in two detachments.

The rain had ceased, but threatened, so that I thought prudent to retain my defenses. An immense hill only remained to ascend and descend, for Cartago is on the bank of the river we passed.

Ascending the hill, I saw the Bihai (Heliconia Bihai), a cannate herb, that supplied leaves for shelter to travelers before tambos were built. The leaves are of that characteristic Scitaminate form shown in our gardens by the Indian-shot (canna), and in pictures by those of the plantain and banana. They are from one to two feet long, whitish beneath, and are hung by a notch in the petiole to horizontal strings passing over the poles that make the roof of a rancho. Each peon and carguero was bound to carry his quota of these from this place going eastward, and the traveler might have to sleep nearly a fortnight under a thatch thus transported.

From the top we had the first good view of the Valley of the Cauca. It was not level, but rolling, as they say at the West. Its vivid green contrasted beautifully with the dry plains of Ibagué and Espinal. I can scarcely believe that there can be a more beautiful scene than that where the plain breaks in upon the view. Around you still is the rugged scenery of the mountain, while in the blue distance are the Caldas mountains, which I fear I shall never cross. It would be more beautiful still were the Cauca visible; but, as its right bank is lined with uninterrupted swamp and forest, it is not to be seen but by penetrating to it. We had obtained a single glimpse of the valley the day before, not long after leaving Lagunetas, but it was only through a narrow opening of the trees.

Soon after coming in full sight of the plain the duties of the silleros ceased. At the first pool below, they put themselves in their best trim to make their appearance in Cartago. Camisas were drawn forth from some safe storage, and hats and ruanas, added to the simple costume of the mountains, made them into ordinary peasants.

At length we reached the plain, but when we made the change from primitive formation to the alluvial I cannot tell. I doubt even if the line is capable of being determined, so strongly do the soils of the two resemble each other.

The expense of the trip I cannot tell exactly. The cost of beasts was fifty-two dimes each, including peon service; the subsistence may have been half that sum, but we kept no separate accounts. Our expenses will be found rather below the average cost of crossing the Quindio, unless the losses from petty thefts are to be reckoned in. My chief loss was a hatchet having two chisels deposited in a cavity of the handle, a towel (not that crash one), of course, as much rope as they could easily lay their hands on. We arrived in good season on Saturday, but our baggage did not get in till too late for mass the next day.

Cartago is a town of about the size of Ibagué, but much lower and warmer. Cartago has much more of tile and less of thatch than Ibagué. The place is old, but not entirely finished, for I saw one house of tapias still going up. They put together a frame, with sides of strong plank, shovel in earth, and beat it down. Bars that hold the frame together leave holes through the wall, but these can be stopped. The work is rather slow, but as no frost ever attacks these walls, they are as good as brick, and in an earthquake even better. By whitewashing occasionally, they are as beautiful at a distance as marble, and much cheaper.

I searched the churches for anything of note, and found only a Saint George—San Jorge—mounted over one of the altars, with his dragon beneath his horse's feet, of course. This saint is rather rare in this country.

Cartago stands on the La Vieja, but opposite the town is a large grassy island, with a small and safe arm on this side, and a stream beyond that would be navigable for a small steamboat. It is two or three miles from the banks of the Cauca, as, indeed, are all the towns. This little branch is a favorite bathing place, and Sunday is a favorite day, so I found the little stream swarming with all ages, both sexes, and a variety of costumes and colors. The stream was now so high that a girl of twelve or fourteen had just been rescued from drowning, they said. I saw her adjusting her hair very composedly, and the danger, if it had been real, seemed to have made no impression.

On a subsequent day I visited the jail. It is like any other house. One chap was making pictures, or paintings, he called them, of such a desperate character that I think he ought not to be turned loose without formally forswearing the brush—I will not say pencil. Another held undisturbed possession of the front sala and the adjoining bedrooms. His windows opened out on pleasant balconies, in view of the plaza mayor. One of his frequent visitors proposed to the alcaide to put a ladder up to one of the balconies, and save himself the trouble of letting him in and out.

The girls' school seemed to be in a remarkably fine condition. The patio was full of flowers, better cultivated than anywhere else probably in the whole province. The children seemed more lively and cheerful than ordinary; the result of zeal, I think, in the teacher, who seemed more than usually qualified for the task. Give her books, and her pupils would become ladies. I went to looking over their reading books, and found one reading lesson of so singular a nature that I could not resist my desire to possess it, so I went home and tore in two a number of *El Día*, a Jesuit newspaper. I selected a half which had a long string of verses, beginning, "I, the President, am an Ass, and my master, Faction, rides me." This I gave her for a reading lesson in exchange for hers, which was a small electioneering handbill, containing all the names of the candidates of both parties, with a footnote to each, praising those of one party, and bringing scandalous charges against the others. A picture of the Goddness of Silence in the room is the work of Señor Santibañas, one of the best native artists now extant; small praise, I allow.

I called at his studio, and saw there some clamshells, a thing so rare that I have known no others in all New Granada. He directed me to a pond where I found two species alive. The pond had no outlet, and the bottom is quite muddy, but it is still resorted to for bathing by some who do not like the brisk, clear water of the river.

I attended in Cartago the best ball that I saw in all the country. I cannot deny that it was dull, but the participants appeared quite like gentlemen and ladies. Still, there was a restraint and stiffness in the affair that we do not see in our best society at the North, and which I should not expect in a southern race. One event of the evening struck me too strongly to be easily forgotten. A young gentleman entered the room about eight, radiant with smiles of satisfaction; he was cordially received, and entered into the dancing with great spirit. I found that he had lain all the week in jail for debt. It was only since dark that he had gained his liberty, and he did not seem at all mortified at the occurrence.

Imprisonment is abolished for debts contracted since a certain date, but the old laws were even too severe. No amount of security would suffice to liberate the debtor against the will of the creditor—nothing but the money. The creditor is to allow the prisoner a real a day for subsistence.

They had just had a grand time in Cartago before my

arrival. The plaza had been fenced in for bulls. The
favorite game of Horned Monkey (Cachimona), in which
dice are used and coins change owners, had disappointed
some and elated others. But the only thing of interest that
I lost was some open-air plays on a stage of guaduas, that
was still standing in a corner of a plazuela, in an angle
made by a church and the sacristia.

# XVII

## CARTAGO

Just as we reentered Cartago we passed one of the numerous bridges that cross the brooks and ditches which are plenty in the plain around. The old wooden structure had given way, and let in a gentleman's carga mule. A part of the load had been a live guinea pig, brought for some days from up the river, which, when on the threshold of a new home, had thus finished its mortal journey. We crossed the ditch—brook I ought to call it, I suppose—without being much bespattered, and in a moment more were in the plaza, and, entering a portón, soon found ourselves in the patio of a casa alta.

As we filed up the stairs, at the head there was another file to meet us. Don Eladio found himself first in the arms of his widowed mother, Doña Ana Murgueitio de Vargas, a woman of nearly sixty, something like her daughter Elodia, though hardly as dignified as she will be at her mother's age. I wish it were more common for old women to be pretty here, but that cannot be without education. But of really old women there cannot be many in the country. I cannot think now of an octogenarian of either sex.

Next in order came a pretty girl of about seventeen—Mercedes. Of her parentage or relations I know little, except that Eladio whispered to me, at the first opportunity, "She is the daughter of a white man." I should think her mother, too, might have been as white as his.

With two more embracings Eladio's salutations were finished. These were with a venerable Negro cook, and another servant, a few shades lighter, and a little cleaner in dress. In all these huggings I had no part. The first half of them, or even less, would have pleased me as well as the whole; indeed, I was contented with the matter as it was.

The house had originally been one of magnificent dimensions. It occupied three sides of a square, and covered ground enough for a large hotel. But it had been inherited by two children, who proceeded to run a wall through the middle, with a portón on each side, and in the same way the front and back patios were divided. Evidences of diminished magnificence in this way are visible over all the towns of the Cauca, but in this case it was an advantage; for, had the furniture of the family been scattered over double the space, it would have cost them much unnecessary walking to go from article to article.

In addition to the interior corredor, we have balconies overlooking the plaza, and an exterior corredor on the side that overlooks a church patio filled with a dense mass of weeds. This corredor is our dining room, and a pleasant one. The kitchen is still farther from the street, a large, desolate room, without a table or chair, and, withal, somewhat dilapidated in its walls. The tinajera, the forgelike cooking place, and the grinding stone, are all that the room contains. The transit from the sala to the dining corredor cannot be made without passing through the principal dormitory of the family or through this kitchen. The road by the dormitory, even had it been the longer, would be better to travel in going to dinner.

One article of furniture surprised me. It was a spacious and elegant iron bedstead from Europe, with a wide, thick, and soft hair mattress, that might have made a bed for the president, had he been a Conservador and their guest. As it is, it seems rather an article of curiosity, for I do not know that it has ever yet been covered with sheets, unless it be to keep the dust off; nor is it of any use except to show what Sybarites the temperate zone harbors. How we all sleep here is more than I can say. The ground floor in the rear is a stable, and in front it is rented to a family. The servants sleep in the kitchen, or on the floor of the principal dormitory. I assign the smaller dormitory to the queenly, pious Elodia, sprightly Manuela, and Mercedes, the white man's daughter. And Eladio, his mother, wife, two children, and their nurse, with the two other servants, could find plenty of room in the large dormitory. My inseparable friend, the hammock, hangs in the sala, a luxury by day and a necessity at night.

But Susana Pinzón de Vargas has the earache. She is distracted with it. It is worse after dinner. She can hardly sit still long enough to nurse her babe. And a ball is coming off tonight. It is not a hacienda ball, such as we are yet to see, but a town ball, from which it seems that neither the sick nor those in prison can be spared; for Susana went not distracted as I feared, but, needing some distraction in her agony, went to the ball, and, as I could not attend this evening, I saw her no more till morning.

In the morning she was no better, and the doctor was called. He prescribed cupping, and the barber was accordingly sent for. He produced a scarificator, and Doña Susana was surprised that so ingenious a piece of mechanism should have strayed beyond the walls of the Inquisition. But the proposition of trying its multiplied knives on her was simply absurd. And, indeed, scarification in any form, however proper for others, could never be permitted on her. The physician was gone, and when Eladio proposed, as a compromise, that she be bled in the arm, she assented, glad to be thus rid of the barber, and he assented, glad thus to gain his fee and be off.

An accidental discovery here looks worse than it is; let no lady faint over it or scream audibly. I happened in the dormitory one morning before Señor Vargas had risen. He was late, for the Señorita Manuela Pinzón, his sprightly sister-in-law, was already dressed and conversing with him when he began to rise. He sat up in bed stark naked, except so far as covered by the bedclothes, for, like Jaques Couche-tout-nu in the *Wandering Jew*, he denudes himself entirely when he goes to bed. I do not know whether this custom prevails out of the Cauca; I should not have discovered it if it had.

I cannot tell what people do in Cartago. It is a quiet place for one in its position. It stands where four great

ways of commerce meet. Above is a grazing country, that
yields horses, mules, beef, and pork. Beef is cheaper on the
vast plains of the East, in Casanare, for instance, but there
they have no demand for it. Below Cartago is the gold
country of Antioquia, including also part of the province
of Cauca, where little food is raised. Rough, steep, and
rocky, it looks to the plains above for its beef and pork,
horses and mules. I estimate this digging population at
249,822, most of whom eat some beef and pork, and use
some beasts of burden. West of here is the gold-washing,
fish-eating province of Chocó, with a population of 43,639.
Enough of these see beef and lard once a year, or oftener,
to make the population dependent on the pastures above
Cartago a quarter of a million.

Some horses and mules are driven over the Quindio,
but no beef. Dried beef is sold for this journey. Most of the
salt used in the upper Cauca comes over the Quindio, and
a large part of the imported goods. Most of the hides of
animals raised here are put to uses unknown at the North,
as mats, beds, baskets, trunks, packing boxes, chairs, cord-
age, harness, fence, doors, and other uses too numerous to
mention; so there is no hide trade. A tobacco trade is
springing up. The cinchona of the province of Popayán
passes through Cartago, and over the Quindio, to avoid
the risks of Buenaventura. Tobacco makes its exit in both
directions. Cacao is raised above, and sent through here
to the mines. Rice might be. Indigo might be exported.

With all this, I am surprised to see so little in the
streets of Cartago. The most active doings I see are the
movements of the water boys. They are mounted on a
mule, a horse, or the ruins of either, while yet the vital
spark remains. To the four corners of the sawhorse that
serves as a saddle are hung four tarras of guadua. The imp
to whose mercy the quadruped is abandoned rides deep
enough into the arm of the La Vieja to dip up his water
without dismounting. He ought to dip it up only on the
upper side of the horse, with no other water boy above
him, nor any groom washing down horses, nor any bath-

ers, but you cannot make such a scapegrace careful. His mind is all bent on running races with water boys as wretchedly mounted as himself. Now he is stopped by a woman that offers him a cigar if he will hang on her two tarras, and return them to her full. He asks no consent of his beast or his employer. So a water boy knows no want of cigars.

I cannot take leave of Cartago without mentioning the most numerous, and by far the most active part of its population. The flea is a beautiful object when secured in balsam between two plates of glass for the microscope. Trained to drag a chain or draw a carriage, as these little hexapods are said to have been, they are worthy of the attention of the curious. And organize them into an army, and the sharp, slender claws, so beautifully exhibited in the microscope, show themselves admirable for clinging to you, and the curious lancet is a most perfect instrument for perforating the human cuticle.

But to all these good qualities there are two drawbacks. One is his nullibiquity—*nirgendheit* our German cousins would call it—his *no-where-ness* "when you put your finger on him"; and the other is the hardness of his cuirass. It would take me till night to tell you of all the adventures which have taught me the extent of these qualities. One time I will "put my finger on him" really. I crush him, ruin him, pulverize him, and take up my finger to feast my eyes on his mangled carcass, when lo! he bounds off eight-hundred times his length, and I can almost imagine a tiny derisive laugh at the idea of his getting a broken leg or a sprained ankle so easily. I can find another more easily than catch him again.

Another time I wet my finger before I put it on him; he shall not fool me so. I rub him till I have broken every bone in his body, and almost the bones of my finger besides. I stop and deliberate whether I will let him up yet. No; I will make assurance doubly sure by giving him one more crushing. Then I take my finger off, and lo, "he isn't there!" Of course I look foolish. But no mortal can stave off his fate when his time comes; so I find recorded in my diary, "Paila, 9 July, 1853. Had a capital day. Dreamed of home last night; had recent beef for dinner; got a new plant, caught a butterfly, and *killed a flea*." The flea that died that day met, doubtless, an accidental death; but my last visit to Cartago initiated me into the art of flea-catching by incessant practice. I killed dozens of them. It was almost worth a journey there. Once I went down the La Vieja and bathed. I turned my clothes inside out, and with unpitying eye saw no less than six ejected, far from any house, to take the chances of the weather; and all the way home I was the sole tenant of my vestments.

# XVIII

## ROLDANILLO

Don Eladio Vargas and I had been riding from Cartago to Zaragoza, when we fell in with Belisario Cabal. He is a young LL.D., who lives I know not how, unless it be by his interest in the hacienda of Chaqueral. Law pays little or nothing here. I was, as usual, trying to extract from him any information that he might possess about the resources and elements of wealth of the country. He stated that he had great hopes of vanilla. I remarked to him that any export worth a dollar or more a pound would be likely to be able to bear the costs of getting to the ocean; but no cheap ones, at present. He said that he had 10,000 plants of vanilla already set out, and hoped yet to increase the quantity. I was glad; hoped they would succeed; should be very happy to see them; I had seen none but spontaneous vanilla plants. He hoped I would call at Chaqueral some time when he was at home. After more talk of the same sort we arrived at Zaragoza, and Belisario went on.

When Belisario had gone on, Eladio told me that all he had been telling me was a string of lies.

I stopped, and looked hard in his face. Couldn't I understand Spanish?

"He has not a single root of vanilla in cultivation," said he. "It is all lies."

So, when I had proceeded up from La Cabaña to Las Lajas—Flat Stones—River, I turned off to the east toward Chaqueral, not to see a vanilla plantation, but a liar. A gentleman liar would be less of a curiosity now; but my readers will excuse me—I was green then, and believed what gentlemen told me. A man needs to be a year in a country before he can begin the study of the character of its inhabitants to advantage. I wanted to see how Belisario would look, what he would say, when I insisted on seeing his vanilla plantation.

Leaving to my right a house on a pretty knoll, on the right bank of the Río de Las Lajas, I passed through a hill by one of those hoof-worn cuts so common on the Cauca, even on plantation roads. I entered on a plain beyond, or the valley of a brook. Here I met young Belisario, who was very glad to see me. He was going up to Libraida on business, but he would turn back and introduce me to his aunt and cousin (that noun was feminine—prima), and would be back to a late dinner. In fact, he does not live at the hacienda, but at Buga, where he attends to his business. It was fortunate that I found him near home.

So we turned round, and proceeded in toward the mountains by an unending series of knolls, plains, cuts, and little precipices of six to ten feet. We bent northward, too, till I began to think that he was leading me by a roundabout way to Victoria, and that there was not even a Chaqueral, an aunt, or a prima, any more than a vanilla field. At length we saw the house of a tenant, a field for fattening cattle, and then the house. It was a mere cottage, on the top of a steep knoll, not far from the right bank of that troublesome Río Hondo that I found south of La Cabaña.

The house was a cottage of three rooms. Along the front ran a corredor, and before it was a fence half-down the hill, with an entrance gate. Behind was a smooth, well-swept area, that might be called a patio; but there were no buildings around it except a shed to cook under, in place of the kitchen that had been burned down.

Of course, the central room we entered was the sala. On the north end (left-hand) was the family room (very small), and on the opposite end was a room for Belisario, or, in his absence, for Don Modesto Gamba, his uncle. Opposite the front door was the back door, that opened out on a diminutive piazza or corredor, with two small closets, or pantries, at the ends. Such were the reduced halls of the vanilla planter. Don Modesto seemed to be a sort of partner or tenant of the young lawyer. He was now out, probably at work with his own hands. Doña Paz Cabal de Gamba was sitting at a table, making cigars. The prima, Isabel Gamba (Cabal), was sitting by the door on the floor, making a gown. Her cousin introduced me, and wished me a pleasant time till his return.

All hopes of vanilla being postponed till after dinner (most probably at night), I began to make the best of circumstances. I was evidently not unknown to them, though I had never heard of them. Isabel was about eighteen, and wore the peasant dress, which suited her very well. If there is some Negro blood in her veins, it is not perceptible. The gown she was making was for herself —she dresses, then, sometimes as a lady. A novel, translated from the French, lay on the table. She loved reading, but never had any education. Cousin Belisario lent her books. Her brother, a student in Bogotá, had given her some.

Here, then, was an intermediate link between the aristocracy and the peasantry of the country. She belonged rather to the latter by birth, but, although she had never been educated, she had contrived to pick up enough to make her really quite attractive, as more than one aristocratic Caucano would acknowledge, if he dared speak his mind. My own opinion, at this distance of time and place, is this, that she is just the most agreeable native lady that I have found in all New Granada. Her father and mother are plain, good people that seem quite contented with their girl, and hope the best for their absent son.

All their domestic help consisted of two little black mute girls of perhaps eight and ten. They are not idiots, and are very lively, can hear as well as anybody, understand all you say, but do not speak more than a syllable or two. I have watched them closely, and even studied them, as in many points they resembled those remarkable dwarfs exhibited in the United States as "Aztec children," the remains of an extinct race. I had busied myself with those "Aztecs," and had fortunately discovered, by a letter from Granada, their history, and that they were dwarfed specimens of a mixed race of ordinary size. The

little mutes at Chaqueral scarcely differed from them
except in size. They were lively, active, cheerful, ready to
do anything that their strength permitted, but could not
be made to speak a word.

I spent the day very pleasantly reading and talking,
with one or two strolls along the margin of the stream. In
one of our chats Isabel looked up from her work, and asked
me if I had any children.

"I never was married," I replied.

"Belisario told me that you was a bachelor, but I
thought quite probably you might have children never-
theless."

"Were I so unscrupulous as to be a father before
marriage, I should be enough so to deny it also. Were I
suspected of such a thing, I have not a friend that would
not close his doors against me. Such persons are not
admitted into the society that I frequent."

"Were we to be so particular here," says Doña Paz,
"we should have to live without society."

They thought with me that it was a great misfortune
that things were so, but she did not know that their religion had anything to do with the laxity of their morals. I
had been before asked in the same way about my children
by a gentleman who had already invited me to an intimacy
with his amiable family.

At night Belisario returned from Libraida, and his
uncle from his work, and we three sat down, I at the head,
and they at the side of the coarse, long, substantial table.
I had the post of honor there in the armchair; they sat on
the poyo. Isabel stood and looked on, to see that we wanted
nothing. After we were through, the dishes were removed
to the ground at the back corredor, where she and her
mother sat down and ate.

On another occasion, when they had with them Belisario's sister, Virginia Cabal, and the gentlemen were both
away, I protested that I was not used to eating alone, and
they must eat with me. Two more plates were put on, and
the young ladies sat down, but they refused to eat. They

conversed till I was through, and then dined with Doña
Paz on the ground in the corredor. I think the custom of
the women eating apart from the "lords of creation," and
on the floor, is giving way a little. The best families in the
Cauca do not practice it.

In the morning, the first topic was vanilla. The plantation was too distant to visit, but we would go and see
some spontaneous specimens. But the cultivation of the
precious plant was so important that I would grudge no
time to see it with my own eyes; so after breakfast we
mounted, and went inward toward the mountain. We
went in farther than I have ever since seen any occupied
land, except near Tuluá. We came to a pasture that is
shut in mostly by a ravine and a stout fence; beyond this
we entered the woods, so that there was nothing but a
forest between us and the neighborhood of the Magdalena.
Here he showed me three plants of a vanilla that he assured
me he had planted. I examined them, and pronounced
them likely to live. I happened to know that we had
already passed over his line into the property of another
man. I thought it inhuman to carry my vanilla hunt any
farther, and "was fully satisfied." It is with great reluc-
tance that I leave the family of Señor Gamba.

Let us now look at the town residence of Don Ramón
González. The village of Roldanillo stands in a nook of the
Caldas chain, or western cordillera, below the mouths of
the La Paila and Las Cañas, and above that of Lajas,
Hondo, and Micos rivers, all of which come in from the
east, and are variously and incorrectly laid down on the
maps. Río Frío comes out of the western mountains, and
empties into the Cauca above the village. The census
tables, which give the population of districts only, give a
clue to the comparative size of villages. With rare excep-
tions, the more populous a district, the larger its village.
Thus, Roldanillo district, with a population of 4800, must
have at its "head"—cabeza (which is also the cabecera
[capital] of the Canton of Roldanillo)—a population of
some 4000. Here we may expect physicians, schools, balls,

and respectable festivals. It is not strange, then, that the
González children were all born here, are to be educated
here, are to dance here, and to spend their money here.

Indeed, we would in charity hope that here is their
residence, and that it is only occasionally that they occupy
for a few weeks the mud cottages of La Vega. It is not so—
cannot be so. Don Ramón has no faithful mayordomo—
overseer—as may sometimes be found east of the Quindio.
He must see with his own eyes, and be present constantly,
or everything stops and goes wrong. Still, the town house
is much more respectable in size, material, and furniture.
It is large enough, if not with rooms enough. It has but
five rooms indeed, including kitchen and stable; but all
these are spacious, and all, except the stable, in the upper
story of an adobe house. The bedsteads and table are
movable, and as elegant as might be expected from the
hands of a rough carpenter in a land where the lathe is
unknown.

In fact, the only approximation to a lathe I have seen
here is a contrivance to make an object revolve three or
four times in one direction, and as many in the contrary.

Don Ramón has also a chest of books here. I think
one volume has been added in his own day, the *Colmena
Española—Spanish Hive*. It appears to be a translation of
the *Penny Magazine*, and, were copies plenty, would have
done a good work for the rising race. I did not see any
book that I thought had been purchased by his father, but
previous generations appear to have been much better
patrons of the bookseller. Thus all the books had passed
the minimum point, and age now only adds to their value.

On the Sabbath I drew from this treasury a Latin
work on Jewish antiquities, which, if compiled from the
knowledge and traditions of the Jews in Spain, ought to
have a peculiar interest at this day. There was a rope-
dancer to exhibit that evening, and, all the rest of the
family wished to go. Imagine me, then, seated at the table,
with a tallow candle in the candlestick, bending over the
old parchment-bound Latin volume, and resolved to have

a Sabbath evening to myself. At eleven the family returned, bringing their chairs with them. On all such occasions the spectators must find their own seats, and it is
so even in the theater of Bogotá. Thus closed my Sabbath
in the family of Ramón González.

Filial irreverence runs wild in New Granada. I have
seen a girl of eight, the daughter of a most respectable and
high-spirited mother, strike her and call her the vilest
names known in any language, and that with impunity. I
am not prepared to assert that family discipline is known
at all here. Less would be needed than with us, by far. As it
is less called for, it is not so strange that it is in almost
entire disuse.

I visited the boys' school at Roldanillo, but saw nothing worthy of remark. I saw also a select school for girls.
Select it was, for the number was only five. In intellectual
advantages this was no way superior to the average of
public girls' schools, if even so good; but the pupils were
more out of the way of learning bad language. The teacher
was the sister and housekeeper of Priest Elias Guerrero,
the most amiable member of the clergy I have seen here.
He is without the charge of any church. I could not but
feel sad to think of so affectionate a brother that could
never be a husband; so intelligent and worthy a man exposed to the sins that are (humanly speaking) inseparable
from forced celibacy.

I stayed a night at the house of Padre Elias. He had
to say mass the next morning. I proposed to accompany
him. He assented, only requesting me, if my conscience
did not permit me to kneel in mass, to stand where my
nonconformity could not be seen; so I stood in the sacristy.
The church is quite a large, desolate concern, not over-
rich in pictures and statues; but it has an organ. I went up
to try it. A man tried to blow it, but it would take two men
to do it; and you could find no two pipes in harmony in it;
such a shrieking, growling, squalling, and squealing as it
made was almost diabolic.

After breakfast Señor Guerrero went to work examin-

ing a peculiar book, that had been made by adding leaf
after leaf of stamped paper to a nucleus of two or three
sheets with which it had begun. It was a criminal trial—
proceso. A man had been charged with some crime, and
had been denounced. The denunciation was page 1. Page
2 stated that he was not guilty. Page 3 was from the juez
letrado del circuito—the circuit judge—ordering the
judge of the first instance to take the evidence of A, B, C,
and D. These made up documents 4, 5, 6, and 7. No. 8 was
from the accused, demanding that someone be assigned as
his counsel, as he was too poor to employ a doctor of laws.
No. 9 was from the judge of the first instance, ordering
Reverend Elias Guerrero to defend the accused. In No.
10 my friend had asked that B and C be reexamined on
certain points, and E and F examined; 11, 12, 13, 14
contained the results of these examinations.

If it shall seem to the personero (prosecuting attor-
ney) that the case is made up, he will demand, in No. 15,
an interview at a proper time between the juez letrado,
the accused, his defender, six jurors—jurados (sworn men)
—and himself, in which these documents will all be read,
and the case argued. We may then hope that No. 16 will
contain the vote of a majority of the jury, and No. 17 the
sentence of the judge.

Such is the outline of the French, Spanish, and Granadan process, as it seems to me. It is much more dangerous to men of bad character than our blessed English
system, which yields a more perfect protection to the
criminal than any other ever invented. I tried to describe
our process to him, but I fear that he did not believe all I
said.

From Roldanillo I had arranged to go to Libraida or
Zarzal, directly across the river. I parted with the good
priest with no little regret.

## XIX

### GRAZIER LIFE

Beyond the river the road bears to the west, to avoid some very high hills. We proceeded to the base of the first of these, and found ourselves at the ancient hacienda de la Paila. The hacienda extends from Las Cañas River to the River Murillo, which formerly bounded the provinces of Antioquia and Popayán. The width there is seven miles. The length, from the Cauca to the summit of the Quindio, may be thirty miles, and the whole cannot contain less than five hundred square miles, and may well be a thousand. During the good old regime of tyranny, when prosperity was the lot of the rich, and unrequited labor that of the poor, the hacienda is said to have boasted thirty-six thousand cows and eight hundred mares; now the mares are greatly reduced in number, and the cows cannot be a tithe of what they were.

I cannot pretend to conjecture the number of houses on the estate. They are scattered from the road to the river, but there are none far east of the road. A line of houses skirts that large plain north of the La Paila called the Medio. The inhabitants there are mostly white. There is a group on the south bank of the river, half a mile below the ford; the inhabitants of these have a good deal of Negro blood in their veins. On the south end of the road, across the estate, there are no houses. These families of herdsmen, of every color, have been a great study for me.

The chief exports of this tract are young bulls, young horses, and hogs. The latter are raised by the inhabitants of the river forest, the others by the family. Some of the tenants owe personal service for rent. This is generally rendered on Friday and Saturday, and most of it performed on horseback. The others pay a ground rent of from $1.60 to $3.20 per annum. All have their estancias, or fields, in the forest. They contain from half an acre to two acres, enclosed by an elliptical or circular fence of split guaduas. Those who live in the open land have often quite a distance to go to their fields, but, as they work only occasionally, it makes little difference. But the grazing interest demands our more particular notice.

The horses themselves are the most obedient and well-broken I have ever seen. The slightest intimation of the bridle will guide them. They will patiently gratify your whim of flower-gathering, even at the expense of running their head into a thornbush. You may stand on the back of many of them, leaving the reins at your feet, or, throwing the reins over the high pommel of the saddle, leave them for some time. Their gait is generally very easy. They are not large, nor is much regard had to parentage.

The bridle was made here. They would not like to trust to a bit made abroad. The Caucan bit is a formidable affair. The saddle is a study for an anatomist. The co-jinetes are a cover over the whole, made of a leather resembling buckskin. It is often padded and embroidered with silk. It has two huge pockets, each capable of con-taining a pair of shoes, or two hundred dollars in silver. It would have saved me some labor had I been told by my books that in New Granada a high-pommeled saddle and an armchair are silla; a low-pommeled saddle, a side-saddle, and a fresh-water turtle are galápago; a common chair, taburete; easy chair, poltrona; ottoman and stool, cojín; sofa, sofá; lounge without a back, canapé; bench with a back, escaño; bench without a back, banco. Saddle, bridle, sudadero, stirrups, and halter (jáquima), con-stitute a montura. A traveler here ought always to own his montura, and watch it well. Horses, cows, and goats will eat his sudadero, and dogs will eat all the rest but the tanned leather, wood, and iron; of these last, including the contents of the cojinetes, the peons will rob him; his clothes are victimized by the washwomen, and his skin by mosquitoes, fleas, and niguas. Happy is he if he can save his bones and his conscience (particularly the latter) undamaged, and, leaving his cash and much of his flesh, return to his native land with his credit and his constitution.

I think the idea we have of skill in the use of the lasso is exaggerated. Even in the corral it is well to catch five horses at ten throws. One assured me that one hundred throws would catch eighty or ninety horses. The next six throws caught but one.

The outer corral has two entrances; a horseman is stationed at one, and a ruana on a stake at the other, and we start off for the wilder herd. Our way is riverward, over beautiful valley land, sprinkled with clumps of trees and thorny bushes of acacia. Silence! We steal along at a walk, curving our course around an unseen center. Now Cristóbal starts forward at a gallop, with his head bent down to the horse's mane. We follow, and the herd find us shouting between them and their refuge. A few desperadoes plunge with a crash into the thorny thicket behind us, the rest gallop in the opposite direction. A bushy ravine extends across our course near the corral. Instead of crossing it, almost the whole herd pass our ranks, and disappear toward the river—all but now and then one arrested by the lasso in her flight. Those who have not thus caught a prize beat the bushes, dislodge an animal, and catch him as he runs. In this way we secure at least a delegation from the wild herd; we will hope to do better next time.

Now begins the business of the day. What calf has not his earmark? What youngster of two months has not his little brand on his cheek? What yearling not branded for life on his side? A lasso on his head, another on his heels. A fire is burning by the division fence, and the irons are hot.

Now comes the turn of the horses. They are subject to many more infirmities than the cows, are of more value per head, and, besides, are to be trained. Hence they are reviewed much oftener and more carefully. Owing to this, they are not so wild.

This life would not be without its perils were not the vaquero so tough. He is riding at full gallop, and his horse puts his foot into a deep hole covered with grass. He comes to the ground as from a railcar. He picks up his guasca, and, if his cow has not got clear, off he starts again in the chase. His girth breaks when he has a bull tied to the pommel of his saddle. He manages to escape unharmed. I have known but one serious accident, the dislocation of a shoulder joint.

Both horse and rider enjoy the sport highly. It is severe sport for the horse, who will injure himself before showing any sign of flagging. A curious scene closes the rodeo. A vaquero catches a wild colt which he is to break. He manages, amid his struggles, to exchange the guasca for a halter, and binds the infuriate youngster securely to the tail of his horse, who goes homeward from the corral with the meek resignation of a deacon who has a dissipated son.

From the superior whiteness of the inhabitants of the Medio, the balls here are rather attractive to the Paileños. I went to one myself, which I found, as usual, stupid. I must, however, give some account of it. There were no seats, or not enough, for the women, so they sat on the ground at the sides of the room. Men stood in two groups just within the doors, and some also were permitted farther in. Cakes and aguardiente were for sale in the corredor.

The bambuco I have not yet described, although it was performed for my instruction at Fusagasugá. One couple needs the whole floor in the bambuco. It is decided that he is to dance it. Then they wonder who she will be. He bows to her. She borrows a pocket-handkerchief (mine, perhaps), and steps out. She moves to the music, but ad libitum as to the direction, and he follows her motions as faithfully as a mirror. If she moves east, he dances west; when she goes north, he goes south; when she turns a little, he turns as much, and in the contrary direction. Thus they advance, recede, turn side to side, or even entirely round; so they dance without ever touching each other, till she becomes tired, drops a courtesy, and sits down. He thinks he has acquitted himself extremely well; his carelessly turning up his ruana, to show the brighter colors of the underside, is not bad. But his chef-d'œuvre was that kick of the dog, without losing either time or place. The quadruped, surprised and indignant, looks round, and, could he speak English, would ask, "Why I?" But his partner appears unconscious of this achievement; not that she is insensible to it, but it is beneath the solemnity of the occasion for her to be betrayed into a smile.

The torbellino or whirlwind is another dance after the bambuco plan, only, as the name implies, more violent in its action. I saw at this ball the queerest couple I have seen yet. A little girl of under ten was called out—sacada —to dance the bambuco with the tallest vaquero of the hacienda. To see her little body directing the movements of the whole of his reminds one of a battle between a kingbird and a crow.

On the south side of the river, in the edge of the woods, lives Sánchez el Manco—the one-handed. He is the most thrifty tenant on the estate, and has horses, cows, swine, and rather extensive fields, including a cacagual, or cacao orchard. Now and then he sends me word that he has a raceme of bananas ripening, and then he is sure of a call from me.

This side of Sánchez el Manco lives Timotea, who gains an honest penny by making palm-leaf hats, and sudaderos or saddlemats of rushes. I engaged a sudadero of her for two dimes. I went at the appointed time, and it was not done. I went again, and she had finished it and sold it. She promised me another. I went for it, and, as I asked why she had not done it, I was whittling a fruit with my penknife. She had not finished it for the want of two pieces of hide to protect the rushes from being worn by the girth. "Cannot find two bits of hide?" said I; "here are two." So saying, I picked up a piece of hide on which a girl had been sitting to braid, cut off a projecting corner, and cut it in two. Timotea was surprised. She evidently had not thought of that; it ruined the seat. The next time I called my sudadero was ready.

In one of these houses I saw a corpse. It was that of a man. It was decently extended on the earth floor, with a sort of robe on, with a girdle of new rope of cabuya. Several candles were burning around, being stuck into masses of mud, shaped so as to answer for candlesticks. A large number of persons were gathered around, quiet and thoughtful. One was saying a string of Paternosters and Ave Marias in Spanish. I was there when they carried him out on a bier made on the spot by tying slats of guadua together with bejuco. The burial ground is not far from there. It is in a desolate condition, and the fence has entirely fallen. The grave was five feet deep, of ample width, but shorter than the body. An extension, or place for the head, was dug in at the southern end, so that when the body was properly placed in its last resting-place, it occupied the whole grave, and in filling it no earth would be thrown into the face. It was altogether as respectable a burial as you would find in the same class in life in a western state. All the religious ceremonies (simply prayers of laymen) were finished before the burial began.

Deaths had been frequent, and particularly in this family. It was decided to be an epidemic, and the remedy was concluded to be a procession in honor of Santa Barbara—a rogación to her. She is the patroness of the little chapel at La Paila. I had visited said chapel once before, when, one Sunday, the piously disposed went in there to pray. Short work we had of it, for our orisons were scarce begun when the service was adjourned. The cause was that the niguas had taken possession of the holy place, and were concentrating on the defenseless girls their myriad hosts. I washed half a dozen off my legs on coming out. Now, however, it had been sprinkled and swept till it would do to worship in very well.

The priest came in the evening, bringing with him his wafers, a chalice wrapped in a cloth and tied under his arm, and a vial of wine with a paper stopper. During the mass the next morning a poor fellow was attacked with epilepsy in the church. They took him into the sacristy, and, to recover him, they concluded to apply wine to his nostrils. The wine in the bottle is unconsecrated; so they turn the vial up till the paper stopper is saturated, and rub it on the nostrils and lips of the patient, and then put it back into the vial. After the consecration came the procession, on a very humble scale, with an image borrowed for the occasion. The hostia must be carried under an umbrella for want of a canopy, and in default of a better I lent them mine. It was whole when I closed it last, many months before, in Bogotá; now I find it broken, no one knows when, where, or how. After the ceremonies were over, I found a cork that I could spare, and whittled it down to fit the vial of wine, and threw away the wad of paper.

I went once to visit Bernabé, the district judge. He is a Negro, with a mulatto wife, Dolores, and two or three children, that seem a little lighter than she is. I may be deceived, but, again, perhaps Bernabé may be. The judge cannot read. He lives on the base of a knoll overlooking the pasture of Guavito, and his house is supplied by a small brook that flows down a ravine, and is often almost dry, or with no running water. There always happens in the beds of these brooks to be some water in the charcos or holes, and as you advance toward the source you find a very little running in the channel. Cattle understand this, and, when impelled by thirst, follow a dry brook up till they come to water.

I found Dolores in the kitchen, and she sent a little girl to tell me she could not leave it just then. I went out for the sake of seeing a Caucana fairly busy. She was distilling aguardiente. A large tinaja was standing on tulpas (three stones), in the middle of the floor, with a fire under it. It contained some fermented cane juice. The condenser was a brass pan or kettle (paila) that covered the mouth of the tinaja. Under this condenser was a peculiar earthen plate called an obispo—bishop—so constructed as to receive the drops that fell from the under surface of the kettle, and permit them to run off. To keep the condensing kettle cool was Dolores' present occupation. She dipped it full of water from a trough, and then dipped it out again into the trough, and thus continued filling and emptying it incessantly, while the drops of the dearly earned fluid fell deliberately into a junk bottle placed beneath.

I went back to Libraida, the head of the district, to see an election. A series of them, four days apart, and about six in number, were coming off. It was under a new law, which was exceedingly rigid in securing the rights of the citizen to a secret vote. The elections must fall on different days of the week, and of course only one of them on the Sabbath. All votes in the same province must be of the same precise size, about six inches square. Three officers sit in a room, and no man can come in except electors, one at a time, with a ballot once folded between the thumb and index of the right hand. The loss of either of these organs disfranchises him. He holds it out horizontally; an officer takes it, unfolds it face downward, drops it into a box, and the voter goes out at the back door, where no persons are permitted to remain, and jumps over the fence in the rear. The counting was a great ceremony. The declarer held the ballot aloft in both hands, so that all around could see both sides of it, and then read it while others recorded it.

Now all the gentlemen aforesaid, and not a few minors—menores de edad—have been anticipating the advent of San Juan. It is not the saint, however, but the day they seem to expect as eagerly as any schoolboy his holidays. The eventful day was Friday, 24th June; but these events love to be anticipated. On Tuesday a couple went to Libraida to be married. Their return on Wednesday noon was celebrated and announced by a sufficient number of these rocket crackers. This was also the signal for the commencement of a day ball in a cottage near the gate. In the course of the afternoon I went down, and came back with a description of the dress of the bride, put on, of course, after marriage, for nothing but somber colors are allowed in church.

The hair was short all over the head, but, being as crisp as wool, retained without difficulty a side comb of gold and some artificial flowers on each side, and a complete garland behind. The earrings were of gold, quite original in their pattern, reminding me of the top of a steeple, the ball being represented by a stone of the size of a cherry. On the neck was, first, a chain of gold going twice around; second, a string of pearl beads; third, another gold chain. The camisa was of fine white muslin; sleeves of another muslin, shot with red, reaching below the elbow; collar of the same, two-fingers broad, falls down from the top, which is so low in the neck that it hangs off one shoulder, but, per contra, probably does not extend halfway to the feet; enaguas of de laine, slate color, with two flounces. A belt of material resembling that of gentlemen's braces passes twice round the waist and tucks in. Below this, the skirt sags in front three inches. In the mouth, a cigar; on the hands, four gold rings with emeralds; on the feet, nothing, with pantalettes of the same.

The ball, after lasting some sixteen hours without intermission, closed early on Thursday morning. After a ball or other fatigue a swim is very refreshing. My affairs brought me accidentally in contact with a swimming party this morning. It consisted of the whitest and handsomest girls of the Medio, the young men of the "house," and vaqueros. I believe I have described the bathing dress of gentlemen and ladies. I will repeat, however, that the men wear a pocket-handkerchief—never more nor less. The girls wore less than ladies do, only a skirt and a handkerchief tied around the neck at top, and confined at the bottom by the skirt. I fancy they profess not to go in at the same place, but ni two places, say five rods apart; but they do not fail to invade each other's bounds. The women use a profusion of soap.

After my return home it was announced that a party of Sanjuaneros was approaching the house. Demetrio loaded the gun, and Mother Antonia hastened to place cake and aguardiente on a table in the corredor. The party advanced with whoopings and rockets, to which Demetrio responded, setting fire with the wad to the thatch of the cane mill. In the party I counted twenty-six females, every one of them astride of a horse, a mare, or a gelding. Without dismounting, the wineglass of raw spirit, without sugar or water, passed the whole cavalcade. The men drained it, the women only sipped. They went as they came, on the gallop. I joined the party some time after at the lower cottages. Many had flags made of a handkerchief, and adorned with ribbons. All the women wore shawls on their heads under their hats and ruanas.

Arches were erected in front of two houses, ornamented with cloth, etc., and fruits, as plantains, slices of a huge species of Citrus (called cidra), and a pineapple. Under the arch you find a bench and a table, with aguardiente for sale. Now you find them all gathered before a house. Fulgencio, ex-judge of the district, has bought a bottle of spirits there, which must pass from mouth to mouth till it is empty. Owing to the time lost in pouring into a glass, a bottle is drunk in less time without one, and, what is surprising, is emptied by fewer persons.

This was followed by a race between two horses, in which the stakes were from a dime or two to perhaps three dollars. My conclusion from all this is, that the beloved disciple was fond of horse racing, dram drinking, shouting, and gunpowder; but perhaps it is John the Baptist that is to answer to these charges.

Saturday brought no remission, unless it be that the cohetes had been nearly all let off. Toward night there was a bullfeast in the front yard, but quite a different affair from those of a higher grade, as at Fusagasugá. On Sunday again there was horse racing, and we had another bullfeast. I have not spoken of the balls, though there has probably been one every night. It is really amazing to me to see so much drinking, so little drunkenness, and no fighting, especially in a people where drunkenness is not very disreputable, and where they have a civil war every ten years.

I wish to give a more accurate picture of domestic life among the first families in the Cauca. For this I have selected the Vargas family, as I wish strictly to avoid entering the domain of fiction by combining the occurrences of two or more families. I write this in the earnest hope that no reader will recognize the originals, or, if unfortunately it should be otherwise, that the discoverer will be so good as never to make known their name or residence to any inhabitant of South America.

It will be recollected that when I introduced Señor Eladio Vargas to the reader, I mentioned that, in the times of slavery, they were wealthy. Besides this estate of La Ribera, and their mines in Chocó, that now yield not a dollar, they have two haciendas in this valley, though there is a lawsuit with an adverse claimant to one of them. La Ribera alone could support them handsomely were it well managed, but their chief desire seems to be to keep things along here, and to spend in Cartago all they can scrape from this estate, while I doubt whether the others yield anything at all.

We are not early risers at the house, as the family residence is denominated by the cottagers; but, as the hour of six approaches, also approaches the sun to the horizon, and would be visible soon after but for the clouds, that render a rising or setting sun a thing unknown here. As rises the sun, rises also Pilar, the "mistress of keys," crosses herself, and, I conjecture, dresses herself—perhaps washes her hands and face. She sets herself to sweeping the back corredor, the sala, and front corredor, a task hardly worthy of the chief housekeeper when perchance goats or cows may have made the front corredor their dormitory. Escolástica rises from a hide laid on the ground, leaving sprawling naked there the son of (she says) Dionisio, and, without any dressing or washing, sets herself about something that bears the semblance of work. Three negritas, naked from the waist upward, one with her skirt rent in three from top to bottom, come and place themselves astride the wall of the corredor—pretil—to see if anybody passes in the distant highway. This mode of sitting appears more agreeable to the negras than in a chair: Escolástica and others older find it convenient at times. Estefana, the cook, rakes open the kitchen fire, and lights her cigar; or, if the fire is out, strikes a light with flint and steel as readily as you would put on your coat. Her tinder is the huge pith of the Fourcroya—maguey.

Roso, the negrito, the happy possessor of his nudity and not a thread more in the world, comes from his nest, and, without any fear of wearing out his clothes or blacking his skin, sits down on the floor to play. Joaquina leaves her lair, and sits down till milking time. Josefa rises and walks about. The menservants make their appearance from various nooks where they have passed the night. Manuel goes to his smithy, that he may not be seen about the house idle.

Manuel, Esteban, Dionisio, some shades lighter, and Jacinto, many shades darker, also take their seats on the pretil, a bench, and my table, and appear to be busy with a part of a saddle, a bridle, and a halter. Aureliano, Cosme, and Gregorio, three white boys, who, under the name of servants, contrive to escape with half the work one boy ought to do, post themselves in the corredor to watch the operations of three dogs. Volcán and Enamorado, led by Folía, selected, at five o'clock, one of the milch cows for their amusement, and they have worried the poor thing ever since; but they are all cowards, and dare not bite her. Ramón, a larger boy, neither whiter nor blacker than the other two, creeps, as if with sore toes, to the enclosed pasture—potrero—and drives several horses into a yard; throws a lasso over an old white horse, which is too lazy or too well-bred to run, and goes off to an estancia to look for plantains for breakfast.

Carlos Vargas, the youngest of the gentlemen, catches another with more difficulty but more dexterity, and calls Jacinto from his busy idleness to saddle it, and also another for himself. They start off together to the open pasture, and will return at breakfast time or a little after. They go to see if anything has happened there. Toledo (this is his surname), the horsebreaker, has tied each "hand" of a colt to the corresponding foot, and is riding him round and round in a very small circle in the sugar mill. Pepe Gómez, a relative living in the family, has ridden off to the cacagual, or chocolate orchard, to see if any cacao needs gathering, and to see if the hogs have broken in. Pepe and Antonio come forth from No. 1 or No. 2, as the case may be, and, without attending at present to their ablutions, sit down in the corredor to read a Spanish translation of a French novel, published as a sort of extra by the *Correo de Ultramar* in Paris. I have not particularly introduced these younger brothers of Don Eladio. Of Pepe I will only say that he is worth any two of his brothers in business, energy, and reliability, and only inferior to the pious and dignified Eladio. Antonio, who is but seventeen, has quite an active turn of mind, that loves to exercise itself in horse racing, dancing, cockfighting, in the administration of baptism and medicine, and other useful offices.

Prompt washing is not the custom here, and I have been led gradually to defer my ablutions till near breakfast time. I have gone to the tinajera, and found there a bowl and water, but no dipper nor servant; half an hour after I would find a dipper, but no bowl; and the next time all that I wanted except water, for now the tinajas are all empty. Soap is sometimes imported—that made here is black and pasty. In all cases it is dear.

But breakfast is ready. Some dried beef—tasajo— has been boiled in water to make a soup—sopa—thickened with cakes of maize, or with plantains roasted and crushed. The meat, reduced to a form resembling oakum, has been fried. It is so dry that, if laid on a sheet of letter paper instead of a plate, it possibly might neither wet nor grease it. It is rather insipid. The borders of the platter are covered with slices of plantain, fried. When perfectly ripe they are delicious; a little earlier they are insipid and hard; green, they do not fry them. Generally, a roasted plantain is found by each plate. Entirely ripe, they are very good; a little short, they are mealy and insipid; green, they are

hard and (to me) uneatable. Unfortunately, the peasantry
and the servants generally eat up the ripe ones, and leave
us with green ones. But there is another dish; and of this
you must take the testimony of an enemy, for I detest it.
It is called sancocho, and is the staple of both meals, and
with the peasantry generally the only dish except roasted
plantains. For this dish, take any quantity of tasajo (that
which did not spoil in drying is best), with or without
bones, fat or lean; put it in an earthen pot—olla—with a
pailful or less of water; add shreds of green plantain, and,
if you have them, pieces of squash and yuca root (Manihot
utilissima). Potatoes, turnips, carrots, parsnips, onions,
and beets would be admissible, but the first cannot grow
here, and the others are universally neglected. Sweet potatoes—batatas—inferior to ours, so that I doubt their
identity, are sometimes added, and tomatoes. This mixture is then boiled. The bogas eat it with spoons of totuma
from the shields of tortoises; the peasantry from broken
ollas and totumas with spoons of wood or totuma; the
respectable families eat it with heavy ancient spoons of
massive silver from soup plates of the old "willow pattern"
of our early days. A fried egg or two, or as many as there
are covers, may be found on the table. If boiled, they are
eaten with salt only. As you are closing your meal, a small
cup of thick chocolate is set upon your plate, or offered
you on another plate. Saucers are seldom used as such.
Your chocolate contains about two cubic inches of cacao
and brown sugar—panela—ground together on a warm
stone.

The tables are not well attended here, considering
the disposable force of a family. More than half this charge
may fall upon the ama de llaves—"mistress of the keys."
I ought to add that breakfast concludes with water. Two
or three tumblers, or silver cups, are brought in on a tray.
They are successively filled from small tin cups till all
have satisfied their thirst. Then, if a priest be present, but
never otherwise, the "Lord's Prayer" and some others are
said by way of returning thanks.

It is now about half-past ten. How, or when, or where the servants have breakfasted I know not, only that it is not together, nor at a table, nor with knives and forks. Things wear as quiet an aspect after breakfast as before. Viviana has caught every hen that has shown a disposition to lay, and shut them up to secure the eggs. The negritas now set themselves down in the corredor of the storeroom to sew, under the direction of Josefa, or to read, taught by Pilar. Private instruction here is no better than the schools; and a mulata, a slave eighteen months ago, just able to read, is no better than the public teachers, nor much worse. The first book is the *Cartilla*. It contains the alphabet, and *ab's*, and some prayers. This is followed by the *Citología*, no more interesting to youth. I have looked at every book in which children learn to read, and have not yet found a child who had anything to read that could interest him. An old lawbook; *Artillery Tactics*; the *Theory of Human Liberty and Constitutional Rights*, a Protestant tract —anything that is not damaged by being worn out, or missed if lost, is good enough for a reading book.

The dinner begins, as the breakfast did, with soup. The everlasting sancocho is sure to be present; but in addition to, or in place of, the meat oakum, perhaps you may find a guisado, much like baked beef. It is often very tender, and, I think, superior to our ordinary New York cooking. After the meat comes a teacup or small bowl of boiled milk, eaten generally with roasted plantains; to this succeeds sliced brown sugar (panela), sirup, or sirup and milk boiled together, or some other sweetmeats. The varieties of these, from squash to fig, are innumerable. With these and with chocolate, they never fail to mingle their extemporaneous cheese; or, if this be wanting to their chocolate, they substitute its principal ingredient— salt. After the dulce comes water, served as in the morning. During a meal they rarely or never drink, unless it be wine or aguardiente.

The calves are now shut up. Escolástica goes out and collects weeds (Sida—escoba) for a new broom. The negritas set themselves to playing at marbles with corozos, the seed of a thorny palm, in the front corredor. A peasant from a little distance comes to the house. Five dogs bounce out upon him; the peon coolly draws his machete; Volcán, more zealous than prudent, receives on his "hand" a machetazo, which, for a day or two to come, will make him put down three and carry one. A boy brings in three eggs tied in a cloth to exchange for a candle, both bearing the value of a cuartillo. Ramón brings in a load of cane on a horse. The packsaddle has two horns—one before, the other behind. To each of these is hung a hook on each side, and on two of these hooks rests the cane. He tells me his load has not slidden off the hooks more than once in coming. All the cane for the cane mill is carried in this way or on human heads. A horse draws four guaduas at a time (six if seasoned) with one pair of hooks, the other ends resting on the ground. If a single guadua is wanted, it is tied to the horse's tail; the boy mounts his back, and rides home in triumph. Sometimes a man on horseback draws a guadua for a quarter of a mile only with a lasso.

It begins to grow dark. A cricket—chillador—in a corner of the room makes a distracting noise, incredible to one who has not heard it, and we are compelled to kill him. The wind, which blew from the sea all the morning, is now blowing seaward, bringing from the woods an ample delegation of mosquitoes. Viviana comes from the kitchen with a furnace of fire on her head. She sets it in the corredor, and with chips, cobs of maize, and fragments of guadua, makes a smoke to drive away the mosquitoes. The family sit on a bench, some heavy armchairs, and the pretil or railing of the corredor. Antonio has his guitar. Jacinto has his tiple in the back corredor, where the women are smoking. Two negritas are waltzing "on the sly" in the dining room.

At length a lighted candle is placed on the dining table. A Negro comes to have a demand written; for such things the family good-naturedly find time, and paper, and pens, and ink, and law. Pepe Gómez brings in the writing case and makes out the document. Pepe is reading aloud in the *Piquillo Aliaga* by Scribe. Toledo and others are listening, and at every surprising passage they exclaim "Caramba!"

Pilar carries the dishes to the inner closet, leaving behind two knives, and a definite number of cups, spoons, saucers, and plates, and two tumblers. She spreads the tablecloth, puts on the plates, a knife, a piece of "cheese," and the spoons. Some green plantains, fried, and then flattened between two stones, come in. Next enter three cups of chocolate on a plate. Each of these is set on a plate by itself. The rest are brought in in the same way. A plate or bowl of dulce is set on the table, and the saucers to eat it from. Last comes the water; and the tumblers are filled and refilled, some drinking from the tin cups, till all are satisfied. This ends the eating and drinking for the day.

It is now nine. The men soon retire for the night to beds and benches, which pass into each other, as the naturalist says, by imperceptible gradations. Then is heard the voice of the women in praying the Rosary, a sound easily recognized after hearing it once. Another day has passed without making any more change in the Valley of the Cauca than on the face of the ocean. And so have passed generations.

I cannot better continue my picture of this family than by faithfully noting the actual events of a single Sabbath. On Saturday night the bells of the chapel rung a little—just enough to say that there would be mass in the morning. The good cura leaves San Vicente occasionally for a day, and comes and spends the Sabbath with us; and well he might, for more than half his salary comes from this hacienda. I went to church in the morning, as I always do when I have the opportunity. Well, in the first place, we had one baptism and two fractions; that is, two of the babes had received just enough baptism to save them from hell had they died before this time, but not enough for decency.

The priest met the unbaptized at the door of mercy,

or side door of the church. One assistant held a little plain wooden cross, and another a lighted candle. After the prayers he put salt in the babe's mouth, and went to the font, an excavated stone, on a pedestal, with a hole for the water to run off. Here awaited the other two babes. One was held on the left arm. "Put the head there," said the priest. The woman turned herself, so as to bring the head to the required spot; the feet of the babe were more out of their place than ever. An exclamation of impatience from the fasting cura led an assistant to aid in placing the babe on the right arm. First he put spittle on the ears and nostrils of each; then he completed them one by one. He took from his portable baptism box a silver vial, with a rod passed through the silver-capped cork, and some cotton. With the rod he made a cross on the breast of each, and another between the shoulders, and wiped the oil off again with the cotton. The dress of one tried the cura's patience again. He exclaimed, amid his prayers, "Better bring your babe naked than with a dress tight at the neck." I held it away with two fingers as well as I could. Then the babe's head was held over the font, face downward, and holy water was poured from the little silver teapot on the crown of the head. Another cross was made on the crown of the head with the oily rod, the head covered for a moment with a white cloth, and the task was done. These prayers would occupy a Protestant clergyman about two hours, but our curate dispatched them very soon. If he skipped a word, or pronounced it wrong, he left it for next time.

He went back to the vestry, put on different robes, and, again accompanied by the cross and candle, met a marriage party at the door of mercy. These were more awkward than the mothers. First, the groomsman, who happened to be the husband of the bridesmaid, placed himself next the bride. Then the bridegroom tried to insinuate himself between the bride and bridesmaid, apparently intending to be married to one of them at least. When the parties were placed aright, the priest read them a long address, telling them, among other things, that it was their duty to endeavor to raise up heirs, not so much to their goods as to their religion, their faith, and their virtue. The bride, though never married before, need not excite his anxiety on that point. Not only were two of her children witnesses of the ceremony, but, besides, she was visibly in a state which is here designated by the word embarazada. I must add, then, that the older of her two children appeared to be three-fourths black, and the younger three-fourths white. The mother was a mulata, the other three adults of pure African blood. All were barefoot; the females wore that plain dress which alone is permitted to rich or poor in church—the head covered with a shawl, the body with a dark-colored skirt (saya).

The address through, the priest directed them to join their right hands. This was accomplished after much delay. When the priest asked the bride if she was willing to have this man for her husband, she made no answer. He repeated the question; no answer. "Say yes or no," exclaimed the priest; she said "yes." Two rings were taken from the small silver tray used in the mass. The priest put one on the finger of the bridegroom, and the latter put the other on the little finger of the bride. It was large enough for her thumb, and she instantly removed it to another finger. Then the priest took eight or ten reals, half francs, and dimes, from the tray, put them in the hands of the bridegroom, and he in those of the bride. In the course of the subsequent prayers the fasting priest fairly lost his patience at their awkwardness, as might be seen by the angry tones and snappish accent he gave his Latin. Then he stopped short off, and administered a rebuke in plain Castilian.

These prayers over, their hands still joined, the priest passed the band—estola—of his robe round the man's wrist, and led the pair, followed by the other pair, to the altar. They knelt, and mass commenced. Two golden chains, united by a ribbon, were put on their necks. Two yards of white cloth, with a fringe, was spread over her head and his shoulders. Regularly, they ought to have partaken of the Eucharist. I afterward asked the priest why they did not; he informed me that the bride's situation did not admit of the delay and fasting that were necessary to prepare them for that sacrament.

Mass over, everyone is at liberty to amuse himself as he pleases, for Sunday is a holiday, and it is a sin to work more than two hours, but no sin to play. At night I found that an extraordinary activity had prevailed in the kitchen; fresh pork and chicken appeared on the dinner table, and a bottle of aguardiente. At the head sat the cura, and a vacant space opposite me was at length filled by the four who had figured so conspicuously in the morning. I was not prepared for this. If I must eat with Negroes, I will do it with a good grace, but I could well have spared the company of an "embarazada" bride. During the dinner we had the music of two octave flutes and a drum.

This was ominous of the evening; in short, bad as was the weather, we had a ball. When I went for my chocolate, I found the good cura, with his gown tucked up, dancing the bambuco with unusual grace with one of the nymphs of the pastures. As I was making my retreat, young Carlos, about sixteen, was waltzing with an aged manumitted slave that had been his nurse, and that of all his brothers and sisters before him. Later in the night was a scene yet more curious, as I am told. The pretty little Mercedes, of seventeen, the white man's daughter, waltzed with the Negro blacksmith, Miguel. He appears over seventy, is very tall, very grim, and is the most pious man on the plantation. It must have been a sight. I tried to persuade her to it again at a day ball, but she would consent only on the condition that I should first waltz with her. She even dismounted for this purpose, after being ready to start for home; others seconded her proposition so eagerly that I could only get off by protesting that the Presbyterian Church did not permit dancing.

In the morning, when a crevice of my window shutter let in unquestionable evidence of day, I arose to see the last of the ball. The dance was the bundi, a Chocó dance.

Two couples, very black, and past the summer of life, had the floor. The four were slowly revolving about the room in a large circle, while each couple alternately rushed toward the center, and receded as the other advanced. This is the theory, but the manner defies me. The man commences his centripetal movement as if he had "broken loose," and you feel a fear that his partner will be demolished in a collision. And then the ad libitum steps of his retreat! But the music! One was drumming with his fingers, the other thumping a bench with a broomstick with all his might, and both, with others, were singing "Ai ke le le" obstreperously. So furious was the fun, that I thought every minute someone would have to give in or drop dead. Set after set danced the bundi, and the last to leave the floor was our cook, an aged Negress, who, having been busy in the kitchen all day, wore a camisa that had seen eight days' service in a kitchen without a chimney, and, further, had two holes worn in it just where it should be whole.

I must not forget to add that the bride kept up all night, and in the morning I saw her sitting watching the dancers with the gold chains still about her neck. One of her children had his head in her lap, the other was sitting by her side smoking a cigar. Saturday night she was up all night at a ball. Tonight is another ball, and probably tomorrow night another. This is not all. She has her fasts to go through, and to commune, before the marriage will be so complete as to permit them to sleep together. I wonder how she lives through it all!

A few days afterward, the pretty Mercedes, who danced with the tall, grim old Negro Miguel, received some letters from Quilichao, where she had been at boarding school. She offered them to me to read. The first was from a schoolmate, and began, "Mi querida negra"— "My dear Negress." I was astonished. She was "a white man's daughter," then; but whose? and what Negress was her mother? She cannot be darker than a quadroon. As I write, I am infested with the idea that she is a very

near relative to Don Eladio. The other letter was from
her teacher, and contained this expression: "I hope, my
dear Negress, that you are enjoying your visit at La Ribera." Such terms of endearment are not new to me, but
I select this case as unusually authentic.

They say that the tobacco of this region is as good as
that of Havana. I do not rely upon that opinion. I do not
believe that better coffee can be raised than in some parts
of this valley. The cacao tree is said to be indigenous to the
Cauca. Indigo might be raised here in any quantity, and
cochineal. Both these articles will pay transportation, but
they require too much labor and care to suit the disposition of the Caucanos.

What more could nature do for this people, or what
has she withholden from them? What production of any
zone would be unattainable to patient industry, if they
knew of such a virtue? But their valley seems to be enriched
with the greatest fertility and the finest climate in the
world only to show the miraculous power of idleness and
unthrift to keep a land poor. Here the family have sometimes omitted their dinner just because there was nothing
to eat in the house. Maize, cacao, and rice, when out of
season, can hardly be had for love or money; so this valley,
a very Eden by nature, is filled with hunger and poverty
from Popayán to Antioquia.

## XX

## To Buga and Palmira

A project had been hatched up to hunt for cinchona in the forests, high up the River Tuluá. It was now Friday afternoon, and it was proposed to reach Portazuela that night, and La Ribera next day, in time to make all necessary arrangements so as to take to the woods early on Sunday morning. To this I would not assent, but agreed to the plan, with two modifications. We were to leave La Ribera on Monday, and not to travel the succeeding Sabbath; and paper must be taken for me to collect plants in.

All this was assented to. I had an hour at La Paila to arrange matters for a week's sojourn in the forest. I took a fatigue dress, hunting shirt, hammock, flannel nightdress, encauchado, bayetón, a little Greek Testament, a needle book, pocket compass, thermometer, machete, pocketknife, comb, and a ream or two of printing paper. All this, except the paper, I accommodated about my saddle. The object of the expedition was a secret. Some of the party had mules at pasture that they wished to see; the others went with them to have a hunt.

After leaving La Paila, we stopped in Guavito at the house of Bernabé, the Negro judge, who was skinning a goat; then, again, at Murillo, and at 7 P.M. were seated at a comfortable dinner at Dr. Quintero's table at Portazuela. There was other company there, and the house was full. My hammock was ingeniously hung by passing the ropes over the tops of two opposite doors from the sala into inner rooms, and tying to them two cobs of maize, so that they could not draw through. My weight rendered the opening of the doors impossible till I rose.

In the morning, the thongs of rawhide to tie my hammock over the pockets of my cojinetes had disappeared. Dr. Quintero charged the theft upon the dogs of a guest. "My dogs do not eat rejo," said their owner. Dr. Quintero, who happened to be cutting rawhide at the instant, threw a strip to one of the accused, which pleaded guilty by swallowing it instantly; not a word was said.

After breakfast we all went to La Ribera. Here they told me that they had again concluded to start on Sunday morning. "Very well," I said; "leave me a guide, and I will come on after you on Monday." Finding me firm, they concluded to have a hunt on Sunday, and start as agreed; so I rested, according to the commandment, and the party, some of whom had slept in Tuluá, met and killed a deer. Damian, the young lawyer, whose energy makes amends for Don Modesto's slackness, had joined them, and had pledged himself to eat the hides and hoofs of all the deer they killed that day. They were so pleased with their success that they excused him from the task. The mode of hunting is to post themselves in ambush near where deer are likely to pass when pursued, and wait while the thicket is beaten with dogs and peons.

Opposite the little town of San Pedro is a hacienda, to which my mind runs back with delight. I am sorry I have not had better opportunities to become acquainted with the peculiarly amiable family that occupy it. Here, as at La Ribera, the ladies sat at the table with us. Our dining room was the back corredor; my bedroom was the other, with my hammock extended from a window grating to a pillar of the roof. A curious screen separated the dining room from one of the nicest gardens in all the country. I did not at once discover that it was a thick matting of a Passiflora with a very small flower. There are several such species here. This formed a dense curtain, capable of shutting out the sun and admitting the air—a perennial veil of leaf and flower.

Directly under the eaves of the house ran a cheerful rill in a channel of burned bricks. Water for the table was dipped up at the upper end. The plates, as taken from the table, were set in it farther down. Most operations which are done in dishes and pails of water in our kitchens are

here done in the acequia, if there be one. There seemed to
be a mystery about this acequia, for I could not tell where
this water could come from. The house was west of the
road, and the water must cross it; but, apparently, the
house stands higher than any point of the road that I could
see. I have spoken already of the acequeros' skill, the
results of which here puzzle me.

In the morning we were astonished with a breakfast
at six! It is little short of a miracle, being, perhaps, two
hours earlier than any other I ever heard of in all the land.
The family can be no ordinary people certainly. Here I
filled a bag with oranges, which were as abundant and as
good as man could desire. They have also cocoanut trees,
which, if they do not yet bear, are majestic ornaments,
and keep up a very pretty music in the night breeze by the
rustle of their leaflets. They need twelve years here to
grow in.

We were off earlier than most families could have
sent us away with chocolate only. A little above, I saw
some trees rather taller and more slender than most apple
trees. I thought at first they were deformed by dozens of
hornets' nests. I looked again, and really the supposed
nests were the fruit. It was the guanábana (Anona muri-
cata), called in Jamaica soursop. The flesh is firm, slightly
fibrous, so as to eat beautifully with a fork. Elegance of
eating is a high recommendation to a fruit. However
delicious the flavor, you cannot enjoy a fruit that smears
fingers and face, clogs the teeth, or keeps you on the alert
to separate eatable from uneatable. The guanábana is as
large as the largest pineapple, slightly acid, and not quite
sweet enough, and with no aromatic flavor. The pulp
separates in morsels, and is free from the rind and seeds.
Two other Anonas are to be mentioned. The A. Chiri-
molia, the chirimoya, is smaller, of less regular shape, more
fragile rind and tender pulp than the guanábana. It is by
many reckoned the best fruit in the world, and by others
rejected in disgust. Its flavor is almost exactly that of its
congener of the valley of the Mississippi, the Anona or

Asimina triloba, there called papaw. The Anona squa-
mosa is of the size of a large apple, much like the chirimoya in physical constitution, but inferior in flavor.
They call it anon. The guanábana, which I prefer, is
undervalued here, just as our northern papaw is abandoned to Negroes and opossums.

After picking from a guanábana all I wanted, dropping seeds along the road for a mile, and eating with my
fingers without unfitting them to handle white satin, I
threw away the rest. Soon after ordinary breakfast time,
we were rattling, in a long single file, over the pavements
of Buga, the capital of the province of Cauca. After turning various corners, the head of the column rode into a
house, and we all followed. We dismounted in the patio,
and soon were seated in a parlor more civilized than
usual. I received no introductions, but the conversation
showed that I was known to them. In explanation, I was
told that one of the young LL.D.'s with whom I crossed
the mountain was a cousin to them. Some dulce and
water were served, but no cigars offered. Per contra, they
had some curious articles of vertu, images, etc., made of
tobacco: they were exposed to the inconvenience of needing to be moistened with aguardiente from time to time.
I always knew that tobacco and rum were allies. On the
table were books, and a portfolio of drawings, and guitar
music. All these looked strange to me, so long had I forgotten them.

Buga is on the right bank of the Piedras River, a
broad, shallow stream, over which they think of throwing
a footbridge of guadua. It has less volume than the Buga-
la-Grande and the Tuluá, and nearly the same as the
Paila. A vacant space of stony ground here separates the
town from the riverbank. The shore is lined with washerwomen and garments spread out to dry.

I mounted my horse at the Piedras, and rode through
the back streets of Buga. I passed a place where they had
killed a cow, and were pinning the hide to the ground. On
the fence were half a dozen gallinazos, waiting for a

chance to pick up a morsel of meat; then they looked at my horse, and, by a wicked leer, seemed to insinuate that I was trying to cheat them. Somehow I felt guilty, for they looked at poor Rozinante with the eye of a gratified connoisseur. I could have knocked them off the fence with a good will.

We left Buga about eleven. By one we had crossed the Zonza, a small river, with a few houses south of it. Here the sun became intolerable; and had the day been as long as in northern summers, it would have been nearly as severe. We stopped at a venta, where a billiard table occupied the sala. I went back to the river to swim. The water then, about 2 P.M., was at nearly 100 degrees F. It had a strange effect on coming out. I was dressing myself in the shade, and I found it too cold. I had to step into the sun to warm myself. I started a little before the others, and stopped to see them building a church with adobe. In all New Granada I have seen no new church in the process of construction except at Zonza and Overo. All the others are either finished or abandoned. I rode on, and stopped on a gentle rise to wait for the company. Never have I seen, and never expect to see, in this mortal world, another place so beautiful. The ground was gently swelling; clumps of trees were scattered here and there in every direction. The Quindio range in the east terminated in plains at some miles distant, and the river forest, too, had retired far from the road.

Before sunset we were at Cerrito, the only regularly laid out town (with a plaza) this side of Cartago, except the paved towns and Libraida. In the center of the plaza stands a ceiba (Bombax Ceiba), the most glorious shade tree I ever set my eyes on; in size it is equal to a large elm, in shape a little more regular, the trunk almost smooth enough to varnish, and the thick green leaves already varnished.

I visited the boys' school here for less than five minutes one day. I do not always learn as much that is new by a longer visit. It is conducted on the Lancasterian principle, as are all the public schools here. Monitors were at this moment passing around, examining the toes of the boys, cutting their nails, and extracting the niguas. This is a part of the regular business of Saturday afternoon, and wisely enjoined, so neglected are too many of these children at home.

Here we turned at a right angle to the east, passed the mercy door of the church, and, as we left the village, entered the estate of Aurora, the property of Señor Miguel Cabal, late gobernador of the adjoining province of Buenaventura. We were soon seated at a plain, prompt dinner. I found our host a man of unusual intelligence, and, what is more, of a candor that leads me to rely more on his statements than on those of any other one man in all New Granada. He is a Liberal, and, therefore, I thought it a good time to get information on the Conservador presidents Herrán and Mosquera. I rely upon little here that does not come in the way of admissions, and sometimes very reluctant ones.

We stopped a while at a venta on the banks of the Sabaletas, a larger stream, over which there is a bridge of guadua. It requires some courage to venture across this frail fabric, although some of them are said to be strong enough to bear a mule. A sprightly girl here seemed greatly to attract the fancy of my companion, who wished her to go home with him and live with his wife, but why, or in what capacity, I could not guess. She promised to go at a future time, but my conjecture was that they did not mean anything, or that either supposed the other in earnest.

We had passed below here a robber, as they said, in custody of two armed men, all on foot. They were on their way to Buga. It is quite common to go armed here, either with a pistol or sword, but it is entirely useless. The chief reason why no more robberies are committed is, that they are not eager for money, and, therefore, lack a motive. I have never wished myself armed, or protected by the arms of another, for a single moment.

I know of no place of the size of Palmira that excels it in the population of its jail. To this bad preeminence I think the administration of López brought it by giving it wicked rulers; but of that we shall see more presently. The jail is miserably insecure. It is of unburnt brick, and the windows open on the street.

The only public institution which I visited besides was the boys' school. I was then making my investigations on the amount of arithmetic learned in the common schools. Here I proposed this sum: A boy bought a cage for twelve cuartillos, paid five for having it mended, and sold it for nineteen: how much did he gain or lose? It was given to the best boy in a large school, but he could not do it.

I was invited to dine with a family here. It was a Friday in Lent, and I had to do without meat. This is the only instance in all my Granadan experience where the lady would not allow any meat on her table. I have seen one lady and one child fast, but no more, except this family. The priests are supposed to fast.

Between here and the river lies some of the worst road in the world on account of mud. The distance between Palmira and Cali is given as eighteen or nineteen miles, but it is as far as a horse ought to travel in a day. At one place we had to unsaddle our horses and walk across a slough on logs, holding them by the halter lest they drown.

## XXI

## Cali and Vijes

We are on the left bank of the Cauca, and about four miles east of Cali. For some distance the land is liable to be overflowed, but at length we come to soil that is capable of cultivation. There are one or two haciendas near the road. At length we see before us an immense compact grove, with palms rising here and there above the rest of the foliage, and, above all, some steeples, and the bodies of two churches, one of them crowned with a fine dome. That grove covers Cali.

A nearer view does not belie the pleasing prospect at a distance. It stands on the right bank of Cali River, on dry, open ground, half a mile perhaps from the foot of the western or Caldas chain of the Andes. It may be regarded as the seaport of the Cauca Valley. It is the capital of the province of Buenaventura, and, while that port has but 1986 inhabitants, Cali, the fifth town in New Granada, has 11,848. It is one of those old towns that I love to meet with, where most of the architecture is solid, and few indeed of the roofs are thatched. It has a sufficient supply of suppressed convents for hospital, colegio, and other public uses, and one still in operation, a Franciscan convent of monks, besides a beatería, or place for the special devotions of females.

This convent of San Francisco is probably the richest west of the Quindio. Its church is exceeded in size only by the Cathedral of Bogotá and the church at Chiquinquirá. It is really the finest church I have seen here. They say it was built of old clothes. From some notion of the people, they love to be buried in the robes of a Franciscan friar. An old robe is preferred to a new one, and some say the older the better; so a friar cannot afford to keep his clothes till they get shabby. A man not acquainted with this custom became alarmed once for the extinction of the order. Every day or two he met a Franciscan going to his last home. On discovering his mistake, he wondered if the devil could be cheated as he was.

At a high mass here I was surprised by hearing a priest that could really sing; it was a great treat. I was so much interested in him that I sought an introduction to him, and called on him. He proved to be an Italian. He had refrained from making music a special study, he assured me, because he was desirous of preaching, and if he became a chorister it would interfere with his bent. I never heard him preach, but urged that he could not render a better service to religion than by rendering the musical parts of it endurable. He told me he was also engaged in image-making, and showed me some Jews that he was making for the processions of Holy Week. I told him that I thought a priest's time better spent in making Christians out of pagans than making Jews out of gypsum. He asked me to dine with him, but I deferred it till another occasion. When I next visited Cali he had moved to another convent.

San Pedro is a parish church of Cali, but is not equal, in either size or splendor, to San Francisco. It glories in a suite of large, new pictures, apparently all by the hand of the same artist, and a very industrious one. I am wicked enough to like new paintings, and, though this artist will never equal Vásquez, I looked them over with great satisfaction.

They had a great procession here, in which some image of the Virgin went from her home through a large number of the streets and back home again. Great preparations were made at some of the places it was to pass, to ornament the houses by hanging out calico, and whatever they thought ornamental. After the procession was over I was permitted to see Our Lady of the Queremal.

I visited the colegio. It was, perhaps, my most profitable visit to a school. I introduced myself to the subdirector, who seemed anxious to enlighten me in their modes of teaching. I was curious to hear his boys conjugate a Latin verb. From Latin I set them to parsing Spanish, and got them on that untranslatable phrase, Qué tal le ha ido a usted (what so to him has it gone to your majesty), which means how have you been. My chief objection to the system of education in this colegio is, that it is too speculative, and undervalues practical knowledge, as geography and chemistry; and too ambitious, having too much of calculus, and too little of arithmetic. Everything is attempted, and, therefore, little is mastered.

I visited the primary girls' school. It occupied the whole of a casa claustrada—a quite needless amount of space. It was a well-ordered school. I expressed a wish to obtain their hymn book, which they assured me I could do at the gobernación. "We have enough to spare here," added the directora; "but, as they are receipted for, it is impossible for us to give away or lose one without being held accountable." When a teacher resigns, a clerk of the gobernador comes, counts all the property of the school, and gives it over to the successor, taking a receipt.

I saw a loom in Cali. It is the only one I have seen. A rude affair it was, far inferior to any of our old handlooms. There are no arts that need introducing here more than spinning and weaving. Spinning must precede weaving, which cannot flourish while spinning is done in the antique mode, and spinning wheels are unknown. Had half the expense spent in introducing factory machinery into New Granada been spent on domestic machinery, a new era would have dawned here. Neither spinning nor weaving has been introduced into New Granada by Europeans, though possibly this loom may have been patterned after those of Spain. The manta, or native cotton cloth, made from an indigenous shrub, was one of the riches of the aborigines before the conquest, and the mode of spinning cannot have improved any since that day.

I am sorry to say that I heard one sound in Cali that reminded me of home. I am ashamed to tell what it was, but as a faithful, conscientious traveler I have no alternative. It was a man quarreling with (I suppose) his wife. For how many months has this been an unknown sound to my ears! I heard two women quarreling in Bogotá, and came near seeing a quarrel of two bogas on the Magdalena; but these men are of a degraded race and mixed blood, ignorant and half-civilized, wear machetes to cut bushes, and not a bowie knife to fight with, and do not even whip their wives.

There is a hospital for lepers here. I was anxious to visit it, but my friends protested; so much would they dread the introduction of elephantiasis into their families, to gratify my curiosity. I cannot think the disease so contagious as they imagine, for I do not hear of those who live with lepers contracting it.

I attended the funeral of a General Borrero—not, as I then supposed, the candidate for president in 1847. He was a member of La Tercera, the third order of St. Francis, and accordingly was buried as a monk. "When the devil was sick, the devil a monk would be." His body lay, the night before the funeral, in a chapel of the convent. The next day they sung the mass of the defunct, with the accompaniment of the best musicians and vocalists that could be hired in Cali.

Then marched forth a long procession through the streets, with hats off, and candles thirty inches long and two in diameter, dropping wax in the street. They went to a small church, or chapel, at the northern extremity of Cali, adjoining the old cemetery. Here some further singing and praying was performed, and the procession proceeded eastward, out of town and over the plain, to the new cemetery, where as yet no chapel has been built. I did not enter the cemetery with the procession, nor see the body deposited in its last resting-place, owing to a little accident in leaping one of the stagnant brooks that cut the plain in every direction; I had landed in a soft spot, and covered myself with rich black mud nearly up to my knees. When I had got it washed off, and had entered the cemetery, the body was already placed in a brick bóveda, or oven, about three feet high, and they were building up the mouth. Burnt bricks are always used for this work.

One other great affair came off here, the celebration of the triumph of the Liberales, on 7th March, 1849, when President López was elected president. The affair was official, and, frankly to speak my sentiments, therefore in bad taste. Especially it was adding insult to injury to require the Franciscan monks to celebrate an event that grieved the heart of every fanatic.

The celebration began, of course, with the vesper of the day, on Sunday night; this was by an illumination. As there is no window-breaking mob here, and no windows to be broken, the affair suffered in brilliancy accordingly. In the plaza there were but thirty-one lights, and most of these were in the balconies of government offices.

On Monday there was a grand mass in San Francisco. Artillery and infantry were drawn up in front of the church. At the proper time, when all the bells rang, the drums also beat, and the rattle of musketry and the thunder of cannon added wings to the devotion of the dense crowd that filled the vast and beautiful church. Soldiers on parade do not kneel or remove caps at mass.

An accidental circumstance led me to call on Dr. Manuel María Mollarino. I supposed him at the time to be an M.D., but, judging from his library, I infer that he is (as are most of the doctors here) an LL.D. I little foresaw then that the supreme power was so soon to be placed in his hands as vice-president. He is an intelligent gentleman, and speaks very good English; better, I think, than anyone I have met who has not resided in an English country, or, as Vice-President Obaldía, on the Isthmus. He is a Conservador, but not of an ultra stamp, and, had he any power in his hands, would use it well; but the president is too much like a head clerk to sign papers.

I left Cali in company with Señor Triana and Señor Monzón, director of some mining operations which we wished to visit at Vijes. We crossed the Cali over a brick bridge, the longest and best bridge, as well as the last, that

I have seen in all New Granada. It is wide enough for a carriage to pass, and consists of seven arches. You would forget where you are while looking at the bridge; but look above at the washerwomen that line the bank, or the swimming boys and swimming girls below, and you will see that you are in New Granada yet.

One strange peculiarity of Vijes is that the lands here are common property. Some man in times past owned all this plain, and, of the hills adjoining, a quantity unknown to me; from their steepness and aridity it would seem the less the better. When he died it fell to his heirs without division. Some may have sold half their share, and in this way there are more than a hundred owners of this property. There are many cases of this kind in New Granada, and laws to regulate the improvement of the soil and other questions that must arise under this cumbrous coproprietorship. It will be a very difficult thing to bring about a division. At present no one wishes it, for large parts of this fertile plain are yet untilled, and there are considerable parts of it which I have not, in these many days, explored either on horseback or afoot. It includes one or two detached hills in it. All the rest is level and fertile.

The population of the district is 1160, most of whom live in the village, and nearly all of them near it on the plain.

Once in the memory of man this people attempted a new church. They fairly began it and stopped. The cura, I believe, has not yet given up all hope of getting them at work on it again, but I see little prospect of it. He is the best preacher I have heard in New Granada, where preaching is so rare, and preaching talent still rarer. At the time I heard him he was holding a protracted meeting, as we should say, that is, preaching every evening for more than a week, preparatory to the separation of Church and State. If it makes every priest work as hard as he did, the new arrangement will keep them from eating so much of the bread of idleness.

Can a railroad be put here? As a physical question of

grades and curves, I answer, I have little doubt of it. Will
it pay? That is a serious question. I answer, not at once;
and never while the government is what it is. That the
time will come when the Cauca will be connected with the
Pacific, and the Magdalena by railroad, I strongly hope;
but there are great difficulties in the way.

The most formidable physical difficulty is in the un-
healthy nature of the Pacific coast. It is a network of
muddy creeks and islands, as bad, perhaps, as the west
coast of Africa. If a town could be located west of it all, it
might be healthy, and from such a point cultivation might
spread to the east. Bad as Buenaventura is, its business
must increase with the growth of Panama, Oregon, and
California. Could the Cauca have peace, and I now hope
it will, the productions and trade must also be stimulated
from this source. Here I stand, not three days from Panama, and the valley behind me has held a population
equal to all that New Granada now has. Even west of me
are fertile and healthy lands not occupied. The population of the whole canton that lies on the Pacific is 3338. The
belt of malaria must be broken—it shall be.

But there is a moral difficulty. This people love to
dance, but they hate to work. How will you induce them?
With gold? The line of the road may run through the
richest gold deposit of the world. How can you hire cutting
and filling done where the earth contains an ounce to the
bushel? Hunger cannot urge them, nor cold, nor naked-
ness; and among the rights most sedulously guarded by
the theories of the ultrarepublican is the right to be a
vagabond. These theorists are in favor of exempting the
improvident and indolent from all burdens. He buys no
land, and often pays no rent. He votes, and pays no taxes.
The nation is bent on repealing, as soon as they are able,
every tax that now yields anything. They have abolished
tithes, of which it cost four-fifths to collect the remainder.
Excise on spirits and tobacco have gone. Salt and stamps
must go. The vagabond gives no notes and eschews law,
so he pays no stamp tax. He must eat salt, and here he pays

a tax of a cent or two a year. The plan for the future is to assess all taxes on incomes that exceed a certain amount. This will let him clear. A poll tax is a barbarism. So little does he use of foreign goods, that, even while the impost system remains, almost nothing is exacted from him under it. The gross revenue of the nation is less than half a dollar a head, and this by loading the wealth of the nation as heavily as it can bear, while unthrift and indolence go scot free.

Again, there is no stability in the government. I do not now speak of revolutions, for the last two were unsuccessful, and I think we have seen the last of them; but the theory of their government is against stability. Whether there ever was a worse Constitution than the present I know not. Its adoption was an infamous lie of the Obando administration, to which the nation assented. The Liberal Congress of 1851 made a Constitution which the Congress of 1853 had a right to adopt or reject. It did neither; it altered it till it lost its identity, then voted that it was the same, and adopted it. Then the nation shouted for joy, and cried, "At last the true republic has come!"

The executive is shorn of its powers. Both houses are chosen on the same ticket, and their deliberating in two chambers is a farce, for the absolute majority of the whole Congress voting in joint meeting carries every point against the will, it may be, of all the Senate, and in spite of any executive veto.

And changes the most stupendous, such as it would take twenty years to bring about in England, are the work of a single week, perhaps. In England, neither the size, shape, nor number of the counties has changed within a century. If there has been a year without a variation of the provinces of New Granada, I am not aware of it. It would be harder to abolish the troy pound in England than to overthrow twice the whole metrical system of New Granada.

What will be the end of these things? I conjecture bankruptcy. The expenditures are double the revenue;

but they are not to be so when their plans are perfected! I see no remedy but to plunge back into the barbarian darkness of the United States, or even beyond them. But to restore poll taxes, imprisonment for debt, passports, and vagrancy laws, ordaining that the labor of man shall build roads, bridges, schoolhouses, ay, and prisons too, even though he have no wish to travel, learn, nor yet to be imprisoned, would be enough to make a theorist like Samper rave; and I fear it will not be done till they have suffered greater calamities than they have felt since the Spaniard left their shores.

Such conclusions grieve me, for I love the Granadan race. These pages testify to an uninterrupted series of kind acts of them toward me—kindness that I can never repay. I can hardly mention a single reasonable request of mine neglected—not one refused. Even many unreasonable ones, as I afterward knew them to be, were granted, often at an inconvenience that I greatly regretted. The authorities, too, have been as kind as private individuals. All sorts of documents have been furnished me, even by offices that had to send to Bogotá to replace those spared me. Nothing has been withholden me that a traveler could ask.

I have not made them the returns I would have wished. I would have gladly pointed them more directly to a purer religion that can remedy the evils they are struggling with; but while I could profess to be a communicant of a Protestant church, circumstances rendered it unadvisable to do more. And now, in enlisting the sympathies of our own people, I am doing what I can.

To tell the truth of them, I have been obliged to speak of their faults and deficiencies. But, after all, I here boldly declare the Granadinos a highly moral people. I speak not of the Scotch and English standard of morality; that is not fair.

Again, as to the crimes against life, I suppose, in all the nation, there are not a fifth as many murders as in New York City alone! Probably a single year in California has witnessed as many murders as have been perpetrated in

New Granada, among two million and a quarter of all races, since it has had its place among nations. I have more than once had to blush for the ruffianism of the scum of our nation, like which nothing can be found in the very worst population of New Granada. But again to figures. I cannot estimate the murders in New Granada at more than three per million per annum.

Say I not well, then, that the Granadinos deserve a high place among the nations of the earth in point of moral character? And we, especially, owe them our respect and esteem. The conduct of the government at Bogotá in relation to our Isthmus transit has always been more than generous—it has been noble; and to us they look for examples of government—to us for their closest allies in trade. And, lastly, we two, of all the nations of the earth, are without any established church, granting equal rights to all men of all creeds. Long may we remain so, but not long alone. VIVA, PUES, VIVA LA NUEVA GRANADA!

| | DATE DUE | | |
|---|---|---|---|
| | | | |
| | | | |
| | | | |
| | | | |
| | | | |
| | | | |
| | | | |
| | | | |
| | | | |
| | | | |
| | | | |